Policy and Practice in the Justice System

Policy and Practice in the Justice System

C. Aaron McNeece
Florida State University

Albert R. Roberts
Rutgers University

Nelson-Hall Publishers
Chicago

Senior Editor: Libby Rubenstein
Typesetter: Fine Print
Printer: Capital City Press
Cover Painting: "26th and California" by Marcia Danits
Illustrator: Corasue Nicholas

Library of Congress Cataloging-in-Publication Data

McNeece, Carl Aaron.
 Policy and practice in the justice system / C. Aaron McNeece,
Albert R. Roberts.
  p.   cm.
 Includes bibliographical references.
 ISBN 0-8304-1417-7
 1. Social work with criminals—United States.   2. Prisoners—
Services for—United States.   3. Juvenile delinquents—Services
for—United States.   I. Roberts, Albert R.   II. Title.
HV7428.M35   1996
365'.66—dc20   96-11325
                                                                        CIP

Copyright © 1997 by Nelson-Hall Inc.

Manufactured in the United States of America

10 9 8 7 6 5 4 3 2 1

Contents

Part III ▸ Direct Practice, Advocacy, and Outreach

Part IV ▸ Educating/Preparing for the Future

Foreword

Frank B. Raymond III

The entire justice system in the United States is in a state of flux. While the system has changed continuously throughout its history, in recent years its shifts have been more dramatic in scope and direction than during any previous time. These changes have resulted, on the one hand, from the system's response to changing societal conditions and ideologies. On the other hand, the system has been reshaped not only in reaction to external forces but also in response to its own shifts in philosophy and the development of new knowledge.

It is now common knowledge that the numbers of individuals entering the U.S. justice system have grown dramatically in the past several years. While some would argue that this increase is due to social factors such as the breakdown of the family, the influence of mass communications, and the entertainment industry, there is no doubt that our societal definitions of criminal behavior have also contributed to this growth. For example, the U.S. war on drugs is considered by most criminal justice experts to be the single, most important factor in the rising rates of arrest, conviction, and incarceration.

Not only have societal beliefs about what constitutes crime affected the size of our justice system, but our changing philosophies about how crime should be dealt with have resulted in the burgeoning of that system. There seems to be a national thirst for punishment, which is undoubtedly one of the reasons the United States now incarcerates a larger proportion of its citizens than any other industrialized nation. The U.S. prison population, which broke the 1 million mark in 1993, exceeded 1.1 million in 1995, as state and federal prisons recorded their largest population increases since record keeping began in 1923. In addition to this increase in incarceration, other components of the justice system have experienced tremendous growth. Furthermore, as these programs, such as probation, parole, or other forms of "aftercare," have expanded, their focus has shifted from rehabilitation toward control.

As these changes in the U.S. justice system have taken place, social work's participation in the system has likewise changed. The relative number of social workers employed in the criminal justice system has decreased significantly. Perhaps this reduction is the result of the shift of our justice system from a treatment to a punishment approach. The roles that social workers are expected to perform have changed, and there is a greater emphasis on the "control" function of social workers, as opposed to the "helping" function. Relatedly, there has been a sharp decrease in the percentage of students enrolled in master of social work degree programs who plan to work in the justice field. Because it is so difficult to recruit and retain professionally trained social workers, numerous states have declassified social work positions in the justice system. Many nonprofessionals are being hired to fill the positions previously held by professionally trained social workers. Given the changing context of their work environment, those social workers who are committed to working within the justice system and using their professional skills to make a difference in the lives of individuals and in the structure and functioning of the system itself are often frustrated and confused about their roles.

How does one make sense of all these changes in the justice system and in the role of social work within the system? What will be the future of the justice system in the United States? Will social workers have a place in the justice system of tomorrow, and, if so, what will they be expected to do? This book provides answers to these questions.

In explicating the justice system and interpreting the evolving roles of social work within the system, the authors of this text use several unifying devices. First, each chapter presents an excellent historical overview of the subject at hand. Each component of the justice system is discussed from its evolution to its present form. New programs created to serve special populations or to respond to particular social problems are also presented in terms of their historical development.

Second, the impact of changing social philosophy is considered. The authors demonstrate how the changes in the philosophy and consequent structure of the criminal justice system over the years can be understood only within the context of the prevailing societal ideologies. In recent years, for example, the shift from a deterministic conceptualization of human behavior to a "free will" perspective has resulted in a movement from the rehabilitative ideal of the earlier Progressive Era. The shift in social thought during the past several years has led to an approach to crime more closely akin to that of classical criminology, which dominated in the Western world throughout the eighteenth century. Now, as earlier, within broader society and within the justice system itself, there is an emphasis on law and order and the application of punishment as the appropriate response to crime. In discussing this recent trend the authors describe the shift from treatment to punishment. They discuss the substitution of the medical model with the justice model. At a broader level, they illustrate how the growing commitment to social control is manifested not only in the recent increase in the population of our criminal justice system, but also in more punitive regulations for means-tested social welfare benefits. Present attempts to transform the justice system into a low-cost, retributive, custodial system that relies heavily on incarceration are paralleled by the efforts of legislators and policymakers to reform the entire social welfare structure. In other words, the authors make it clear that past, present, and future changes in the justice system do not occur in a vacuum; rather, they must be interpreted in the context of larger social changes.

The third theme is the role of social work in the changing historical context of the justice system. The authors describe the expanding involvement of the social work profession in criminal justice when the rehabilitative ideal was more prominent. They discuss the problems experienced by social workers when confronted by the conflicting demands of the control and rehabilitative models. They explain the retreat of social workers from the justice system when the correctional systems began to abandon rehabilitative goals in the 1970s. On a more positive note, however, the writers also discuss present roles for social workers in the justice system at both the micro and macro levels of practice. They remind social workers of the unique contributions they can make within the justice system. They challenge social workers to assume leadership and use their professional knowledge and skills to help shape the justice system in a manner consistent with the values and ethics of the social work profession. The book is indeed a "call to arms" for social work.

This book will prove useful to a variety of audiences. College students who major in the liberal arts can benefit from reading it. It will provide them with a better understanding of our justice system, the relationship of that system to the broader society, and the challenges and dilemmas currently faced by the system. *The book should be required reading for all persons preparing for roles in the justice system, especially social workers.* Knowledge of the structure and functioning of the present system, its historical development, and the system's relationship to the broader social structure is important for all who plan to work in this field.

Those who are already employed in the justice system can also profit from reading this book. Given the magnitude and velocity of the changes that have occurred within the justice system, both newcomers and old-timers struggle to comprehend what is happening and to anticipate what the future may be like. This book will provide them a better understanding of this complex, ever-changing system and their roles within it.

The authors of the various chapters have lived up to their reputations as outstanding scholars in the justice field. Their writings reflect a sound knowledge base built on years of experience and research. Each chapter presents a thorough coverage of the subject and an extensive review of the relevant literature. Without overwhelming the reader with trivia, figures, and unnecessary detail, the writers succeed in presenting a complete picture of where we have come from, where we are, and where we are likely to go in the justice field.

Preface

If we haven't reached a crisis in our justice system, we are very close. The United States incarcerates the highest proportion of its population of any major industrialized nation. We currently have over a million adults in federal and state prisons and over 400,000 in local jails. Approximately 90,000 juveniles are now in detention or training schools, and another 100,000 juveniles are being admitted to adult jails each year, despite decades of reform efforts. While incarcerated, many of these inmates (both juvenile and adult) are experiencing filthy, dilapidated, unsafe facilities with inadequate food and medical care and weak or nonexistent supervision. Boredom, racism, corruption, and violence are facts of prison life. State inmates spend an average of fourteen hours per day in their cells; federal inmates, eighteen and one-half hours per day. Of the 508 jails in the United States with an average daily population of one hundred or more inmates in 1991, 136 were under court order to reduce overcrowding, and 257 were under court order to make improvements ranging from additional staff to medical services.

And this represents only a small piece of the "justice" system. The great majority of clients in the justice system are maintained in the community on probation, parole, "aftercare," or some other status that less severely restricts their liberty. As many as one in ten minority males may expect to find themselves in the justice system at some point during their lives. (More African-American males are in the justice system than are in college!) Perhaps 5 percent of *all* males may be in the justice system at one time or another in their lives.

Social work has a long tradition of involvement in the justice system, with some social workers tracing the roots of this area of practice back to John Augustus, a Boston shoemaker generally credited with developing the practice of probation in the eighteenth century. Somewhat later the social work profession's connection to the justice system was officially acknowledged in the creation of the National Conference on Charities and Corrections in 1915. In recent years, however, social work has drifted away from justice system issues and clients. We see this book partly as a "call to arms" for social workers, hoping to stimulate their interest and renewed involvement in the justice system. By providing the reader with a number of descriptions of social work roles in various components of the justice system, we hope to convince students, faculty, and working professionals of the need to pay more attention to justice system issues.

As of the mid 1990s there were over four hundred Council on Social Work Education (CSWE) accredited B.S.W. programs and one-hundred-twenty M.S.W. programs. However, only a small number of programs—approximately 10 percent or fifty-two programs—offer an elective course in correctional or justice social work. More promising are the six universities that offer students the opportunity to enroll in a twelve- to eighteen-credit concentration in offender rehabilitation; social-work-in-justice settings; or victims, offenders, and the law. Part of the problem stems from many social work students being interested in working only with highly motivated clients or patients in hospitals, mental health centers, and family service agencies. In fact, there is a large number of students in every M.S.W. program throughout the United States whose career goal is to eventually have an independent or group private practice. These health and mental health social workers are in for a rude awakening within the next ten years. With the proliferation of managed care organizations, HMOs and PPOs, the number of clients seeking reimbursable treatment will be slowing down considerably. Except for the wealthiest Americans, most people will not be able or willing to pay for more than a few sessions of psychotherapy out of their own personal funds.

Where will the jobs for social workers be in the year 2010? We predict that the most promising specialties will be in the fields of crisis intervention and brief treatment, case management with families and the elderly, chemical dependency treatment, domestic violence, juvenile justice, juvenile and adult probation, and victim assistance. Many of the clients in justice and crisis management settings are involuntary. As a result, social workers will need the knowledge base and specialized skills to engage and motivate somewhat resistant clients. It is critically important, therefore, for social work and criminal justice educators to keep abreast of the emerging multiple employment opportunities in justice and crisis management settings. A strong linkage between faculty members, field instructors, and agency administrators can optimize appropriate changes in both course content and new curriculum options.

Substance abusers, battered women, juvenile and adult offenders, and violent crime victims are some of our most neglected vulnerable populations. According to recent prevalence estimates there are over 8.7 million women battered by their intimate partners annually, and there are over 15.1 million substance abusers in the United States (Roberts, 1996a; 1996b).

In recent years a small yet growing number of social work professors and administrators have made a commitment to change the status quo. Three significant changes need to take place in order for the therapeutic and rehabilitative needs of victims and offenders to be met:

1. State and county personnel standards and job descriptions need to be changed so that entry-level probation officers, police social workers, addiction treatment specialists, victim advocates, and therapists are required to have a minimum of a B.S.N. degree or a bachelor's degree with a major in criminal justice or psychology. An M.S.W. or M.S. degree in criminal justice and three years experience should be mandated for all supervisory positions.

2. All B.S.W. and M.S.W. programs should be required by CSWE accreditation standards to have at least one course on policies and practices within the justice system. One of the missions of social work education is to prepare students for work with vulnerable and oppressed minority populations. Recent reports by the U.S. Bureau of Justice Statistics reveal that minorities, the poor, and substance abusers are highly overrepresented in both victim and offender populations.

3. We should continue to focus professional attention on justice system issues by continuing to have special symposia at professional meetings (such as the APPA annual conference, and the CSWE's Annual Program Meeting) and special commissions (especially in the National Association of Social Workers) to advocate for the interests of justice system clients.

This book is divided into four parts. Part I deals with juvenile justice policies and programs. Part II concerns a special aspect of justice system issues—drugs and the justice system. Part III includes chapters on direct practice, advocacy, and outreach, both juvenile and adult. Part IV examines the education of social workers for justice system employment and speculates about the future of social work practice in the justice system.

References

Roberts, A. R. (1996a). *Helping battered women: New perspectives and remedies.* New York: Oxford University Press.

Roberts, A. R. (1996b). "Epidemiology and definitions of acute crisis in American society." In A. R. Roberts (Ed.), *Crisis management and brief treatment.* Chicago: Nelson-Hall.

PART I

Juvenile Justice Policies and Programs

In chapter 1 Mark Ezell examines social work roles in administration, the context for administrative roles in juvenile justice, and the structure of juvenile justice administration. The overall picture he paints is one of imminent crisis. Diane Dwyer provides us with an overview of juvenile corrections in chapter 2. She sees reasons for us to be more hopeful, if not optimistic, based on the recent passage of federal legislation that will provide "an infusion of funds." At the same time she warns that it is incumbent on practitioners to adopt an aggressive policy regarding the value of social work theory in prescribing solutions to the current plight of juvenile corrections. José Ashford describes juvenile aftercare in chapter 3 as "the neglected phase of the juvenile justice process." He also criticizes the dearth of special training of social workers for justice system employment and examines the theoretical bases of aftercare supervision.

Chapter One

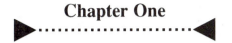

The Administration
of Juvenile Justice

Mark Ezell

Glick (1986) said that "the organization and administration of youth programs for juvenile delinquents is both an art and a science that has evolved into a technological discipline" (p. 219). Whether artful, scientific, or technological, the process of organizing and managing systems, programs, and staff to work with delinquent youth, their families, and their communities is an important challenge for social workers. Often it is difficult to feel much compassion for a youth who has robbed someone at gunpoint, stole and destroyed a car, or broken into a house. Social workers in the criminal justice system should be able to see that many of these youth were passed over or failed by the child welfare, mental health, health, or perhaps the school system. Many of these youth have already been served by programs that we designed and for which we had high expectations. But for some reason things didn't turn out as we had hoped, and these youths have gotten themselves into trouble. We are not accustomed to failure nor do we like to stare our failures in the face. This, to a large degree, is the situation in the juvenile justice system, and this is one of the reasons social work should not turn its back on it.

There are incredible highs and devastating lows to be experienced while working in the juvenile justice system. The problems in juvenile justice systems and the high-profile cases of youths with long records have frustrated communities and contributed to a media blitz that has raised the fear of youth crime to an all-time high. Legislators and other policymakers are attempting to transform the juvenile justice system into a low-cost, retributive, custodial system that relies heavily on incarceration. New direction and leadership are desperately needed, and the profession of social work should be striving to train administrators and policymakers for the juvenile justice system.

This chapter focuses on the different ways that state juvenile justice systems are structured and administered, as well as on the long-standing debates over how these systems should be organized. The reader should not expect to find a single answer that indicates the "right" or "best" way to organize and administer juvenile justice. Even though "the answer" is not included in this chapter, all sides of the arguments are outlined and weighed. In addition, this chapter provides a framework for analyzing management positions in the juvenile justice system, and it describes many of the large number of administrative roles available to social workers in juvenile justice.

The Context for Administrative Social Work in Juvenile Justice

Before analyzing specific administrative roles available to social workers in the juvenile justice system, a couple of definitions and a context-setting discussion is necessary. This discussion will put some reasonable, and hopefully understandable, parameters on this chapter; but more importantly, it should underscore the understanding that the structural and policy context of the juvenile justice system is critical to effective social work administration. This knowledge is indispensable when it comes to understanding and working with funding streams, budget calendars and process, personnel recruitment and policies, lines of authority and accountability, planning, and interagency relationships, among other things.

For the purposes of this chapter, the juvenile justice system is defined as *the network of agencies, programs, actors, policies, and practices that delivers services to, administers sanctions on, and exercises authority over children, youth, and their families.* The operation of this system relies on federal, state, and local law as well as federal and state constitutions for its policy underpinnings. Law enforcement, court intake, detention, prosecution, defense, probation, adjudication, sentencing, and rehabilitation or punishment programs are the primary juvenile justice functions subsumed by this conceptualization.

"Administration" is another concept that is important to define. This term and "management" are used interchangeably; they involve the tasks of planning, fund-raising and budgeting, organizing, staffing, supervising, coordinating and controlling, representing, evaluating, negotiating, and information processing (see Patti, 1977 and 1983, for full descriptions of these functions). The nature of managerial activity is dependent on several factors, especially the size of the agency or program. Patti (1983), for example, distinguishes between three levels of management: (1) the executive management level, which includes those social workers "who carry the overall responsibility for directing the organization or a major portion thereof" (p. 43); (2) the program management level, which includes those in charge of major agency units, who are generally referred to as "mid-management"; and (3) the supervisory management level, who are those administrators who have daily contact with direct service workers.

There are clear distinctions between the activities of managers at these different levels, and as noted above, managerial functions also depend on the size of the agency. For example, the program manager of a small program (e.g., less than ten direct service staff) is likely to have supervisory responsibilities in addition to program management tasks. When necessary and appropriate, distinctions between management levels are discussed throughout the chapter. All levels of management in juvenile justice can be staffed by social workers, even though other fields such as public administration, criminal justice administration, and business administration are increasingly competing for these jobs.

Context for Administration

In most states and jurisdictions, juvenile or children's courts are at the hub of the juvenile justice system; in others, family courts are. The difference between a juvenile and a family court is one of breadth of jurisdiction. Juvenile courts have jurisdiction over matters such as delinquency, status offenses, and child welfare, whereas family courts have additional jurisdiction over divorce, paternity and/or child support, adoption, domestic violence protection orders, and intrafamily misdemeanors (Rubin 1991). There are disagreements over which approach is best, but many would argue that the family court can accomplish better case coordination, especially if the same judge hears all the different types of cases for a particular family. Advocates for family courts argue that in the absence of a family court, a family's cases could be scattered among civil, criminal, juvenile, probate, domestic relations, and traffic courts. This is a reasonable argument, but the day-to-day reality of court operation is rarely this simple, and there is no empirical evidence to indicate which approach is more effective. On the other hand, family courts may be asked to deal with too wide a range of civil and criminal matters. (Agreeing on a definition of "effective" is the first challenge, much less conducting such complex research.) As of 1991, when the most recent survey was done, only eleven states and the District of Columbia had a single court with broad jurisdiction over all these matters (Rubin, 1991).

As previously mentioned, the operation of the juvenile court is largely dictated by a state's constitution and laws, which articulate the position of the juvenile court in relation to other local and state courts (e.g., municipal, county, district, circuit court, and so on). The court design may not be consistent throughout the state; it is common for big cities and counties to have different arrangements than less densely populated areas. Juvenile judges are administratively responsible for the operation of the court and in some cases detention and probation. State laws and constitutions articulate how judges are appointed and/or elected to these positions, and local court rules and practices describe how one becomes a juvenile judge, for how long, and the specific duties of the chief administrative juvenile judge. All social workers in administrative positions in the juvenile justice system should be intimately familiar with these laws, policies, and practices. (Unfortunately, few are likely to find this training available in professional schools of social work.)

Another important contextual factor that social work administrators need to understand is the trend for state and local agencies to purchase services from private providers. This trend is the result of many related factors: (1) the widely held belief that the private sector can do things more efficiently and less expensively than the public sector; (2) efforts to "reinvent" or "downsize" government; and (3) efforts to increase programmatic flexibility similar to the results achieved in Massachusetts (Young, 1981). Whatever the reason, administrators need to have negotiating and contracting knowledge and skills. They will be challenged to concretely define the products and outputs desired from each contract, and further, to design and implement monitoring and accountability mechanisms for use with the contracted vendors. Fiscal accountability is only a part of the challenge, possibly the easier part, when compared with accountability for program outcomes for individual youth.

Employee unions also represent a significant source of complexity for those who manage juvenile justice programs. Sound personnel policies and practices are critical whether unions are involved or not, but they seem to get more attention and to be the subject of deliberations when unions are involved. Negotiating wage and benefit packages is complex work. Fortunately, unions are invested in their members' training so that they can effectively carry out their responsibilities. All too often, management views unions as adversaries instead of effective partners.

A final contextual factor that strongly influences the management of juvenile justice programs is the availability of funding. Simply put, funding bodies are asking for more but paying for less. This pattern is not likely to change. In fact, the funders and the public seem to be demanding better performance despite increasing numbers of clients, some of whom are more violent, more chronic, and more troubled than in the past. As a result, efficiency, custody, and security become higher priorities than treatment, and programs are forced to operate with leaner staffs and underqualified personnel. It has been over a decade since managers have used annual budget growth as a criterion of their effectiveness; the best administrators now point to their success at either maintaining last year's budget level or avoiding and minimizing sizable cuts. Even if juvenile justice goes the way of adult corrections and experiences a construction boom, funds for operations are likely to be lean and stretched across more programs and facilities.

The juvenile justice system is funded by multiple sources. Almost no federal money is expended by juvenile courts to support ongoing operations, but demonstration projects are funded with grants from the Office of Juvenile Justice and Delinquency Prevention (OJJDP) and the U.S. Department of Health and Human Services. This appears to be changing somewhat under the Violent Crime Control Act of 1994, with $377 million available in Fiscal Year 1996–2000 for crime prevention programs sponsored by local governments. This money will also be administered by OJJDP. Other provisions of this act may also make federal funds available to courts for general administration ($150 million). Another $36 million has been authorized for "delinquent and at-risk youth" programs. A few private foundations also fund innovative programs for short periods of time. Juvenile justice operations are financed primarily by a combination of state and local dollars, and the amount contributed of each varies by state and locality. For example, the state of New York reimburses New York City for 50 percent of the costs to detain delinquents; the state of Washington provides funds to counties based on a formula for what used to be a probation subsidy program but is now more of an early intervention and diversion program. Bond issues are generally used to fund the construction or renovation of state or local facilities.

Administrative Debates

There are three ongoing debates about the best way to administer juvenile justice that justice system administrators need to understand. The first debate concerns whether the executive branch or the judicial branch should operate juvenile justice programs and functions (Pettibone et al., 1981). This debate stems from the fact that "the original juvenile court was conceived of as a social service agency in a judicial setting, a fusion of social welfare and social control" (Feld, 1993, p. 280). Although too simplified, one position is that juvenile judges need administrative control of the resources necessary to fully serve the best interests of youth, their families, and the community. The opposing position is that judges are neither managers nor program specialists, and that the administration of juvenile justice should best be left to local or state agencies. The particular arrangement in a locality is a result of historical and political forces rather than research and evaluation. This is a complex matter involving issues of fairness, funding, due process, conflict of interest, separation of powers, and philosophy (Pettibone et al., 1981). Young (1981) explains that although the juvenile court has historically functioned both to care for and to control children and youth, the combination of these two is recently at issue. "The now familiar criticism is that when responsibility for social services and social control is lodged with the same individual or organization, the proper provision of each is contaminated by the other and the end result is the worst of both worlds" (p. 491). We believe that the juvenile court has not functioned well as a social service delivery system because it is trying to be all things to all people—counselor, protector, mediator, disciplinarian, and so on—with inadequate resources, structure, and management.

The second debate concerns whether juvenile justice agencies in the executive branch should be operated by the state or local level of government. This issue is slightly less complex than the judiciary versus executive argument with its due process and separation of powers variables, but it is equally arguable. As noted below, even when some juvenile services—typically probation—are funded and operated by local agencies, others, such as institutions, are operated by the state. Many argue philosophically that troubled youth are the responsibility of the communities in which they live, and they are hopeful that local government programs can and will be responsive and accountable to local communities. Many states have long histories of strong local control and are not about to relinquish control to a centralized state agency. On the other hand, not only can states rely on a much broader tax base than can local government, but state agencies can maximize statewide program consistency instead of having a few counties that operate model programs while others struggle to fund juvenile services. The lack of resources to operate appropriate and necessary programs is particularly acute in many rural areas.

The third debate on the administration of juvenile justice has to do with the location and structure of the responsible state agencies. Currently, juvenile institutions are the responsibility of state executive agencies in all fifty states (Hurst and Torbet, 1993). According to Hurst and Torbet, at the National Center for Juvenile Justice, states use one of four administrative approaches for determining who is responsible for juvenile justice (though governors and legislators frequently propose changes to these arrangements for political and other reasons): (1) the state human or social services agency (twenty-one states); (2) the corrections agency (eleven states); (3) a separate state agency for children and youth (six states); or (4) a separate juvenile justice agency (twelve states).

The untested argument for placing juvenile institutions in a broad human or social service agency is that most delinquents and their families have multiple social services needs (some already being handled by other divisions of the agency) and that a package of integrated services can best be delivered by a single, unified agency. On the other hand, it is argued that a separate department for children and youth or for juvenile justice can give priority to the needs of children and juveniles and avoid the fierce competition for limited funds with other needy client groups. The recent change in Florida, for example, where all juvenile justice functions were taken out of a large public welfare/health bureaucracy and placed in an independent department, was largely due to two factors: the perceived inability of the Department of Health and Rehabilitative

Services to competently administer delinquency programs and the public perception that the "worsening" juvenile crime problem required this rather drastic action. Even though the major change made by states in the last decade is to move away from unified adult and juvenile corrections departments, legislators have argued that correction agencies have successfully managed large prisons for years and are better prepared to manage delinquency institutions.

The administrative structures for probation and aftercare are not as simple as the ones for delinquency institutions. The most frequent arrangement for the administration of probation is through the local judiciary (sixteen states). But fourteen states have some mixed design where local and state judicial and executive agencies share responsibility. Administration of aftercare is slightly less complex, with the executive agency in thirty-seven states bearing responsibility.

Most state executive agencies, however, are decentralized to some degree and are divided into service regions or districts of different sizes with varying degrees of policy and administrative authority. If a great deal of policy and program authority is delegated to a region, it may seem that juvenile justice programs are locally administered. In addition, most states have implemented structural and operational service integration mechanisms intended to ease access to services (Ezell & Patti, 1990). In 1975, when Florida reorganized and decentralized its human services agency, for example, there was an effort to implement a single intake system for delinquent and dependent youth so that all intake workers would be able to investigate reports of child abuse and to conduct court and detention intake interviews for alleged delinquents. The intake workers, who had come from distinct professional backgrounds of juvenile justice or child welfare, resisted the change to a generalist type of caseworker, insisting that specialized skill and experience was required for the different types of cases. As have other states, Florida also worked to co-locate many of its services in order to achieve "one-stop shopping." This policy seems to have had better success than single intake did.

Each state has developed a unique formal division of labor between state agencies, local governments, and their court systems, but informal agreements, policies, practices, and funding patterns have emerged over the years to solve long-forgotten practical or political problems. In addition, the private sector plays an increasing role in juvenile justice as purchase-of-service vendors and policy advocates. Knowing only the formal structure is not enough to guarantee the success of social work administrators when they seek funding, policy changes, advocating for a client, or negotiating an interagency agreement.

Given all this complexity, it is more than reasonable to ask what administrative arrangement is most effective and efficient. While arguments abound, and the debaters offer many "facts" to support their positions, no one is able to declare one arrangement the best. Each approach has its own strengths and weaknesses. A rigorous evaluation of their effectiveness and efficiency has yet to be conducted.

Social Workers as Managers

While little or no systematic data exists, there is general consensus that social work does not have the presence it once did in the juvenile justice system. Very few courses are offered by the schools, and only a small number of social work students are assigned to field placements in juvenile justice. Only 1.3 percent of the students in masters programs in 1993 focus their studies in the area of juvenile or criminal justice (Lennon, 1994). The author's experience at the University of Washington indicates that interest tends to be greater among B.S.W. students than among M.S.W. students, but interest is low in both groups. It wasn't too long ago that the M.S.W. was the minimum education required to become a probation officer or to hold other juvenile justice jobs.

Scolding the social work profession and schools of social work for their declining interest in the juvenile court is one strategy, but "guilt-tripping" is not known to be an effective recruiting technique. In addition, many dedicated social workers are employed in juvenile justice agencies, doing important work—we should applaud them and not minimize their roles. Perhaps if we understood the reasons why these workers chose to work in juvenile justice— the intrinsic and extrinsic rewards and the nature of their jobs—we could improve our recruiting.

There is an infinite number of challenging roles for social workers at direct service, supervisory, management, or policy levels. Social workers have traditionally been employed at all these levels in agencies responsible for intake, detention, probation, residential and nonresidential programming, and after-care. Since the 1970s and the boom of alternative diversionary programs, social workers have increasingly been employed by nonprofit organizations that also work with delinquent youth—usually under contract with the state or local agency.

This discussion will focus on social work roles at the three administrative levels outlined earlier. While it is not a comprehensive listing of all the administration jobs available to social workers in juvenile justice, it is meant to give some examples of the numerous opportunities. The heuristic framework used to organize this discussion (not every cell will be discussed) is shown in figure 1. Because of size history, design, and other reasons—many of which were discussed above—real juvenile justice agencies and jobs do not fit neatly into the cells, but the framework is useful to guide our discussion. In fact, it could be made more realistic—but more complex—by including at least two more dimensions: (1) agency auspices (public, private nonprofit, or private for-profit); and (2) level of government (local, state, or federal).

Many juvenile court administrators throughout the country are professionally trained social workers. Whether accountable to a county executive or to the chief juvenile judge, they have to work very closely with the juvenile court

**Figure 1.1:   Framework for Discussion of Social Work Administration
                in Juvenile Justice**

| | Level of Administration | | |
Juvenile Justice Function	Supervisory	Program Management	Executive
Court administration			
Probation			
Detention			
Intake			
Prevention			
Diversion			
Defense			
Residential dispositions			
Nonresidential dispositions			
Law enforcement			

judges. They are usually responsible for probation and detention, which commonly have their own directors, thus putting the court administrator at the executive level. In large urban areas, the juvenile court administrator could have a staff in the hundreds and a total budget of several million dollars. Staff members can be very important actors in the policy arena and have the opportunity to encourage a great deal of innovative programming. Social workers at the supervisory level are likely to work directly with those doing court intake to ensure that court policies and procedures are followed and to assist or consult on particularly difficult cases. Intake workers may testify in court, and since their reports are part of the court record, it is important that they be accurate, fair, and comprehensive.

Chief probation officer is another executive level position occupied by some, but available to even more, social workers. Probation officers/counselors conduct intake interviews, do family studies to prepare predisposition reports, make disposition/sentencing recommendations, and supervise youth placed on probation. In addition, probation departments frequently design and implement innovative programs for youth and their families when they recognize a shortcoming in the existing array of programs and services. Probation departments also can be quite large, with complex staffing patterns and sizable budgets. There are countless opportunities for social workers to exert leadership at all levels of probation departments.

The executive level roles in detention centers are usually referred to as superintendent, deputy superintendent, or assistant superintendent. "Detention" mainly refers to facilities used for holding youth awaiting trial, disposition, or post-disposition placement. In addition, some detention centers incarcerate youth as part of their sentence. These are complex jobs that require advanced management and organizational skills. Operating a secure facility, which may hold upwards of two-hundred-fifty youth or as few as twenty, involves food service, educational programs, recreation, laundry, transportation, and health and mental health services, to name just a few. Arranging visitations by attorneys, families, and friends are a challenge by themselves. Each of these services may have a director and numerous staff, not to mention the staff who supervise the youth day and night. Most funders and policymakers grossly underestimate the skills, knowledge, and experience necessary to keep such a facility operating smoothly and ensure safety for both the staff and juveniles.

In addition to the detention facility itself, many communities operate a variety of detention alternative programs, all of them with staff who need supervision and programmatic oversight. These alternative programs range from nonsecure detention (e.g., small group homes with high staff-to-youth ratios), day reporting centers, electronic monitoring programs, and home detention (youths are placed in their homes with different types of monitoring). All the alternatives have to be well-coordinated with the secure facility and must ensure that youths appear for their hearings and remain crime-free while awaiting their appearances.

Prevention and diversion programs are frequently operated by community agencies in conjunction with the juvenile court. There are numerous types of delinquency prevention programs in which social workers could serve in administrative roles: community mobilization programs; school related programs; substance abuse programs; social services for children and families; or family mediation services, for example.

There are too many types of diversion programs to fully describe here (see Ezell, 1992, pp. 48–49). but they can be operated by nonprofits, probation, court administration, the prosecutor, or the court itself—and all of them need directors, middle managers, and supervisors. When diversion started to become popular in the 1970s, diverted youth were typically referred to youth service bureaus (which had and still need social workers in administrative positions) where their needs were assessed and the youth then referred to counseling, recreation, tutoring, or other types of service programs in the community. If the needed services were unavailable, the youth service bureau would either provide them or work to have another agency offer them. In recent years, however, it has been much more common for diversion programs to be retributive, such as in restitution and community service programs. One of the most difficult challenges for a social worker in a diversion program is to define and identify a target group of youth without widening the net of the juvenile court and possibly labeling undeserving youths as deviants.

It is becoming common for public defender offices to employ social workers who prepare dispositional studies, make recommendations, and generally help in getting the youth the most appropriate services and/or placement. These social work units are usually small but still require a great deal of planning, staffing, training, coordinating, and supervision. Facilitating the delivery of services to these youths, many of whom have been bounced around from one agency to another and failed by the system, is incredibly rewarding. Families of these youths are frustrated, want help, but do not know where to turn.

Managing a residential facility for delinquents, whether a relatively small group home, a medium-sized halfway house, or a large institution, is somewhat similar to managing a detention facility. The level of security can range from open, where youth can come and go in accordance with program rules; staff secure, where the staffing ratio prevents youth from leaving; semisecure, where doors and windows may be locked at night, for example; to highly secure with lockdown capabilities, video monitoring, and a fenced perimeter with razor wire. Besides such maintenance services as transportation, feeding, and supervision, residential facilities operate individual and group counseling, substance abuse, educational, and vocational programs. Once again, social workers can serve as supervisors of direct service staff, program managers, and directors.

Besides some of the traditional jobs held by social workers in the juvenile justice system, there are many others in which social workers can perform administrative tasks. First, although rarely discussed in the literature, some social workers get law degrees and therefore prepare to become juvenile judges, prosecutors, or defense attorneys. Whenever there are several juvenile judges, public defenders, or prosecutors, one or more of them serves as the administrative leader with the full complement of managerial duties (probably in addition to carrying a case load).

Second, we are witnessing growing interest by states and communities in removing categorical barriers to service delivery and promoting "blended" or "wraparound" services, especially to multiproblem youth. Many of these service integration pilot programs have targeted delinquent youth and their families. Social workers are an excellent choice as case coordinators or managers. These types of programs require social workers with many skills: planning, coordination, needs assessment, case management, advocacy, budgeting, and so on. Social work managers must have intimate knowledge of the local service system, funding sources and policies, and eligibility requirements.

Third, many delinquent youths have problems with drugs and alcohol, health and mental health issues, learning deficits, as well as developmental challenges. If more social workers were involved in designing and administering high-quality services to address these needs, either within or adjacent to existing juvenile justice programs, the juvenile justice system would function better and the youth would be much more likely to stay out of trouble.

Finally, not many would deny that the juvenile justice system continues to have structural flaws, policy inadequacies, and operational problems. These deficiencies create a great need for social workers to do advocacy work, from inside or outside of the system, at the case or class level (Ezell, 1994). The voices for progressive change in juvenile justice are too often drowned out by special interests and fearmongers. There are excellent models of advocacy organizations at the national level (e.g., Children's Defense Fund), state level (e.g., Kentucky Youth Advocates), or local level (see Coates, 1989). Social workers have played key roles in starting and managing these organizations, and more such workers are needed if there is going to be any balance in the public policy debates about youth crime and what to do about it.

Other Macro Roles for Social Workers

Before concluding this chapter with a brief description of a few of the challenges facing social work administrators in the next decade, brief attention should be given to other nondirect service jobs in juvenile justice. Many readers might consider these administrative in nature, and to some degree they are right. Most of the time they do not involve any supervision, however. Job titles and actual functions frequently bear no resemblance to one another, so it might be difficult to identify some of the following jobs by name or description. Also, a planner in one agency, for instance, might have totally different duties than a planner in another agency.

Many agencies employ professional planners whose jobs involve program planning and development, needs assessment, grant writing, and the writing of rules and regulations. Sometimes planners develop Requests for Proposals (RFPs) and play a role negotiating service contracts. The job of a "policy analyst" can be considered somewhat similar or overlapping. State agencies sometimes use this job title, as do governors' offices, and policy analysts devote a good deal of their time preparing and analyzing legislation.

In addition to these two roles, social workers have filled important jobs in the budget offices of state and local agencies. As commonly acknowledged, the budget is the key policy document for a jurisdiction. Planning, evaluating, monitoring, negotiating, and other management skills are important to social workers in these roles. The author has worked with budget staff as well as many other social workers who are on staff with the legislative committees responsible for juvenile justice legislation and appropriations. They analyze and draft legislative proposals, monitor the implementation of laws passed by their committee, educate legislators on the operation of the juvenile justice system, and conduct studies on issues of interest to their committee.

There are two final macro roles for social workers in juvenile justice that will be mentioned here. Many juvenile justice agencies used to have evaluation staffs, and some still do, but it is more likely that they contract for this service. In fact, the author began his juvenile justice career as a "planner-evaluator" for a state juvenile justice agency. Social workers who conduct evaluations are generally trying to determine how well a program works, how much it costs, and whether it is reaching the most appropriate youth. Not only must they be competent researchers, but they must be skilled and diplomatic report writers and they must understand the program they are studying so they can develop practical, implementable recommendations. Finally, there are opportunities for social workers as designers and managers of computerized management and client information systems. Well-designed systems can help to track youth as they make their way through the system, can help direct service staff with case management and report writing, can facilitate coordination when multiple programs are working with the same youth, and can provide management with information useful for monitoring the operation of their program and assuring the quality of its services.

None of these jobs are reserved for social workers. Many of them required an M.S.W. at one time but have since been declassified so that other degrees are sufficient. None of these jobs, however, are beyond the reach of a properly trained, competent social worker. At any given moment, the social worker in any of these jobs might find them exciting or mundane, in the middle of the action or tangential. Notwithstanding these ebbs and flows, the jobs are always important and central to the goals of the social work profession.

Challenges for Juvenile Justice Administrators

We are seeing large increases in media coverage of youth crime and violent crime in particular. In addition, state and local government budgets are increasingly tight. These are just two of the factors that will make the next decade very challenging for juvenile justice administrators. Programming in the context of increasingly punitive policies and shrinking budgets will be demanding and will require creative fund raising, staffing, and marketing skills.

Recruiting and retaining qualified staff is another challenge. "Of all the human services, juvenile justice agencies, when it comes to personnel, are one of the least regulated. Standards for training and qualifications, certifications, licensures, and the other accoutrements reasonably expected as part of a profession are virtually nonexistent" (Glick, 1986, p. 230). Budget pressures force managers to hire less educated and experienced workers, and then, largely because of low salaries, turnover is a constant problem. In turn, program continuity and quality suffer, which increases the difficulty of demonstrating effectiveness, one of the best ways to attract grants.

Finally, in order to cut overhead costs, especially since privatization of government seems to be gaining steam, juvenile justice managers will be challenged by the increasing number of purchase-of-service contracts. It is important to design fair bidding procedures that allow smaller, and especially minority, agencies to compete with larger ones. Administrative controls, both fiscal and programmatic, become more challenging when dealing with contracted vendors. Coordinating all the subcontractors so that an effective continuum of services exists for delinquent youth requires managers to be creative, planful, and energetic.

Conclusion

This chapter has described the administrative context of juvenile justice and the numerous administrative roles social workers can occupy. Several issues that will challenge managers in the next decade were also outlined. The author's biases about the extreme urgency for social workers to provide leadership to juvenile justice by performing these jobs are thinly veiled. The predictions of catastrophe in the juvenile justice system may not come to fruition, but the conditions of the system and its policy environment continue to decay. Based on plummeting public trust, as well as calls for the system's abolishment by many, it seems to be approaching an imminent crisis. One has only to look at the dramatic increase in the waiver of juveniles to the adult system during the past decade to understand just how close this crisis may be. It is time for the profession to redouble its efforts in defending the interests of those youths caught up in the juvenile justice system.

References

Coates, R. B. (1989). Social work advocacy in juvenile justice: Conceptual underpinnings and practice. In A. R. Roberts (Ed.), *Juvenile justice policies, programs, and services* (pp. 245–277). Chicago: Dorsey.

Ezell, M. (1992). Juvenile diversion: The ongoing search for alternatives. In I. M. Schwartz (Ed.), *Juvenile justice and public policy: Toward a national agenda* (pp. 45–58). New York: Lexington Books.

Ezell, M. (1994). The advocacy practice of social workers. *Families in Society* (Jan.), 36–46.

Ezell, M., & Patti, R. J. (1990). State human service agencies: Structure and organization. *Social Service Review,* 64(1), 22–45.

Feld, B. F. (1993). *Justice for children: The right to counsel and the juvenile court.* Boston: Northeastern University Press.

Glick, B. (1986). Programming for juvenile delinquents: An administrative perspective. In S. J. Apter & A. P. Goldstein (Eds.), *Youth violence: Programs and prospects* (pp. 219–236). New York: Pergamon Press.

Hurst, H., & Torbet, P. M. (1993). *Organization and administration of juvenile services: Probation, aftercare, and state institutions for delinquent youth* (Rev. ed). Pittsburgh, PA: National Center for Juvenile Justice.

Lennon, T. M. (1994). *Statistics on social work evaluation in the United States: 1993.* Alexandria, VA: Council on Social Work Education.

Patti, R. J. (1977). Patterns of management activity in social welfare agencies. *Administration in Social Work, 1*(1), 5–18.

Patti, R. J. (1983). *Social welfare administration: Managing social programs in a developmental context.* Englewood Cliffs, NJ: Prentice Hall.

Pettibone, J. M., Swisher, R. G., Weiland, K. H., Wolf, C. E., & White, J. L. (1981). *Major issues in juvenile justice information and training: Services to children in juvenile courts: The judicial-executive controversy.* Columbus, OH: Academy for Contemporary Problems.

Rubin, H. T. (1991). Child and family legal proceedings: Court structure, statutes, and rules. In M. Hofford (Ed.), *Families in court.* Reno, NV: National Council of Juvenile and Family Court Judges.

Young, T. M. (1981). Locating administrative responsibility for juvenile court services: A framework to guide decisionmaking. In J. C. Hall, D. M. Hamparian, J. M. Pettibone, & J. L. White (Eds.), *Major issues in juvenile justice information and training: Readings in public policy.* Columbus, OH: Academy for Contemporary Problems.

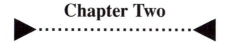

Chapter Two

Juvenile Corrections: Its Implications for Social Work Practice

Diane C. Dwyer

The escalation of violent crime committed by juveniles alarms individuals, communities, and policymakers. A recent national tracking survey (O'Hare, 1994) notes that the arrest rate for juveniles suspected of committing serious violent crimes (homicide, forcible rape, robbery, or aggravated assault) has increased from 305 per 100,000 in 1985 to 457 per 100,000 in 1991 (p. 14). While this measure reflects the criminal activity of a relatively small number of young people—less than 0.5 percent according to Kids Count (O'Hare, 1994, p. 15)—it has become the centerpiece of the public call to reexamine the juvenile justice system in general and juvenile correctional programs in particular. What follows is an explication of the institutional juvenile correctional programs and the implications for social work practice in this setting.

Overview of Juvenile Corrections

Brought about through the efforts of the Society for the Prevention of Pauperism, early examples of institutions for the care and reformation of juveniles were the Houses of Refuge in New York and Massachusetts. Social work philosophy and practice are inextricably tied to the development of juvenile corrections through the efforts of Jane Addams in the establishment and operation of Hull House in Chicago during the late nineteenth century. Acts of juvenile delinquency were seen as symptomatic of broader social problems; that is, poverty, alienation, and intervention were targeted at both the individual and the environment. Notably, in 1880 the U.S. Bureau of the Census conducted the first count of juvenile offenders in public institutions and found they numbered slightly over 11,000. By 1989 this figure had grown to over 54,000 (U.S. Department of Justice, 1993), reflecting a 500 percent increase in just over a century.

Juvenile correctional programs fall into two main categories, which are determined by the level of security (secure or nonsecure) and the sanctioning auspices (public or private). Such characteristics directly impact upon the unique nature of each individual program and consequently alter its goals, policies, efficiency, and effectiveness.

Secure facilities typically consist of detention centers and training schools. Detention centers are temporary holding institutions for delinquent youth prior to and after (while awaiting transfer) adjudication. Such youth are "detained" because their offense is so serious that they pose a threat to the community or their home situation is such that they cannot remain at home. By virtue of their temporary nature and their emphasis on security, treatment is seldom the focus of these programs. Training schools concentrate on security and control as well. They are institutions providing custodial care for those youths sentenced to serve a period of time for their criminal activity. Since the training school placement is more permanent, reforming the delinquent offender becomes a secondary effort. (This goal would be difficult at best given the nature, staffing, and security needs of most such institutions.)

Nonsecure facilities are composed of foster homes, shelters, group homes, and camps or ranches. Neglected children and nonserious delinquents are often placed in a homelike environment with surrogate parents. Here, they presumably receive greater nurturing and closer supervision, thus enhancing their propensity to avoid further delinquent behavior. Shelters provide temporary housing and supervision for children who cannot reside at home while they await more permanent placement. Because the population is transitory, usually there is little emphasis on either punishment or treatment in such settings. Group homes are residential treatment facilities for delinquent youth who reside with houseparents or staff counselors in a group-living milieu. Similarly, camps or ranches are facilities for those individuals requiring out-of-home placement. They stress discipline and personal responsibility, often involving outdoor survival skills and intergroup dependency. As such, they serve as an alternative to the more conventional reform school.

Recent statistics gathered by the U.S. Dept. of Justice (1993) indicate that public juvenile facilities—those operated by state and local governmental bodies and staffed by government employees—number approximately 1,100 nationally. Sixty-two percent of these are secure facilities, with 38 percent being nonsecure. Operating expenditures amount to $1.67 billion for an average daily population of 54,351 youths. The preponderance of these youths (82 percent) are male, and 69 percent have been placed following adjudication. The offense committed was most often a serious property crime (29 percent) or a violent crime (27 percent). Other property crimes and drug and alcohol crimes accounted for an additional 26 percent of confinements. In terms of race, the breakdown is as follows: 40 percent caucasian, 42 percent African American, 16 percent Hispanic, 1 percent Native American, and 1 percent Asian American (U.S. Justice Department, 1993, p. 579).

Juvenile facilities under the direct operational and administrative control of private enterprise can be run by either profit-making or nonprofit organizations. They are subject to governmental licensing and can receive substantial public funding in addition to their private financing. These institutions, numbering 2,032, were similarly surveyed by the U.S. Department of Justice (1993). Private facilities (including detention centers, shelters, reception centers, training schools, ranches or camps, and halfway houses) housed 36,190 youth in 1991. These youths were 71 percent male, 57 percent caucasian, 32 percent African American, and 9 percent Hispanic. Generally they were between the ages of thirteen and seventeen (86 percent), with only 7 percent being less than ten or over eighteen years of age (p. 579).

Unlike public institutions, private facilities provide services for both criminally and noncriminally involved youth. Forty-five percent of the youth served by these private facilities are nonoffenders or voluntary placements. Another 15 percent, while placed by the courts, have been detained for status offenses. Status offenders are those youth determined by the court to need supervision. Their offenses may including running away, being chronically truant, or being generally incorrigible. (Several states have been accused of using private institutions as a way of circumventing federal legislation mandating the deinstitutionalization of status offenders.) The remaining 40 percent are in custody for delinquency offenses ranging from murder to disturbing the peace (U.S. Dept. of Justice, 1993, p. 579).

The number of private-sector juvenile correctional programs is increasing at a faster rate than is their public-sector counterparts (Bartollas, 1993). A greater percentage of white youth, adolescent females, status offenders, and dependent and neglected youth are confined in private facilities. Additionally, these private residents tend to be younger and stay longer than those in public facilities—279 days versus 183 (Bartollas, 1993). While these programs make certain claims about their effectiveness and cost-efficiency, few studies have examined their accuracy. Shichor and Bartollas (1990) examined placements of juveniles in private and public facilities in a large southern California area. They found that although youth in private facilities had slightly more personal problems, and those in public institutions appeared somewhat more delinquent, the two groups did not vary significantly. Still, privatization, the operation and management of a correctional facility or agency by private enterprise, sometimes for a profit, is believed to be a solution to the deterioration and overcrowding common to public facilities. Over the past decade, Florida officials have shifted their confinement priorities to the development of private-sector, community-based facilities (Pingree, 1984).

Given the high costs of juvenile incarceration—approximately $31,000 per person per year (U.S. Dept. of Justice, 1993)—the debate about its efficacy continues. The actual cost of confining a juvenile in New York or California is almost three times greater than the national average. Proponents (Lucart, 1983; Rutherford, 1986) argue that confinement interrupts the delinquent activity by removing the youth from unfavorable associations, at least temporarily. This respite allows for change in the individual or in the environment. Confinement is a logical result of the philosophy that delinquents "deserve" punishment for their actions. This "just-deserts" model fits well with the contemporary "get tough on crime" philosophy, reflecting a disconcerting shift in the underlying assumptions of the juvenile justice system (Dwyer and McNally, 1989). Those who oppose the incarceration of juveniles cite the deleterious effects of labeling. However, Champion (1992) argues that even if these youth were not incarcerated they still would know they were delinquents, and hence try to "live up to" this self-image. According to some studies (Greenwood, 1986), the ages of sixteen to twenty are the peak years for juvenile criminality; hence, incarceration during these years might reduce the delinquency rate. However, one must ask if such a strategy is affordable, even if desirable.

Clearly, any examination of the effectiveness of incarcerating juveniles must consider the age-old problem: What are the goals of juvenile correctional institutions? Various goals, including deterrence, rehabilitation, incapacitation, punishment, and prevention, have been articulated. Troubled by the ever-increasing rates of juvenile crime, the public's primary goal for juvenile corrections is the reduction of delinquent behavior. As evidenced by high rates of recidivism, incarceration has very little, if anything, to do with reducing delinquency. It could be argued that confining the juvenile interrupts his or her criminality. However, this argument is tempered by the fact that the average length of confinement for juveniles in custody is less than ten months (U.S. Dept. of Justice, 1993, p. 585). Therefore, if the protection of society is the espoused goal, simple incapacitation is not working.

There is a strong belief in some quarters that rehabilitation, as rooted in the history of the juvenile justice system, must be the primary goal of juvenile corrections. In his classic research, Martinson (1974) claimed that no program has been 100 percent effective in deterring juveniles from committing delinquent acts or recidivating. His work became the hallmark for the "get tough" policies of the recent past and the discounting of rehabilitation as a reasonable goal of juvenile corrections. Accordingly, punishment and incapacitation have evolved by default as the dominant objectives of juvenile incarceration.

Unquestionably, the security of the community is a legitimate goal, and one that can be met within the parameters of the juvenile corrections system. However, in order to accomplish this, the goal of the correctional program must be to generate behavioral change on the part of the delinquent youth. Confinement, then, becomes a part of the process of behavioral change, not a sufficient end in itself but a necessary ingredient in the total picture. Programmatic design and implementation and the concomitant practice interventions required to achieve this behavioral change are the specific concerns of social work practitioners involved in juvenile corrections.

Social Work Practice in Juvenile Corrections

Social work knowledge, values, and skills contribute a unique perspective to the field of juvenile corrections. Rooted in the past, as demonstrated in the early role of Jane Addams and the child-savers (McNally, 1982) and continuing in the present (Coates, 1989), social work has a theoretical base and a practice history of intervening with children who require confinement. Understanding and building this base is the responsibility of contemporary practitioners. The following discussion considers the state of the art of social work theory and practice and specifically apply it to juvenile corrections.

Zastrow and Kirst-Ashman (1994) have constructed a paradigm, the Systems Impact Model (SIM), which is particularly useful in conceptualizing the juvenile corrections system. They state:

> Social work goes far beyond counseling individual clients at the micro level or working with small groups at the mezzo level. Rather, SIM emphasizes how social workers must often work within the institutional and organizational structure on their clients' behalf. (p. 25)

Often the target must be to change or improve how services are delivered or resources are distributed (p. 25). Predicated upon social systems theory, the SIM (see figure 2.1) illustrates how social workers must consider not only their clients' concerns but also those of other major systems involved in the clients' situation. Consequently, the problem-solving process entails intervention on the micro (individual), mezzo (small group), and macro (large group) level.

In the field of juvenile corrections, the client system reflects the juvenile and his or her family engaged in a direct relationship with the worker system. A worker employs micro and mezzo intervention strategies in attempting to facilitate behavioral change in the client system. Hence, the direct line between the two systems. Moreover, as this model depicts, the client and worker are not operating in a vacuum. Both the client and worker systems are signif-

Figure 2.1

icantly influenced by the organizational and community context in which they function.

The organizational system encompasses not only the institutional correctional program but also the entire juvenile justice system. The ramifications of the arrest and adjudication process, according to this model, influence the client, the worker, and the interaction between the two. Similarly, agency policies and procedures impact the client-worker relationship. It is important to consider many aspects of the organizational system in assessing the outcome of the client-worker relationship. Among these are goal clarity, program design, and adequacy of resources. These aspects are especially relevant to the field of juvenile corrections. The mission of the correctional effort has not been clearly articulated, that is, should it be incarceration or treatment? The jury is out on which program design is most effective in altering the behavior of juvenile offenders. The costs of incarcerating juveniles are escalating, as is their number, and the subsequent strain on federal, state, or municipal budgets is problematic. Thus, rather than fostering success in the worker-client interaction, the organizational system may impede it.

Similarly, the community system has repercussions on the client and worker systems. Communities offer individuals necessary economic and social support. Clients in the juvenile correctional system come from and will return to communities. As such, practitioners must be concerned with the availability of educational, recreational, and employment resources as both preventative and prescriptive intervention tools. On a larger scope, poverty, unemployment, violence, drug abuse, and similar social problems facing communities can affect the implicit and explicit work transpiring between the worker and client systems.

The relationship between the organizational and community systems is also depicted by the Systems Impact Model, as these two macro systems interact with and affect each other. An example of this relationship might be the efforts of a training school's director to have community leaders on her advisory board. The presence of these leaders in the organizational structure might expand the acceptance of the institution in the community. Additionally, avenues for fund-raising, volunteering, advocacy, and crisis management are opened by such a connection. Ideally, these community advisors would represent a cross-section of local interests and be knowledgeable about juvenile corrections, affording the director a viable and constructive sounding board.

Institutional values, those strong societal beliefs about how things should be, comprise the final element in this construct. While these values are frequently in a state of flux at any particular time, they markedly influence the organizational and community systems and subsequently, the client-worker relationship. The contemporary institutional values that most directly influence juvenile corrections include the following:

- Society's need for protection and its belief that rehabilitation doesn't work, hence the "get-tough" policies and the tendency of juvenile programs to more closely model adult corrections (e.g., boot camps).
- Society's need for retribution, hence the need for punishment when norms are violated.
- Society's belief that ultimately the individual is responsible for his or her own behavior, hence the allocation of resources to intervene with the individual juvenile rather than a more macro intervention into the conditions that contributed to the transgressions.

This paradigm is particularly useful in bridging the gap between theory and practice, and it provides a framework for organizing our understanding of the total situation facing the client. In this way, it links systems theory to assessment and to the practice skills necessary in the intervention, be they micro, mezzo, or macro. Social workers assume roles in the helping process based on an agency's function and purpose, the demands of the client situation, and their own philosophy of change. These roles are: conferee, enabler, broker, advocate, mediator, and guardian (Parsons, Jorgensen & Hernandez, 1994).

Regardless of the setting, practitioners in juvenile institutions use these roles on a selective basis in their work with clients. The conferee role, wherein the worker uses the problem-solving process to assist the client, could be exemplified by the worker counseling a youth who has just returned from a runaway attempt. The modeling efforts of the institutional child care worker and her attempts to structure an environment that facilitates change in the delinquent resident would constitute the enabler role. The caseworker who assumed the broker role might collaborate with a substance abuse program to obtain services for an addicted parent of a detained youth. Advocacy, when the worker attempts to secure services or change policies on behalf of a client, could involve petitioning the juvenile court for the early release of a youth in placement. Mediating—assisting in conflict resolution—is a frequently adopted role of the worker who is providing family treatment or dealing with intracottage tension in a residential setting. The role of guardian requires exercising social control over a situation when clients are unable to do this themselves. While the judicious use of this role is within the purview of social work intervention, its misuse poses ethical conflicts. Given the control emphasis of juvenile corrections, the guardian role is frequently exercised and sometimes abused. Too often, in yielding to the institution's control needs, the guardian role supplants the other roles, again emphasizing the competing goals of treatment and punishment.

Social work practice in any setting is guided not only by theory but also by a set of beliefs that define the profession. As articulated in the Code of Ethics of the National Association of Social Workers, these beliefs revolve around notions of the worth and dignity of the individual and social responsibility. Johnson (1994, p. 55) delineates six action principles that flow from these ideas:

1. People should be free to make choices.
2. Individuals are important; individual needs and concerns cannot be totally subjected to community needs.
3. Workers should use a nonjudgmental approach to persons and their concerns, needs, and problems.
4. The social work role is helping or enabling, not controlling.
5. Feelings and personal relationships are important.
6. People have a responsibility for others; for their needs and concerns.

Incorporating these principles into juvenile correctional practice can be difficult. First, many facilities employ a multidisciplinary team approach, so the worker may have colleagues who do not share this value orientation. Second, the need to control behavior, deeply embedded in the nature of corrections, mitigates against fostering client self-determination. This tension, whether direct or more subtle in its ramifications, is sure to impact on the worker. Third, it is a near-Herculean feat for a worker to be nonjudgmental in a system whose policies and practices frequently connote just the opposite. Finally, these six action principles are predicated on a presumption of client maturity. Implied in the juvenile justice system is the notion of diminished responsibility, which easily translates to a paternalistic approach. The social worker must strive to implement these values without the explicit sanction and support of the system. In fact, the opposite is frequently true.

Conclusion

In the near future, juvenile corrections can expect an infusion of funds. The 1994 crime bill, recently signed into law by President Bill Clinton, allocated $150 million for a new grant program to fund alternatives to traditional forms of incarceration and probation for juveniles (*Criminal Justice Newsletter,* 1994, p. 3). Congress also approved $144 million, 35 percent increase over fiscal year 1993, for programs administered by the Juvenile Justice and Delinquency Prevention Act (*Criminal Justice Newsletter,* 1994, p. 6). How these funds are spent and their impact on the problem of juvenile crime in the United States is yet to be determined. No doubt the heated debate regarding treatment or punishment will linger.

Social work theory, pertaining to knowledge, values, and skills, distinctly points to the efficacy of treatment. Despite their current disfavor among policymakers and politicians, behavioral change approaches predicated on sound social work theory offer some hope in addressing the serious social problem of juvenile crime. Perhaps it will take time to demonstrate the efficacy of such a strategy quantitatively and qualitatively, but the status quo is clearly not working.

It is incumbent on practitioners in the field to adopt an aggressive position regarding the value of social work theory in prescribing a solution to the current plight of juvenile corrections. Sophisticated advocacy for the cause of juvenile offenders is necessary. In the current conservative political climate, persistence is warranted as well. Campaigns must be waged for change at the organizational, local, state, and federal level for a more holistic solution to juvenile crime. The road to such change is fraught with pitfalls, but the alternative is worse.

References

Bartollas, C. (1993). *Juvenile delinquency.* New York: Macmillan.

Champion, D. J. (1992). *The juvenile justice system.* New York: Macmillan.

Coates, R. B. (1989). Social work advocacy in juvenile justice: Conceptual underpinnings and practice. In A. R. Roberts (Ed.), *Juvenile justice: Policies, programs, and services* (pp. 246–277). Chicago: Dorsey Press.

Criminal Justice Newsletter. (1994). Washington report, 25, 2-7.

Dwyer, D. & McNally, R. (1989). Juvenile justice: Reform, retrain and reaffirm. In A. R. Roberts (Ed.), *Juvenile justice: Policies, programs, and services* (pp. 319–327). Chicago: Dorsey Press.

Greenwood, P. W. (1986). *Intervention strategies for chronic juvenile offenders: Some new perspectives.* New York: Greenwood Press.

Johnson, L. C. (1994). *Social work practice: A generalist approach.* Boston, MA: Allyn and Bacon.

Lucart, A. (1983). *Juvenile detention: An inquiry into its personal dimensions.* Ann Arbor, MI: University Microfilms International.

Martinson, R. (1974). What works? Questions and answers about prison reform. *The Public Interest, 35,* 22–54.

McNally, R. B. (1982). Nearly a century later: The child-savers, child advocates and the juvenile justice system. *Juvenile and Family Court Journal, 33* (3), 47–52.

O'Hare, W. (Ed). (1994). *Kids count data book.* Baltimore, MD: Annie E. Casey Foundation.

Parsons, R., Jorgensen, J., & Hernandez, S. (1994). *The integration of social work practice.* Pacific Grove, CA: Brooks/Cole.

Pingree, D. H. (1984). Florida youth services. *Corrections Today, 46,* 60–62.

Rutherford, A. (1986). *Growing out of crime.* New York: Penguin.

Shichor, D. & Bartollas, C. (1990). Private and public juvenile placements. Is there a difference? *Crime and Delinquency, 36* (12), 286–299.

U.S. Dept. of Justice. (1993). *Bureau of Justice Statistics sourcebook of criminal justice statistics.* Washington, DC: U.S. Government Printing Office.

Zastrow, C. & Kirst-Ashman, K. K. (1994). *Human behavior and the social environment.* Chicago: Nelson-Hall.

Chapter Three

▶ ·························· ◀

Aftercare: The Neglected Phase of the Juvenile Justice Process

José B. Ashford

In 1978, Gresham Sykes referred to the prison riot at Attica as "a symbol for the end of an era in correctional philosophy" (1978, p. 476). In his opinion, the era of rehabilitation as a key correctional aim was in decline. This viewpoint was shared by others (Cullen & Gilbert, 1982) who were also concerned about the growing crisis in liberal correctional policy. Are there also symbols in our society's recent history that mark an end to the welfare and rehabilitative ideals in the field of juvenile corrections?

In my opinion, the 1980s ushered in a dramatic transformation in our society's view of youth crime. In this period, the serious juvenile offender captured the public's consciousness and triggered significant reforms in juvenile justice policy. "The violent few" took center stage and became the target of most of the policy initiatives. Policymakers engaged in efforts to protect society from serious juvenile offenders. Juvenile delinquents were no longer seen as victims of society who required treatment instead of punishment. This shift toward a punitive posture with respect to youth crime has triggered fundamental questions about the legitimacy of prior justifications for treating juveniles outside of the criminal justice system (Feld, 1993; Hirschi & Gottfredson, 1993). Scholars are evaluating many taken-for-granted assumptions about our juvenile justice system. These policy debates have significant implications for the aftercare component of the juvenile corrections process. In this chapter, I will examine the evolution of policy in juvenile aftercare and how these policy developments have impacted on the role played by social workers in the after-care process.

Aftercare in the Light of History

In the 1800s, reformers in the United States desired to protect children from lives of crime and poverty. Community leaders were concerned about the growing numbers of children who lacked proper parental supervision. In the urban east, the numbers of unsupervised and undisciplined children increased dramatically. In cities like New York, Boston, and Philadelphia, many youths were at risk of becoming criminals or paupers (Clement, 1993). In response to this situation, community leaders decided to create socialization institutions that would provide youths with asylum from their negative environments.

During this period, it was assumed that parents had the duty of molding and controlling their children. Young people were considered highly vulnerable to negative social environments. They required constant observation and supervision. For this reason, reformers assumed that children could be saved from lives of immorality and crime if they were provided protective environments that offered proper dosages of discipline and spiritual guidance (Olson-Raymer, 1993).

At the conclusion of the eighteenth century, children had been recognized in law as being "entitled only to protection and control by adults" (Olson-Raymer, 1993). In many circumstances, children were denied these fundamental rights. Many recent immigrants to the United States were unable to provide proper supervision for their children. Many families were without support systems and many children were without fathers. Some parents died en route to this country or took sick on their arrival, leaving many children without proper care and control.

In the early eighteenth century, most youths were placed in an apprenticeship when they were between eight and ten years of age. This social institution began to decline around the end of the eighteenth century (Clement, 1993), which contributed to a fundamental breakdown in traditional methods of social control. The family and apprenticeships were not providing youths with needed supervision (Clement, 1993). Further, few of these youths attended school. Most had inordinate amounts of time on their hands, which resulted in increased involvement in nuisance activities. They spent their time on the streets, where they often engaged in petty crimes. After being arrested for these crimes, they were processed in the criminal courts and placed in prisons with adults. This treatment of youthful offenders concerned many reformers. The reformers were distressed in particular by the effects prisons had on the youths' socialization, believing that prisons only offered these wayward and delinquent youths education in further criminality.

After visiting juvenile reformatories in England, John Griscom, of the Society for the Prevention of Pauperism, convinced members of a newly formed branch of this organization (the Society for the Reformation of Juvenile Delinquents) to establish the New York House of Refuge (NYHR) in 1825 (Clement, 1993). The NYHR is recognized as the first reformatory for juveniles in the United States (Dressler, 1959). Joseph Curtis was its first superintendent. In his first annual report, Superintendent Joseph Curtis indicated that the mission of this facility was one of "withdrawing young offenders from the vortex of corrupt association for enlightening their minds, changing their habits and inclinations, and restoring them to society prepared to increase the amount of industry, morals, virtue" (Pisciotta, 1993, p. 536).

The average stay for youths in the NYHR was from one to three years (Clement, 1993). While incarcerated they were taught a trade by working on projects directed by outside contractors. The youths were also provided with two hours of academic training each day (Pisciotta, 1993). The final or critical phase of the reformation process was "indenture." "Boys and girls were indentured after they had exhibited order, discipline and self control, and demonstrated some promise of assuming their proper role in the social order." (Pisciotta, 1993, p. 537). Pisciotta (1993) considers the indenture phase of this reformation process the historical precursor of current juvenile aftercare.

Pisciotta clearly describes the functions of indenture. The following description is based on his historical analysis of records from the NYHR. He states:

> Indenture would serve, in theory, a number of positive functions. Most basically, it would provide post release supervision. Indenture to respectable families would provide solid role models and reliable supervision. As importantly, children would learn a trade under the guidance of a master. A good placement would also isolate the child from the temptations of improper associations including, in some cases, unfit parents. Extended periods of indenture (to the age of twenty-one for boys and eighteen for girls) would assure proper guidance throughout the indenturee's formative years. (Pisciotta, 1993, p. 537)

This process of indenture remained intact until its economic viability was challenged at the end of the nineteenth century.

An important component of the indenture process was its handling of a youth's stay at the reformatory. The assessment of a youth's readiness for release was typically overseen by the indenture committee. This committee had many of the same responsibilities that aftercare professionals in current social work practice have (Dressler, 1959). Members of the committee were responsible for determining a youth's readiness for release and for matching the youth with an appropriate release situation. Youths were committed to reformatories for indeterminate periods. Unlike today, few youths were released from these facilities to the care and custody of their parents (Pisciotta, 1993); most were released to an indentured situation. These arrangements involved a contract that specified the duties of both the master and the released youth.

The indenture committee did not begin using visiting agents to check on the success of a youth's placement until around 1863 (Dressler, 1959). This is when the NYHR hired its first visiting agent, who was expected to supervise all youths on release status. Visiting agents also "protected children from abuse and exploitation and society from children who were misbehaving by revoking their placement and returning them to the NYHR" (Pisciotta, 1993, p. 541). The practice of indenture in juvenile reform schools did not decline until the late 1800s. This approach to handling delinquent and incorrigible youth terminated when indenture was no longer considered economically viable.

Aftercare and Its Relationship to Parole

Although indenture disappeared, many of its functions continued in juvenile aftercare. In Pisciotta's (1993) opinion, the beginning of aftercare or juvenile parole is impossible to pinpoint with any degree of accuracy. He states:

> The "discovery" of parole during the progressive era was, in fact, a function of changing job titles rather than job descriptions. Visiting agents became parole officers in the 1890s; their basic day-to-day activities, however, remained essentially unchanged. The indenture committee became the "Parole and Indenture Committee" in 1911 and the "Reception and Parole Committee" in 1913; however, the terms of parole agreements paralleled the terms of indenture. Although the fundamental differences between indenture and parole—i.e., release to parents, friends or relatives as opposed to "masters"—is obviously substantive, parole was, upon close examination, inextricably linked with indenture. (Pisciotta, 1993, p. 545)

Carney (1980) and Dressler (1959) also connect the indenture system to the parole process. However, most authorities consider Captain Alexander Maconochie and Sir William Crofton the founders of procedures in the administration of corrections that led to formation of the parole process. Maconochie is known for having created the "marks system" in about 1840. This system eliminated the traditional flat or fixed sentence and allowed inmates to reduce their time served by redeeming the number of marks assigned against them at the start of their incarceration. "These marks were to be earned by deportment, labor and study and the more rapidly they were acquired the more speedy the release" (Barnes, 1972, p. 145). Offenders in Maconochie's prison in Australia could also obtain a "ticket-to-leave." This legal practice existed prior to

Maconochie's marks system. It "allowed prison officials to exempt a convict from a sentence on the condition that the convict was able to secure and maintain civil employment" (Nietzel & Himelein, 1987, p. 113).

Crofton improved on some of the problems noted with Maconochie's system when he developed the system of release in the Irish prison system. Nietzel and Himelein (1987) point out that Maconochie's system was severely criticized because it failed to provide for supervision of inmates when they were released to the community. They contended that his program ignored the critical rule-of-thumb governing the success of any correctional innovation: "society must be protected" (Nietzel & Himelein, 1987, p. 113). Crofton added supervision to the ticket-of-leave and placed conditions on the offender during this phase of the correctional process. He also introduced grades or classifications into the marks system that involved a process of gradual release to the community. This approach significantly impacted on parole in the United States. In fact, the first system of parole established in the United States was patterned after the Crofton approach. It was implemented at the New York State Reformatory at Elmira in 1876. This facility handled first-time offenders between sixteen and thirty years of age (Dressler, 1959).

Many authorities in juvenile corrections have asserted that juvenile aftercare is "analogous" to parole in the criminal justice system (Kobertz & Borsarge, 1973; Siegel & Senna, 1985). In fact, aftercare is widely regarded in some professional and academic circles as a euphemism for juvenile parole (Keve, 1981). Nonetheless, there are differences in philosophy that emerged with formation of the juvenile court. The juvenile court movement "was aimed at creating a new backup institution to step in where primary institutions such as the family and the school had failed" (Lempert & Sanders, 1986). The theoretical objective of the juvenile court was treatment or "relationship settlement" (Lempert & Sanders, 1986). This differed significantly from the theoretical objectives of the adult criminal justice with its emphasis on "detecting guilt and adjusting the punishment to the crime" (Barnes, 1972, p. 265).

The basis for the authority of juvenile parole is rooted in the *parens patriae* powers of the state and its welfare orientation. In contrast, adult parole derives its authority from the police powers of the state with its attendant focus on crime control and community protection (Ashford & LeCroy, 1993). These differences in aims contributed to the development of competing terminology (aftercare versus parole) and different procedures for processing juvenile versus adult offenders. For instance, because of its beneficent aims, the juvenile system did not subscribe to the level of legal formalism found in adult parole. Although there are strong differences in rationales between the two systems, these differences "are less sharp today than immediately after the inception of the juvenile court movement" (Ashford & LeCroy, 1993, p. 181).

During the Progressive Era (the period from 1900 to 1920), reformers were captivated by the assumptions of positivistic criminology, in which crime was considered a "sociomedical" problem requiring treatment and not punishment (Ashford, 1987; Barnes, 1972). Advocates of positivistic criminology assumed that it rendered the whole notion of punishment "archaic" (Barnes, 1972). This change in philosophy stimulated a shift in policy toward what David Rothman (1986) termed the "power of the expert." The expert gained power in the system of justice administration, shifting the focus in disposing of offenders from their deeds to their needs (Olson-Raymer, 1993). Also, the expert became responsible for answering the critical question: Is the community safe when an offender is at large after corrective treatment (Barnes, 1972)? With this ascendancy of the expert in justice administration, social workers emerged as major figures in carrying out many of the treatment and rehabilitative aims of the juvenile justice system.

The Aftercare Process and Social Work Roles

Many authorities in the early years of the field of corrections considered aftercare and parole as "case work services" (Dressler, 1959). Others maintained that aftercare was essentially a law enforcement function. These competing viewpoints have led to variations in the implementation of aftercare functions. Some states have attached their aftercare functions to family or children service agencies or other appropriate components of the social welfare system. Other states have had the functions of this phase of the correctional process implemented by probation officers or employees of training or industrial schools. This has led to conflicting terminology and approaches for the aftercare process.

Nonetheless, the fundamental aim of aftercare is to reintegrate youths into the community following their release from a treatment facility. In determining a youth's readiness for release, traditional social work skills have been widely recognized for their effectiveness in this area. In developing an appropriate discharge plan, social workers meet with youths and investigate factors in their history, institutional performance, and family environment (Kratcoski & Kratcoski, 1979). The aim of their investigation is to assess the factors contributing to the youth's delinquent behavior and potential success in the community. After their assessment, social workers formulate appropriate release plans. In some states, the same worker is involved in the release decision as in the supervisory phase of the process. Other states have moved to a system involving a more specialized division of labor. In these states, there are separate groups of social workers who handle the discharge planning process and separate groups of professionals who provide supervisory services. In the two key areas of aftercare practice (release decision making and release supervision), there are changes in technology that have influenced how social workers approach traditional aftercare responsibilities.

Innovations in Release Decision Making and Youth Classification

During the 1970s, policymakers began to question the expertise of social workers in making release decisions. They were troubled by the lack of formalism in this decision-making process (Coffey, 1975; Wheeler, 1978). Aftercare professionals had unbridled discretion in making most of the decisions about a youth's placement, levels of supervision in the community, and discharge from the aftercare process (Ashford & LeCroy, 1988). Youths could remain under supervision for whatever periods of time deemed appropriate by the supervising agent. This led to abuses of discretion that troubled advocates of the justice or fairness model (Wheeler, 1978).

The justice or fairness model stresses principles distinctly different from the aims of the early founders of the juvenile justice system (Aultman & Wright, 1982). This newer paradigm challenged the beneficent aims of a therapeutic system of justice rooted in the *parens patriae* powers of the state. It stressed "just deserts," equality in sentencing, and fairness in decision-making processes (Harris & Graff, 1988). The emergence of this new philosophy in juvenile justice triggered reforms in corrections administration that led to increased formalism in corrections decision making. It also stimulated movements that sought the elimination of indeterminate periods of aftercare supervision and the elimination of juvenile aftercare itself (Wheeler, 1978).

Most of the arguments levied against juvenile aftercare mirrored many of the criticisms directed at adult parole. Both processes were challenged on grounds of unfairness and ineffectiveness (von Hirsh & Hanrahan, 1978; Wheeler, 1978). Reformers called for fixed or determinate sentences to compensate for the disparities in parole duration encountered by blacks, women, and younger offenders (Wheeler, 1978). That is, regardless of offense, blacks, females and younger offenders were usually under supervised release for longer periods of time than were other offenders. These attacks against the fairness of aftercare occurred about the same time that scholars (Ennis & Litwack, 1974; Monahan, 1981) were involved in disputes about the validity of clinical predictions of dangerousness.

During the 1970s, debates about the merits of clinical versus actuarial prediction emerged in many areas of clinical practice, including juvenile aftercare. As Clear observed, "Prediction can be overt, as when a parole board denies parole because the offender is deemed a danger to the community, or it may be subtle, as when a corrections officer decides to watch an inmate closely because he thinks 'something fishy' is going on" (1988, p. 1). As Gambrill (1990) points out, accuracy and effectiveness in prediction methods is a critical element of social work practice. It is also an essential component of corrections, including juvenile aftercare. Interest in improving clinical predictions in aftercare prompted a revitalization of research into experience tables (Burgess, 1928) and other formalized prediction methods (Ashford &

LeCroy, 1990). Most of these new methods have focused on predicting offender recidivism and have resulted in the development of "risk classification devices" (Clear, 1988).

The initial work in risk assessment was aimed at providing parole boards (Gottfredson, Wilkins, & Hoffman, 1978) with reliable information about an offender's risk to the community. One common area of confusion was in determining the appropriate criterion variable or type of behavior requiring prediction. In the aftercare experience, workers must make a variety of predictions involving risk: risk of committing violent acts, risk of committing a new offense, and risk of violating aftercare conditions (Clear, 1988). Each of these criterion variables has a different likelihood of occurrence. Most research has focused, however, on predicting further criminality. Baird (1982) found eight factors useful in predicting risk of continued criminal activity among juveniles.

1. age of first adjudication
2. prior delinquent behavior
3. number of prior commitments to juvenile facilities
4. drug/chemical abuse
5. alcohol abuse
6. parental control
7. school problems
8. peer relationships

Similar items are included in many other risk assessment devices used by aftercare professionals. That is, there are other devices in the field that use comparable domains for predicting youth potential for further criminal activity (Ashford & LeCroy, 1990).

Assessment of risk of future criminal activity is just one of the many decision issues confronting aftercare workers in developing care plans for released youths. Workers confront other decision issues in trying to identify appropriate placements and in assigning youths to appropriate levels of supervision in the community. In this area of aftercare practice, there are a number of new decision aids used by social work professionals to clarify their decision tasks. These newer devices try to compensate for many of the simplistic assumptions underlying linear approaches to assigning youths to appropriate supervision levels in the community.

The Baird (1982) approach to risk classification subscribed to the principle that individuals with high risk-and-need scores on classification devices should be assigned to high levels of supervision in the community; whereas youths receiving low risk-and-need scores should be assigned to low levels of supervision in the community. This approach was initially lauded by policy reformers because it increased the consistency and equity in key decisions regarding aftercare. Although this linear approach to assigning youths to supervision was viewed as a marked improvement over clinical judgment, it has been considered too simplistic by Clear and Gallagher (1983). In their opinion, it ignores a number of key factors, besides risk and need, that can influence the level of supervision required to control a youth's behavior in the community. To this end, Ashford and LeCroy (1988) developed a decision-making system in Arizona to address these concerns. Their approach is being expanded by Ashford and LeCroy (1993) in a project for the South Carolina Juvenile Parole Board. Both systems take into account factors in the youth's family environment, the youth's potential for cooperation or responsiveness, and the willingness of the family to cooperate with the parole authority.

Besides formalization of the decision process, it is assumed that these systems can assist authorities in managing resources more effectively. These newer decision devices are not rooted in the medical model of aftercare (Baird, 1982). They differ significantly from earlier approaches to juvenile classification, based on the Interpersonal Maturity Scale (I-Level system) developed by Margarite Warren (1983). This approach to classification focuses on identifying groups likely to benefit from differential forms of treatment. That is, classification in juvenile justice had a different focus prior to the 1970s. The organizing principles of the I-Level system and earlier systems in juvenile justice had roots in developmental theory and treatment concepts. These are not the same principles guiding current classification efforts in juvenile corrections.

Offender classification is not the only facet of aftercare that was influenced by the shift in philosophy toward a justice or fairness model in the 1970s. Supervisory roles also underwent significant modifications. When aftercare first emerged, casework, group work, and community organization principles played a fundamental role in its implementation. In the next section, I will review a number of new concepts that are guiding the organization of the supervisory phase of juvenile aftercare.

Developments in Community Supervision Technology

Since the inception of social work, practitioners in aftercare have brokered services designed to address the individual needs of their clients. Although this practice-of-service delivery is widely accepted in the profession, Melton and Pagliocca (1992) do not believe that it can meet the needs of most delinquents. Delinquents require comprehensive approaches to treatment. Most service systems are not capable of providing the kind of integrated responses required to meet each of the key domains influencing delinquent behavior. Youths are referred to general services that address an identified need in most systems. Melton and Pagliocca (1992) have suggested the "Jericho Principle" as a solution to this problem. This principle assumes that walls ought to come tumbling down between the disciplines involved in the provision of services to children and families (e.g., child welfare and juvenile justice). It also includes the arbitrary, wall-like divisions between mental health and juvenile justice services. Melton and Pagliocca consider these divisions arbitrary because research reveals few substantive differences in the populations being treated in each of these systems.

Given the diversity of problems facing seriously delinquent youths, Melton and Pagliocca believe it unreasonable to assume that these youths are likely to benefit just from weekly office sessions with an aftercare professional. Delinquent youths generally have difficulties in many areas of their lives. "These include: low educational achievement, distorted perceptions of social interaction, impaired problem-solving skills, troubled and delinquent friends, conflictual family relationships, poverty, and deteriorating neighborhoods" (Melton & Pagliocca, 1992, p. 114). These multisystem problems will not be addressed, in Melton and Pagliocca's opinion, unless workers leave their offices to confront the youth's problems in their natural environment.

An example of an approach in juvenile corrections that employs the Jericho Principle is the South Carolina Family Neighborhood Services (FANS) Project. This project "sought to demonstrate that even the most serious juvenile offenders could be treated successfully if services were sufficiently intensive, individualized, and integrated, with attention to the wide array of domains in which serious offenders have severe problems" (Melton & Pagliocca, 1992, p. 116). FANS subscribes to a treatment approach developed by Henggeler and Borduin (1990) known as multisystemic therapy (MST). This approach has many similarities with the family preservation model of intensive service delivery currently employed in the field of child welfare. Other models of integrated service delivery such as the "wraparound" (Behar, 1985) and "individualized care" (Friedman, 1988) models are also beginning to impact the supervision component of the aftercare process. These models assume that individualized care cannot be fragmented, that an integrated system must be designed to meet the distinct needs of youths. That is, these models use an alternative approach to individualizing the care of released youth. Individualization, in these approaches, does not refer solely to developing an individual plan that involves attaching a youth to preexisting services. They call for the formation of an individualized system of total care that can provide services at multiple levels. Unlike other recent movements in aftercare supervision, these approaches were developed by mental health professionals committed to working with seriously emotionally disturbed youths.

Besides experiments in supervisory treatment based on newer principles of individualized care, there are a number of other experiments tried in the field that were triggered by the JIPS (Juvenile Intensive Probation Supervision) movement. This movement emerged in response to calls for accountability and increased crime control in juvenile justice policy during the 1980s. This shift in philosophy culminated in the Model Juvenile Code of the American Legislative Exchange Council (1987), which called for reforms in policy that would hold serious juvenile offenders responsible for their actions. Although few jurisdictions implemented its complete package of reforms, many states did make changes in several areas affecting serious juvenile offenders. Harris and Graff (1988, p. 66) provide a succinct summary of many of the reforms of the 1980s in legislation:

> Reformed codes usually included one or more of the following provisions: provisions which broaden the offense age requirements in waiver, allowing a greater number of youth to the criminal court; lowered ages of jurisdiction, which allowed the criminal court to routinely handle younger offenders without the need for certification; serious delinquent statutes, which ensured the prolonged incarceration of repeat offenders and sentencing guidelines or administrative guidelines governing institutional exit.

Many of these reforms triggered increased commitments of youths to juvenile facilities. The result of this "get tough on crime" approach has been increased overcrowding in juvenile facilities. In order to respond to this problem, institutional systems began exploring methods of release that simultaneously provided security for the community by using intensive forms of community supervision.

Intensive supervision movements are not new in juvenile corrections (Armstrong, 1991). The California Youth Authority experimented extensively during the 1960s with intensive supervision of juveniles on aftercare status. Most of these experiments sought to determine the "magic number" for the average case load. Youths were assigned to special caseloads of twenty-five youths and to intensive caseloads of twelve youths. The results of these experiments indicated that experimental caseloads fared no better than the traditional case loads with less intensive supervision. These results prompted many critics in the 1970s to call for the elimination of aftercare or parole (Wheeler, 1978; Romig, 1978). Such concerns about the effectiveness of aftercare were not limited to high-risk youths. Hudson (1973) found in his research in Minnesota that low-risk youths released without parole supervision fared as well as youths released with supervision. Such findings contributed to a general pessimism about the utility of juvenile aftercare services. By the beginning of the 1970s, most critics were concluding that "nothing works" (Armstrong, 1991).

Thus, the experiments with intensive intervention during the 1960s and early 1970s focused primarily on rehabilitation and habilitation aims. Within this focus, programs sought to achieve a diverse array of personal and interpersonal changes. These themes of personal and interpersonal changes were replaced in the late 1970s with the theme of external control, with its attendant emphasis on developing innovations in methods of surveillance (Palmer, 1991). In addition, life skills became a major component of aftercare programming, and there was less commitment to exposing youths to traditional forms of psychotherapy. Today, most intensive aftercare programs include a broader goal mix than was true of the earlier experiments of the 1960s.

Recent Experiments in Intensive Aftercare Supervision (IAS)

During the 1980s, the Office of Juvenile Justice and Delinquency Prevention (OJJDP) sponsored the Violent Juvenile Offender Research and Development Program (VJO). This program of Intensive Aftercare Supervision (IAS) sought to normalize the behavior of several subsets of violent youths in the serious juvenile offender population. The theoretical underpinnings of this project included social networking, provision of opportunities, social learning, and goal oriented interventions (Armstrong, 1991). The methods used to implement these themes were continuous case management, diagnostic assessment, job training skills, placement in a work setting, and individual and family counseling (Armstrong, 1991; Palmer, 1991). Each aftercare worker was to maintain a case load of between six and eight youths. Youths were to be gradually reintegrated into the home and the community. Palmer (1991, p. 103) provides a concise summary of the fundamental characteristics of this project:

> In each of the four test sites that met the minimum participation standards— Boston, Memphis, Newark and Detroit—program clients (Es) were first placed, for an average of six months in "small secure facilities." After that, they were "reintegrated to the community through transitional facilities via a community-based residence." This stage was followed by intensive supervision, e.g., frequent contacts in small caseloads, "upon return to their neighborhoods."

The VJO program is still being evaluated by researchers; and preliminary studies are too impressionistic, in Altschuler and Armstrong's (1991) opinion, to allow for valid conclusions.

Another project that emerged in the 1980s is the Skillman Aftercare Experiment. This is an intensive aftercare program for delinquents released to their homes after confinement in a secure facility. This project makes clear use of social work skills in its design. It subscribes to social learning and relapse prevention as its integrating concepts. Workers make contacts with youths at the correctional facilities prior to their release.

Case loads of between eight and ten youths are handled by a team consisting of a caseworker and a family social worker. The goal is to have the family visited at least once a week and for the youths on aftercare status to have face-to-face contacts at least twice a day, for a six month period, with team members. In Pittsburgh, a multistage reentry process has been established that involves youths being placed in a group home for one month after they are released from the institution (Armstrong, 1991).

The Paint Creek Youth program in Ohio also has an intensive aftercare component. This private sector facility provides services for serious delinquent offenders. It has an aftercare program based on principles comparable to those in the JIPS program in Delaware County, Ohio. On release from this facility, youths are placed either in their parental homes, an independent living setting, or a group home. Regardless of their placement, the youths are placed on house arrest for the first two weeks but are allowed free movement to attend school, participate in treatment, or go to work. In order to be discharged after six months, they must regularly attend either school or work. Aftercare professionals maintain two face-to-face contacts each day with these IAS youths. Other intensive programs with similar case load and surveillance features are also being implemented in Philadelphia and other jurisdictions across the United States (Armstrong, 1991). They all provide increased surveillance and are geared to protecting the community. That is, their structure has been influenced by the community protection focus that is gaining popularity in juvenile justice policy.

Issues

Some social workers have had longstanding reservations about working in the field of corrections. In their view, notions of social control are alien to the profession's mission. However, this is far from an accurate understanding of social work practice. Although change in the juvenile justice system is seen as a fundamental function of social work, social workers are also involved in fulfilling the other key societal functions of system maintenance and system control (Macht & Ashford, 1991). In fact, social workers are more likely to be employed in settings that focus on system maintenance and system control than in settings that focus on achieving objectives of social change. Nonetheless, unfounded fears about working in the aftercare system increased following the anti-rehabilitation movements of the late 1970s.

As Clear, Byrne, and Dvoskin (1993) point out, there is still substantial controversy in adult parole "about whether the primary purpose of supervision should be to provide help and support for the offender or to establish and enforce controls over the offender" (p. 137). In juvenile aftercare, similar issues are beginning to take center stage. Much of this role conflict is being fueled by a lack of clarity about the juvenile justice system's current mission. Bazemore (1992) has advocated what he has termed a "balanced approach" to the mission of the juvenile justice system. This approach seeks to strike a balance between the following objectives: accountability, competency development, and community protection. In his view, no one objective should take precedence over any other objective. If one objective does, the system is likely to go "out of balance." In an unbalanced system, success is highly unlikely.

Before we can ever achieve balance in the system, however, social workers will need to increase their involvement in efforts to operationalize the diverse array of issues that face aftercare professionals in formulating individualized care plans. The complexity of these plans is what triggers imbalance. Most workers do not have the necessary skills to be effective in working with all types of problems. This has triggered significant discussion in the field about the merits of specialized versus generalist aftercare units (Clear, Byrne, & Dvoskin, 1993). Can aftercare professionals achieve increased balance in their service plans if they have specialized case loads? Traditionally, specialized case loads have been established to meet the needs of serious juvenile offenders. For instance, some states have created special release projects for sex offenders, violent offenders, and offenders with serious substance abuse problems. These units have been praised as well as criticized.

Specialization raises important classification and management issues. Many practitioners have questioned whether specialized case loads will result in increased burnout for aftercare professionals. This question is often raised because workers are concerned about having to deal only with high-need or high-risk youths. Most of them welcome having some low-risk youths on their case loads. However, Clear, Byrne, and Dvoskin (1993) point out that there is little systematic evidence on this issue. "The amount of court work, crisis intervention and 24-hour availability needed to manage these offenders effectively is seen as the problem (though the special identity officers develop when given these assignments may balance the stress, at least for a while)" (Clear, Byrne, & Dvoskin, 1993, p. 142).

Besides having conflicts about how to structure case loads, policymakers are confronting a number of legal and ethical issues vis-à-vis how much discretion aftercare professionals should have in making decisions involving the liberty and life chances of youths on aftercare status (Ashford, in press). In 1988, Ashford and LeCroy surveyed the nation to determine how states were handling many of the policy recommendations of the late 1970s and early 1980s. For instance, the Institute of Judicial Administration and the American Bar Association (IJA-ABA) Joint Commission on Juvenile Standards (1980) established explicit guidelines to address concerns about due process matters. *Standard 4.5* states: "basic concepts of due process of law should apply to a juvenile under correctional supervision. Alterations in the status or placement of a juvenile that result in more security, additional obligations or less personal freedom should be subjected to regularized proceedings" (Bing & Brown, 1977, p. 79). Ashford and LeCroy's survey revealed that sixteen of the surveyed states lacked procedural safeguards for decisions involving administrative alterations in a youth's level of freedom in the community. This includes decisions involving transfers to placements with higher levels of restrictiveness or decisions resulting in alterations in the youth's level of supervision in the community. Sixteen states also lacked formal grievance mechanisms for youths on aftercare status (Ashford, in press).

Although there were numerous calls for justice in aftercare decision-making during the late 1970s, available data indicates that most of the reforms have placed greater emphasis on issues of accountability than on issues of fairness. This is surprising given the recent emphasis on formalization and clarification of decision-making processes in child welfare and other areas of public administration. That is, it was surprising to learn that sixteen states were without standards or review procedures for checking the exercise of discretion by aftercare professionals (Ashford, in press). Furthermore, most states continue to have indeterminate approaches in terminating, extending, and discharging youths from aftercare status (Ashford & LeCroy, 1993). That is, despite the many calls for reform, the system of aftercare continues to be plagued by highly discretionary procedures. Nonetheless, most states have maintained some form of supervised release. However, few states have articulated a coherent policy of sentencing for juveniles that includes the aftercare phase of this process. As Ashford and LeCroy (1993, p. 193) point out:

> Lengths of supervision vary from jurisdiction to jurisdiction; no clear standard of time presently exists for achieving aftercare objectives. States specify from six months to two years as a minimum period for achieving release objectives.

This issue about appropriate limits on the duration of aftercare supervision warrants further scrutiny by policymakers involved in reforms of existing juvenile codes.

Future Directions

Aftercare was considered a key field of practice in the early history of social work. However, it has been virtually abandoned by our profession in recent years. Few schools of social work offer either concentration or specialization in juvenile probation or aftercare. Many states have begun hiring persons with law enforcement training rather than hiring social workers. To some extent, these disturbing trends were triggered by shifts in philosophy about the effectiveness of rehabilitation in correction. However, our juvenile justice system will lose much of its humanity if social workers do not try to reaffirm the system's resonsibility for achieving competency, development, and rehabilitation aims.

Before social workers can reclaim this area of practice, however, they will need to clarify the theoretical assumptions underlying their approaches to aftercare supervision. Altschuler and Armstrong (1991) have expressed significant concern about the fact that theories of delinquency and theories of practice have developed independently of one another. One exception to this rule has been the social bonding approach developed by Hawkins and Weis (1985). This approach exemplifies the previously articulated need for integrated approaches to aftercare. It links several aspects of delinquency theory with new developments in social work practice.

With improved sensitivity to theory-guided practice, there should be increased chances for success, but we must tackle a number of fundamental issues before there will be significant evidence of this success. For instance, social workers must begin to address the issue of what are appropriate standards of care for youths under supervised release. This question cannot be answered, however, without establishing a national data base that tracks youths released on aftercare status. Unlike the field of adult parole, there are no systematically collected statistics at the national level that summarize the rates of successes or failures of youths on aftercare status. This oversight needs immediate attention. In addition, there appears to be an urgent need for establishing a work group in social work that focuses on establishing appropriate supervisory standards of care. To date, there are no accepted standards to address issues of quality of care or appropriate lengths of supervision for achieving relevant aftercare aims. Similarly, advocates for reform in social work need to look seriously at the problem of a lack of due-process safeguards for youths currently receiving aftercare services in many jurisdictions.

In sum, juvenile aftercare has witnessed many changes during its history. In spite of calls for the abolition of juvenile aftercare in the late 1970s, most states have retained some form of supervisory release (Ashford & LeCroy, 1993). Furthermore, the modal type of release remains indeterminate in nature. Unlike in the adult system, few states have implemented approaches to discharge from parole services that adhere to a determinacy model. The only state with a strictly determinate sentencing structure (Washington) still was cognizant of the importance of aftercare services. Policymakers in this state "recommended that youths be entitled to request continued services after completing a length of supervision deemed commensurate with their criminal history, age and committing offense" (Ashford & LeCroy, 1993, p. 192) Thus, supervisory release remains an important component of the juvenile justice process even in states with determinate sentencing provisions.

References

Altschuler, D. M., & Armstrong, T. L. (1991). Intensive aftercare for the high-risk juvenile parolee: Issues and approaches in reintegration and community supervision. In T. L. Armstrong (Ed.), *Intensive interventions with high-risk youths: Promising* approaches in juvenile probation and parole (pp. 45–84). Monsey, NY: Criminal Justice Press.

Armstrong, T. L. (1991). Introduction. In T. L. Armstrong (Ed.), *Intensive interventions with high-risk youths: Promising approaches in juvenile probation and parole* (pp. 1–26). Monsey, NY: Criminal Justice Press.

Ashford, J. B. (1987). Legal criteria and clinical predictions in drug legislation. *Social Casework, 68,* 364–369.

Ashford, J. B. (In press). Protecting the interests of juveniles on aftercare/parole. *Children & Youth Services Review.*

Ashford, J. B. & LeCroy, C. W. (1988a). Decision-making for juvenile offenders in aftercare. *Juvenile and Family Court Journal, 39,* 47–53.

Ashford, J. B. & LeCroy, C. W. (1988b). Predicting recidivism: An evaluation of the Wisconsin juvenile probation and aftercare risk instrument. *Criminal Justice and Behavior, 15,* 141–151.

Ashford, J. B. & LeCroy, C. W. (1990). Juvenile recidivism: A comparison of three prediction instruments. *Adolescence, 25,* 440–450.

Ashford, J. B. & LeCroy, C. W. (1993). Juvenile parole models in the United States: Determinate versus indeterminate models. *Justice Quarterly, 10,* 179–195.

Aultman, M. G. & Wright, K. N. (1982). The fairness paradigm: An evaluation of change in juvenile justice. *Canadian Journal of Criminology, 24,* 13–24.

Baird, C. S. (1981). Classifying juveniles: Making the most of an important management tool. *Corrections Today, 43,* 36–41.

Baird, C. S. (1982). *Classification of juveniles in corrections: A model systems approach.* Madison, WI: National Council on Crime and Delinquency.

Barnes, H. E. (1972). *The story of punishment.* Montclair, NJ: Patterson Smith.

Barton, W. H. & Butts, J. A. (1990). Viable options: Intensive programs for juvenile delinquents. *Crime and Delinquency, 36,* 238–256.

Bazemore, G. (1992). On mission statements and reform in juvenile justice: The case of the "balanced approach." *Federal Probation,* Sept. 64–70.

Behar, L. (1985). Changing patterns of state responsibility. A case study of North Carolina. *Journal of Clinical Child Psychology, 14,* 188–195.

Bing, S. R. & Brown, J. L. (1980). *Standards relating to monitoring.* New York: Institute of Judicial Administration.

Burgess, E. W. (1928). Factors determining successful parole. In A. A. Bruce, et al. (Eds.), *The workings of the indeterminate sentence law and the parole system in Illinois.* Springfield, IL: The Board of Parole.

Carney, L. P. (1980). *Corrections: Treatment and philosophy.* Englewood Cliffs, NJ: Prentice Hall.

Clear, T. R. (1979). Three dilemmas in community supervision. *Prison Journal, 59,* 2–16.

Clear, T. R. (1988). *Statistical Prediction in Corrections.* Omaha: The Robert J. Kutak Foundation and the National Institute of Corrections.

Clear, T. R., Byrne, J. M. & Dvoskin, J. A. (1993). The transition from being an inmate: Discharge planning, parole and community-based services for offenders with mental illness. In H. J. Steadman and J. J. Cocozza (Eds.), *Mental illness in America's prisons.* Seattle, WA: National Coalition for the Mentally Ill in the Criminal Justice System.

Clear, T. R. & Gallagher, K. W. (1983). Management problems in risk screening devices in probation and parole. *Evaluation Review, 7,* 217–234.

Clement, P. F. (1993). The incorrigible child: Juvenile delinquency in the United States from the 17th through the 19th centuries. In A. G. Hess and P. F. Clement (Eds.) *History of juvenile delinquency* (pp. 453–490). Aalen, Germany: Scientia Verlag.

Coffey, A. R. (1975). *Juvenile corrections: Treatment and rehabilitation.* Englewood Cliffs, NJ: Prentice Hall.

Cullen, F. T. & Gilbert, K. E. (1982). *Reaffirming rehabilitation.* Cincinnati, OH: Anderson.

Daum, J. M. (1981). Aftercare: The neglected phase of adolescent treatment. *Juvenile and Family Court Journal, 32,* 43–48.

Dressler, D. (1959). *Practice and theory of probation and parole.* New York: Columbia University Press.

Ennis, B. J. & Litwack, T. R. (1974). Psychiatry and the presumption of expertise: Flipping coins in the courtroom. *California Law Review, 62,* 693–752.

Feld, B.C. (1993). Juvenile (in)justice and the criminal court. *Crime and Delinquency, 39,* 403–424.

Friedman, R. (1988). Program update: Individualizing services. In *Update: Improving services for emotionally disturbed children.* Tampa: Florida Mental Health Institute, University of South Florida.

Gambrill, E. D. (1990). *Critical thinking for clinicians: Improving the accuracy of judgments and decisions about clients.* San Francisco, CA: Jossey-Bass.

Gottfredson, D. M., Wilkins, L. T., & Hoffman, P. B. (1978). *Guidelines for parole and sentencing: A policy control method.* Lexington, MA: Heath.

Harris, P. M. & Graff, L. G. (1988). A critique of juvenile sentencing reform. *Federal Probation, 52,* 66–71.

Hawkins, J. D. & Weiss, J. G. (1985). The social development model: An integrated approach to delinquency prevention. *Journal of Primary Prevention, 6,* 73–97.

Henggeler, S. W. & Borduin, C. M. (1990). *Family therapy and beyond: A multi-systemic approach to treating the behavior problems of children and adolescents.* Pacific Grove, CA: Brooks Cole.

Hirschi, T. & Gottfredson, M. (1993). Rethinking the juvenile justice system. *Crime and Delinquency, 39,* 262–271.

Hudson, C. H. (1973). *Summary report: An experimental study of the different effects of parole supervision on a group of adolescent boys and girls.* Minneapolis: Minnesota Dept. of Corrections.

Keve, P. W. (1981). *Corrections.* New York: Wiley.

Kobetz, R. W. & Borsarge, B. B. (1973). *Juvenile justice administration.* Gaithersburg, MD: International Association of Chiefs of Police.

Kratcoski, P. C. & Kratcoski, L. D. (1979). *Juvenile delinquency.* Englewood Cliffs, NJ: Prentice Hall.

LeCroy, C. W. & Ashford, J. B. (1989). Behavioral approaches in working with the serious juvenile offender. In B. Thayer (Ed.), *Behavioral family therapy.* Springfield, IL: Charles C. Thomas.

Lempert, R. & Sanders, J. (1986). *An invitation to law and social science.* Philadelphia: University of Pennsylvania Press.

Macht, M. W. & Ashford, J. B. (1991). *Introduction to social work and social welfare.* New York: Merrill.

Melton, G. & Pagliocca, P. (1992). Treatment in the juvenile justice system: Directions for policy and practice. In J. J. Cocozza (Ed.), *Responding to the Mental Health Needs of Youth in the Juvenile Justice System.* Seattle, WA: National Coalition for the Mentally Ill in the Criminal Justice System.

Melton, G. B., Petrila, J., & Poythress, N. G. (1987). *Psychological evaluations for the Courts.* New York: Guilford Press.

Monahan, J. (1981). *Predicting violent behavior: An assessment of clinical techniques.* Beverly Hills, CA: Sage.

Nietzel, M. T. & Himelein, M. J. (1987). Probation and Parole. In E. K. Morris & C. J. Braukmann (Eds.), *Behavioral approaches to crime and delinquency.* New York: Plenum.

Olson-Raymer, G. (1993). The American system of juvenile justice. In A. G. Hess and P. F. Clement (Eds.) *History of juvenile delinquency,* (pp. 491–531). Aalen, Germany: Scientia Verlag.

Palmer, T. B. (1991). Interventions with juvenile offenders: Recent and long-term changes. In T. L. Armstrong (Ed.), *Intensive interventions with high-risk youths: Promising approaches in juvenile probation and parole,* (pp. 85–120). Monsey, NY: Criminal Justice Press.

Pisciotta, A. W. (1993). Child saving or child brokerage? The theory and practice of indenture and parole at the New York House of Refuge, 1825-1935. In A. G. Hess and P. F. Clement (Eds.), *History of juvenile delinquency* (pp. 533–555). Aalen, Germany: Scientia Verlag.

Romig, D. A. (1978). *Justice for children.* Lexington, MA: Heath.

Rothman, D. (1986). Sentencing reform in historical perspective. *Crime and Delinquency, 29,* 631–651.

Siegel, L. J. & Senna, J. J. (1985). *Juvenile delinquency: Theory practice and law.* St Paul, MN: West.

Sykes, G. M. (1978). *Criminology.* New York: Harcourt, Brace, Jovanovich.

Trojanozicz, R. (1978). *Juvenile delinquency: Concepts and control.* Englewood Cliffs: NJ: Prentice Hall.

Von Hirsh, A. & Hanrahan, K. (1978). *Abolishing parole?* Washington DC: National Institute of Law Enforcement and Criminal Justice Assistance Administration.

Warren, M. Q. (1983). Applications of interpersonal-maturity theory to offender populations. In W. S. Lauter & J. M. Day (Eds.), *Personality theory, moral developments and criminal behavior.* Lexington, MA: Lexington Books.

Wheeler, G. R. (1978). *Counter-Deterrence.* Chicago: Nelson-Hall.

Drugs and the
Justice System

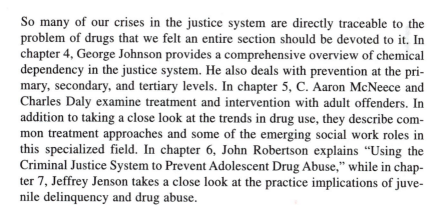

So many of our crises in the justice system are directly traceable to the problem of drugs that we felt an entire section should be devoted to it. In chapter 4, George Johnson provides a comprehensive overview of chemical dependency in the justice system. He also deals with prevention at the primary, secondary, and tertiary levels. In chapter 5, C. Aaron McNeece and Charles Daly examine treatment and intervention with adult offenders. In addition to taking a close look at the trends in drug use, they describe common treatment approaches and some of the emerging social work roles in this specialized field. In chapter 6, John Robertson explains "Using the Criminal Justice System to Prevent Adolescent Drug Abuse," while in chapter 7, Jeffrey Jenson takes a close look at the practice implications of juvenile delinquency and drug abuse.

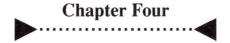

Chapter Four

Chemical Dependency in the Justice System

George L. Johnson

Drug abuse and chemical dependence are social problems. They disrupt the social order. They are behavioral problems that effect the emotional stability of the individual and their interpersonal relationships, and they are health problems from the standpoint of physical well-being. The negative impact of chemical dependence on the social, emotional, and biological condition of the individual, and conversely on society, has been amply documented (*National Drug Control Strategy,* 1994). Furthermore, the prevalence of drug use/abuse in American society is approaching epidemic proportions.

The purpose of this chapter is to consider some of the reasons why chemically dependent persons have generally been unresponsive to prevention and rehabilitation efforts within the existing structure of the criminal justice system and the implications for social work. The chapter also attempts to examine ways in which drug offenders are processed through the criminal justice system and how the rigid application of drug laws tends to mitigate against individualized case consideration. While it is anticipated that this discussion will help clarify the manner in which systems of justice routinely process drug offenders, the primary concern is with the drug abuser whose patterns of use can be considered addictive. Moreover, in this discussion the term "drug" is used to define chemical substances that are ingested, injected, or otherwise taken into the body with the specific intention of altering mood or perceptions (Little, 1989). Issues of routine processing include pre-adjudicatory decisions

and the need for structural and procedural revisions that enhance the effectiveness of the criminal justice system's efforts in addressing the drug/crime
connection. Recommendations that impact social work in processing chemically dependent offenders are considered in relation to primary, secondary, and
tertiary models of crime prevention that are consistent with the framework of
generalist social work practice.

Toward a Criminogenic Definition of Chemical Dependence

Perspectives on drug-use behavior, such as those described above, can be
viewed within the context of four broad frames of reference. Satinder (1980)
identifies the four as mystical-religious, legal-political, medical-psychiatric,
and social-cultural. The assessment of chemical dependence and dependent
behavior can be initiated through the utilization of any of the four, separately
or in combination. In general, much has been written on the assessment of
chemical dependence. Assessment of addiction to a chemical is the foundation
phase of the rehabilitation process (Doweiko, 1993). However, assessing
chemical dependence is not at issue in this chapter. Of concern, rather is the
"street" type of addicts described above and the resolution of their addiction
problems within the justice system.

People use, abuse, and/or become addicted to drugs for numerous reasons.
A person may be given marijuana to treat glaucoma, aspirin to relieve a
headache, medically prescribed morphine to relieve pain, or caffeine to remain
alert during the performance of a tedious task. Commercial ads, social situations, peer pressures, physical conditions, and other factors have been cited as
plausible explanations for why people initially use and ultimately become
addicted to drugs. In American culture the attraction of drugs has been attributed to such factors as the traditional value of individual freedom (laissez-
faire) and the permissiveness of social behavior (inalienable rights). Media
exploitation of people's need to hold themselves in high esteem has created a
myth of glamour and social desirability as reflected in quick-fix remedies to
enhance physical appearance and improve interpersonal skills. Dissatisfaction
with one's physical appearance has been known to result in chronic tension for
which certain drugs have been medically prescribed. Difficulties in relating to
others, including immediate family members, has been found to contribute to
excessive drug use (Cohen, 1981). Both chronic tension states and interpersonal difficulties accompany low self esteem. Studies of personality factors
and patterns of drug use confirm that chemically dependent individuals are
particularly inhibited in their interpersonal relationships and in addition suffer
from intense feelings of inadequacy (Satinder, 1980).

Much of the research suggests that alcohol and drug addiction are family
diseases (Doweiko, 1993). The synergistic relationship between chemical

dependence and criminal behavior link the problem of drugs and the criminal justice system. However, the authoritative and controlling nature of the criminal justice system engenders ambivalence and apprehension on the part of social work and the extent to which professionally trained workers have functioned within that system. In part this may be due to a perceived incongruence between the practice boundaries of social work and the goals of the justice system. Based on a working statement regarding the purpose of social work, the National Association of Social Workers (NASW) affirms that "The environment (social, physical, organizational) should provide the opportunity and resources for the maximum realization of the potential and aspirations of all individuals. Their environment should enhance the dignity, individuality and self-determination of everyone" (Specht, 1988). On the other hand, within the context of the criminal justice system interpersonal relationships are governed strictly by rules that operate primarily to arrest, prosecute, convict, and punish individuals who violate the formal rules of society.

Drug Use

According to a government survey (U.S. Dept. of Justice, 1992), nearly 75 million people report having used some type of illicit drug. It has been suggested that this figure is an underreport because many people in the total population who currently use or have used illicit drugs are overlooked, unresponsive, or otherwise inaccessible to surveys. Nevertheless, this figure is consistent with data from the high school senior survey (U.S. Dept. of Health and Human Services, 1992), which found that 44 percent of all high school seniors surveyed report having used an illicit drug. The same survey also found that, among college students, 50 percent of the respondents reported using an illicit drug at least once. Current estimates show that as many as 40 million Americans have experimented with cocaine. Among those 40 million individuals between the ages of twenty-five and thirty, the estimates of cocaine experimentation are as high as 50 percent and regular use of cocaine occurred in 20 to 25 percent of the survey subjects. This represents approximately 8 million people and, among those reporting regular use, "[c]ompulsive use and the need for treatment will have occurred in 25 percent or an estimated 2 million" (U.S. Dept. of Health and Human Services, 1992, p. 251). To further support the assertion that drug use/abuse prevalence is of epidemiological proportions, consider the fact that 2.4 million Americans have used "crack," a derivation of cocaine freed from its hydrochloride salt commonly referred to as "rock." When rock is inhaled, crack cocaine provides the user with a brief and relatively inexpensive euphoric high. "Crank," which is a combination of crack cocaine and heroin, is another common illicit drug reportedly used on a regular basis by an additional 600,000 Americans (Dash, 1994).

The Negative Impact of Drug Use

For purposes of this discussion, chemical dependence is differentiated from chemical abuse. Although both are social problems, they differ in chronicity and level of severity. Doweiko's model (1993) measures levels of chronicity and severity along a graded continuum ranging from total abstinence through rare social use, heavy social use, heavy problem use, to clear-cut addiction. Based on this model, heavy social users, heavy problem users, and addicted users represent a population of drug offenders whose illegal drug activities and severity of criminal offense should be differentially processed through the criminal justice system. It is at these three levels of chronicity and severity, according to Doweiko, that the onset of drug-related difficulties with the law are most likely to begin. In his study of nonmedical cocaine use, Siegel (1982) identified five usage patterns: experimental users, social-recreational users, circumstantial-situational users, intensified users, and compulsive users.

Although there is a large body of research on patterns of drug use and abuse, beyond the bipolar identification of use/non-use no mutually exclusive classification system of drug-use pattern has been developed. As with many classification schemes designed to describe human behavior, it is difficult to establish one's degree of chemical dependence beyond a predictable level of probability. Some individuals who regularly use and/or abuse illicit drugs are not necessarily dependent. Therefore, while chemical dependence cannot be accepted as justification for criminal activity, offenders who claim "diminished capacity" because of drug use should be carefully screened prior to adjudication of criminal charges against them.

To be sure, it is not uncommon for arrestees to attribute criminal activity to their use of drugs. In many instances the offender is motivated by an attempt to reduce the severity of punishment. Still, many persons who are arrested and subsequently incarcerated actually engaged in criminal activity solely as a means of supporting their drug habits. The compulsive, repetitive nature of addictive behavior among chemically dependent offenders often manifests itself in continued criminal activity as a way to purchase drugs. Chemical dependence has been defined as a "chronic, relapse disorder" (*National Drug Control Strategy,* 1994), and research has consistently supported the assertion that jails and prisons are ineffective methods of dealing with drug offenders. Jails and prisons are not the solution to addiction partly because the compulsive, repetitive behavior continues in spite of the potential for negative consequences. This problem is complicated by the extent to which specific drugs induce different reactions and subsequent behaviors. Moreover, valid criteria for diagnostically distinguishing between drug dependence and drug abuse have not been established.

All drugs, legal or illegal, produce some reaction, and nonmedical use of any drug that is regulated by law is considered illicit. In this context it is interesting to note the following regulatory development of drugs in America:

The original motive impelling state legislatures to control the use of opium was to be found in anti-Chinese sentiment and the early history of agitation for legislation prohibiting the use of marijuana was associated with anti-Mexican attitudes. Similarly, laws governing the sale and possession of cocain can, in part, be explained by the notion popular at the beginning of the century that the use of the drug was intimately connected with the bestial rage of blacks [sic.] involved in crimes of violence. From their origins in an ignorant racism, the various statutes governing opiates, cocaine, and marijuana have become an unquestioned part of American law. (Hamowy, 1991, p. 26)

In this chapter an illicit drug refers to heroin, cocaine, crack cocaine, crank, marijuana, hashish, amphetamines, and phencyclidine (PCP). If there is a unifying element for these drugs it is that biologically they all have been found to act upon "those areas of the brain that mediate feelings of pleasure and reward" (Hamowy, 1991, p. 27). Perhaps the compulsion among chemically dependent individuals to commit crimes in order to purchase drugs can be related to the fact that illicit drugs directly affect the brain reward system. The strength of the link between those drugs defined as illicit and the brain reward system has been amply illustrated by various animal studies. Such studies show that animals will forego food and drink to the point of death or excruciating pain in order to experience a pleasurable sensation similar to that experienced by an individual after using illicit drugs (U.S. Congress, 1993). If an analogy can be drawn from the foregoing regarding the compulsion to use drugs, then the threat of an overdose, of potentially lethal admixtures and/or apprehension and punishment for drug motivated crime are unlikely to deter most drug addicts from committing a crime to purchase drugs.

The Drug/Crime Connection

Aside from the fact that use of the drugs listed above are for the most part illegal in and of themselves, drug users are twice as likely to commit crimes than are people who do not use drugs. Furthermore, it has been shown that involvement in a criminal episode frequently occurs following the use of drugs. In a study conducted by this writer involving three hundred prison inmates, 20.4 percent (N=61) of the respondents indicated they had used some drug other than alcohol prior to committing the crime for which they were currently serving time. (In the same study 71.2 percent or 213 additional respondents reported they had used alcohol prior to committing the crime for which they were currently serving time.) Other studies have consistently shown that as the frequency of drug abuse increases, so does the frequency of crime. This is not to suggest a causal relationship between drug abuse and crime, but "it is clear that the two behaviors are highly correlated and probably reinforce each other" (Weisheit, 1990).

In terms of the drug/crime connection, the structure of the illicit drug market and its link to the criminal justice system obviously derives from the violation of legal codes. Participating in the drug market are dealers and wholesalers whose activities include high financing and whose product is retailed by a variety of merchants, including over-the-counter entrepreneurs and street peddlers. However, drug users and addicts often comprise the majority of people coming into contact with the criminal justice system. The over-representation of addicts in the justice system is a consequence of their addictive behavior and crime-related activities. For these offenders the pleasure derived from satisfying their drug habit is given higher priority than other aspects of their lives. Drug use comes to have greater relative importance than personal, social, and moral values.

President Bill Clinton's *National Drug Control Strategy* requested a budget totaling $13.2 billion for fiscal year 1995 to "[r]educe the number of drug users and the amount of drugs used as well as reduce the supply of illicit drugs entering the United States" (*National Drug Control Strategy,* 1994, pp. 75–85). The president's proposed budget targeted approximately $5 billion toward drug treatment education, community action, and the workplace. Though these figures seem to represent a substantial commitment in combating the national drug problem they pale in the face of the United States' drug laundering money problem, which is estimated at "100 to 200 billion dollars annually from the sales of heroin, cocaine and marijuana" (*National Drug Control Strategy,*1994).

This estimate reflects the continuous "high levels of demand and payment for illicit drugs (U.S. Dept. of Justice, 1993). Thus, despite the fact that approximately $6 billion of the president's drug control budget was earmarked for the Department of Justice, much of the crime research supports the assertion that through the decade of the 90's crime rates will continue to rise and much of this crime will be related to drugs. Indeed, data on drug use and crime shows that drug use is common among individuals arrested.

While correlations do not establish causality, strong relationships are found between crime and drug use. These relationships have been demonstrated through models developed by H. R. White (1990), which outline four forms of the drug-crime relationship. "First, drug use causes criminal activity. Second, criminal activity causes drug use. Third, there is a reciprocal relationship in which both drug use and criminal activity cause one another. Finally, the relationship between the two is spurious with other factors causing drug use and crime."

According to a survey conducted by the Bureau of Justice Statistics (1988), 40 percent of the inmates interviewed reported they were under the influence of drugs or were very drunk at the time they committed the offense for which they were currently incarcerated. In the previously referenced Johnson (1978) study of three hundred prison inmates, it was found that 91.6 percent (N=274) reported having used drugs around the time they committed

the offense for which time was being served. If a strong drug-crime relationship exists, it can be assumed that many chemically dependent individuals
have or will inevitably come into contact with the criminal justice system
(Weisheit, 1990). Indeed, narcotic policing relies heavily upon a cadre of
addict and street peddler informants for arrests and successful convictions for
narcotic violations. Because of the interconnectedness of drug use/abuse and
arrest, the issue of chemical dependence is usually studied within the context
of the criminal justice system. In many instances, just being arrested is the
drug offender's first exposure to drug treatment. Unfortunately the prevalence
and ready accessibility of street drugs results in drugs themselves being more
available than drug treatment. Given these circumstances, it seems as futile to
expect "recovered" addicts to remain straight in the streets as it does to expect
continued sobriety from a recovering alcoholic wine taster.

Although the ingestion of nonmedically prescribed psychoactive drugs is
in violation of law, not all illegal drug use is clinically deviant or antisocial.
For example, the use of marijuana became so popular in the 1960s and 1970s
that today its social use is widely accepted and indeed is considered chic
among many otherwise law abiding persons. Yet there are conflicting reports
on the consequences of marijuana use (Bakalar & Grinspoon, 1987; Jenike,
1989; Schwartz, 1987). Hashish, which is produced from the dried resin of
flowering parts of the same *Cannabis sativa* plant from which marijuana is
derived, is another controversial drug. Based on the available data, there is no
conclusive evidence that cannabis is addictive, that is, produces tolerance or
physical dependence, or that its use inevitably leads to other drug use (Little,
1989). While some discomfort has been associated with cessation of use, for
example, insomnia, irritability, and loss of appetite, the withdrawal effects of
marijuana are mild. Rarely do marijuana users seek treatment and when they
do, there are no well-developed methods for working with them (McNeece &
DiNitto, 1994). Thus, while the pharmacological effects of marijuana are of
major interest to the scientific community its direct relationship to criminal
behavior has not been demonstrated.

There are no universally agreed-upon criteria for defining drug abuse or
dependence. Aside from subjective self reports and observations, neither
behavioral nor social scientists have developed criteria that can be used in
determining chemical dependence. Symptoms that characterize dependence
are difficult to isolate and/or control, that is, they are not mutually exclusive.
Moreover, "the absence of a practice theory in the field of addictions con-
tributes to the confusion that surrounds the assessment of addictive behavior"
(Shaffer & Neuhaus, 1989, p. 88).

Habit-forming drugs, such as cocaine, heroin, and the amphetamines,
form the basis for a strong relationship between drug use and crime. In a report
issued by the U.S. Department of Justice (1992), extensive evidence is offered
in support of the drug/crime connection. Such evidence reveals the following:

1. Crime increases as drug use increases.
2. Criminal activity is two or three times higher among frequent users of heroin and cocaine.
3. Drug users report greater involvement in crime and are more likely than nonusers to have criminal records.
4. Persons with criminal records are much more likely than individuals without criminal records to report being drug users.

Chemical Dependency

The drug/crime connection can be readily understood in the context of the typical street junkie who must seek to satisfy a drug craving by purchasing illicit drugs from street dealers. As Little (1989) has suggested, "The high cost of supporting the illegal habit encourages crime among the addicted" (p. 86). In spite of the consequences for their behavior, most street addicts engage in whatever means are necessary to obtain drugs. It is this chemically dependent individual, the street addict, who is most likely to become involved in the criminal justice system. Police estimate that up to 50 percent of big city crime is attributable to addicts hustling to support their habits, since the overwhelming compulsion to obtain drugs becomes the addict's main goal.

This compulsion takes precedence over concern for any other responsibilities, including health, family, job, food, and so on. The continuous craving for drugs is likely to induce involvement in other deviant or criminal behavior. Although chemically dependent offenders have histories of criminal involvement that precede their addiction, the sustained monetary needs to purchase illicit drugs increases the likelihood of continued criminal behavior. "Unlike the million of alcoholics who can support their habits for relatively modest amounts," many people who are chemically dependent spend as much as $500 or more each day to buy drugs. As a consequence, it is the street addict who is commonly involved in acquisitive crimes, that is, "crimes whose primary intent is to generate income. These crimes include burglary, robbery, shoplifting, con games, forgery, prostitution and drug dealing" (Schober & Schade, 1991, p. 3). Approximately one-third of all heroin purchases are financed by shoplifting, burglary, and robbery (Cohen, 1981).

The legacy of chemical dependence is aptly described by Andre (1987) as being a state of "lying, cheating, manipulating others, dishonesty, and theft. Lacking money to purchase drugs the addict will engage in behavior which invariably brings him/her in contact with the criminal justice system" (p. 42). Several references have been made to "street addicts." To be sure, the stereotypical notion of an inner-city junkie sitting in a crack house is by no means a complete portrayal of the chemically dependent person. Chemical dependence is found among suburban, medically prescribed, pill popping homemakers, the classroom teacher, the police officer making a drug arrest, and the professional athlete. The chemically dependent person may be a physician, a minister, or an adolescent prostitute. Waldorf lucidly describes the typical street addict who has one overwhelming purpose and focus. For this individual:

> Life and existence is oversimplified into a single, overwhelming need that takes precedence over many of the physical and all the social needs which men proclaim are necessary for a reasonable life. Nearly all activity is focused upon the struggle to get the drugs to satisfy that need. Material objects are valued only in their sale for money for the drug. Work becomes nearly impossible, since most persons can never earn enough in a legitimate job to support their ever-increasing habit. Relationships, however close or distant, are inevitably transitory—more often than not, addicts will "burn" their family and best friends long before they rob and steal from other persons. Resources are very quickly exhausted, and soon the addict finds himself without a home, friends or family; and life becomes a seemingly ceaseless struggle for money, drugs and barest existence. Stealing and the sale of drugs becomes the best, and sometimes only, ways in which persons can support the high costs of their addiction. Add to this society's attribution of criminal status to the addict and the resultant arrests, incarcerations, voluntary and enforced treatments, and the sum is a pariah. (Waldorf, 1972, pp. 471–472)

The Justice System

Thus far, this chapter has attempted to examine some of the dynamics of chemical dependence and the potential relationship between drugs and crime. The purpose for that approach has been to establish a frame of reference in which drug abuse and treatment of chemically dependent offenders can be considered within the context of the criminal justice system. As previously indicated, drug-using offenders are responsible for a disproportionate amount of crime (*National Drug Control Strategy,* 1994). As a consequence, a relatively large proportion of offenders who move through the criminal justice system are drug abusers.

When individuals are apprehended for drug violations, the sequence of events after arrest and booking are prosecution and pretrial services, adjudication, sentencing and sanctions, and corrections (Cole, 1989). Consideration to this sequencing of events is needed in order to examine the problem of chemical dependence and the connection to the justice and drug systems.

The administrative structure of the criminal justice system includes four interdependent subsystems—police, prosecution, courts, and corrections (E. H. Johnson, 1978; U.S. Dept. of Justice, 1988). Each of these subsystems assumes separate roles. It is the role of the police to initiate the process through apprehension, arrest, and booking. The prosecution's role is to determine whether arrestees should go to trial. The court's role is to determine which cases brought to trial will be further subject to the correctional sub-system, of which there are two components—first, the various institutional facilities of incarceration and, second, community-based programs employing diverse means of achieving correctional goals (E. H. Johnson, 1978).

Although the availability of drugs and the incidence of drug abuse in correctional facilities has been amply documented (Cole, 1992; Toch & Adams, 1988), the focus of this discussion is on the addicted offender who is diverted from the institutional facility of the correctional subsystem as an alternative to incarceration. (For a discussion of prison based drug treatment, see National Institute of Drug Abuse, 1992). Diversion points may occur prior to police contact, prior to official police processing and prior to official court processing" (Allen & Simonsen, 1986). Allen and Simonsen identify these diversionary points as community based, police based, or court based.

In handling drug-addicted offenders, the criminal justice system is required to deal with the sensitive issue of social ambivalence between perceptions of drug addiction as a criminal behavior or as a dysfunctional disease. As a criminal offender, the addict is perceived as sinful, evil, immoral, and demonic. Consistent with our cultural concept of penance, such behavior should be punished. Thus, a retributivist form of justice is invoked as a form of deterrence. If it can be established that the addicted person is guilty of a crime, then he or she should be punished for both the crime and the addiction. Retribution and deterrence are both used to justify punishment. However, as a dysfunctional disease, the addiction is evidence of a "physical or psychological disequilibrium" (Frans, 1994) and the offender is viewed as being ill. Advocates of a restorative form of justice endorse the disease concept of behavior, which justifies diverting the addict from the criminal justice system to treatment and rehabilitation.

Review of the historical roots of the American criminal justice system reveals that some form of diversion has existed since the colonial era. In seventeenth century America, many settlers were actually persons who were diverted from English jails and transported to the colonies. Currently, diversion is used as a crime-reduction strategy that, among other purposes, is intended to rehabilitate chemically dependent offenders accused of certain types of crimes and divert them from correctional institutions. This, in turn, helps to ease the burden of already overcrowded jails and prisons. Given the drug-crime connection, it is probable that many chemically dependent street addicts will come in contact with the criminal justice system. Diversion is intended to provide more readily accessible treatment to these addicts and has been shown to be more cost efficient, with the potential for eliminating prosecution (Walker, 1994).

The rehabilitation goal of community-based corrections is to restore the chemically dependent offender to a state of law-abiding. To accomplish this, community-based programs include counseling, individual psychotherapy, group therapy, vocational training, occupational rehabilitation, and education.

Unfortunately, these programs are generally given less priority in a system where the primary emphasis is on institutional confinement rather than rehabilitation—on social control rather than community reintegration. Thus, it is important to recognize the distinction between *community-based corrections* programs and *diversion*. In the former, individual opportunity for work, school, or other community activities tend to be coercive, while the latter involves diverting the offender from the correctional system. According to Reid (1985), the more appropriate designation for community-based corrections programs as an alternative to incarceration is "deinstitutionalization."

Intensive Probation Supervision (IPS) is one community-based alternative to incarceration. IPS programs involve alternatives such as house arrest, electronic monitoring, shock incarceration, and bootcamps. The features of these "intermediate punishments" are described by Walker (1994, p. 218) as enforced curfew, urine surveillance, split-sentencing imprisonment (short-term incarceration followed by supervised release), and military-style confinement. These approaches assume the arrest and processing through the criminal justice system for drug related offenses (U.S. Dept. of Justice, 1992). As with other criminal proceedings, drug cases can be dismissed at various stages of the justice process. In cases where chemically dependent offenders are released on probation to community-based treatment, this alternative to incarceration generally must be court approved. Participation in treatment is then a court-imposed condition of probation. If a probationer violates the imposed conditions of the program, he or she may be remanded back to court and ordered to serve the remainder of the period of probation in jail or prison.

Under these conditions, community-based treatment is part of the corrections system. Unfortunately, threat of revocation and incarceration are rarely sufficient to deter the addict who is driven by the compulsion to "get high." Compulsivity, repetitiveness, and lack of self control characterize addictive behavior. Even under intensive legal pressure, there is no guarantee, or even likelihood, that an addict will accept or remain in treatment. Physical withdrawal from drugs is only the beginning of recovery.

Diversion programs, as differentiated from community-based corrections, attempt to redirect the criminal offender from the justice system to the extent that criminal proceedings are halted or suspended in favor of processing through noncriminal dispositions (Callison, 1983). Probably the most widely publicized and ambitious treatment-diversion approach to drug-abusing offenders came out of the Drug Abuse Office of Treatment Act of 1972. Known as Treatment Alternatives to Street Crime (TASC), the goals of these programs include (1) reducing criminal behavior among drug-involved offenders by focusing on rehabilitation and treatment; (2) lowering court overloads; (3) eliminating the negative labeling, brutalizing conditions, and adaptive learning processes of incarceration; and (4) diverting drug-involved offenders to community treatment (Callison, 1983).

TASC programs seek to merge the penal aspects of criminal law with the therapeutic aspects of health care. As an alternative to the incarceration of drug-abusing offenders, TASC program components include "identification of the drug-dependent offender, assessment of the individual's drug dependency and community risk, referral to the appropriate community risk, referral to the appropriate community treatment resources, and case management of the individual to maintain compliance with justice and treatment criteria" (National Institute on Drug Abuse, 1992). As of 1989, approximately 125 TASC-type programs were operating in twenty-five states. TASC program participants are under the direct supervision of the courts. Therefore, restraints on personal liberty, without conviction, are enforced, and pending criminal charges against uncooperative participants can be reactivated. Generally, TASC programs target nonviolent offenders who have been clinically diagnosed as chemically dependent and who voluntarily waive their rights in lieu of prosecution.

Community-based corrections and diversion have both supporters and critics. For example, supporters maintain (1) that community corrections result in smaller parole caseloads and thus, improved chance of success; (2) that community treatment serves to separate low-risk chemically dependent offenders' exposure to other criminal offenders in prisons; (3) that community treatment is noncorrectionally oriented, thus eliminating criminogenic stigma; (4) that "even temporary improvements that occur in treatment are valuable;" (5) that clients who complete such programs are less likely to use illegal drugs and commit crimes than before treatment; (6) that research, although limited, has shown that community treatment has reduced rearrest rates of participants from "87 percent beforehand to 22 percent after three years" (Walker, 1994); and (7) that overall, community-treatment alternatives to incarceration are most cost efficient.

On the other hand, critics maintain (1) that the most effective technique of drug/crime control and community protection is deterrence via incarceration; (2) that community treatment lacks definitive analysis or empirical research to confirm program effectiveness; (3) that community treatment is primarily a prosecutory "bargaining chip;" (4) that program criteria and eligibility requirements are politically motivated; (5) that program personnel rely too heavily upon "reformed addict turned drug counselor;" and (6) that the intent of community treatment is to serve a "population of offenders that [are] mainstream America: middle-class kids charged with shoplifting or possession of marijuana (Matthews, 1988).

These are a few of the opposing views on community-based treatment and diversion debated among criminologists, law enforcement personnel, and health and welfare personnel regarding the efficacy of community drug treatment as an effective alternative to rigid prosecution of chemically dependent offenders.

Implications for Social Work

Organized societies must enforce laws and provide appropriate punishment for those who violate the laws. Yet, the practice of retaliatory incarceration of drug-addicted criminal offenders has had a minimal impact on the drug/crime connection. Constructing new jails and prisons, increasing the number of law enforcement officers, and developing new crime-fighting technologies have not prevented the rise in drug abuse and drug-related criminal activity. Similarly, passage of "tougher" drug abuse laws has shown to be ineffective, largely because they are not uniformly administered or consistently interpreted (Vetter & Silverman, 1978).

Indeed, it has been argued that state and local laws have had the singular effect of overcrowding jails and prisons. Since 1978 the number of inmates serving time for drug possession has more than doubled (U.S. Dept. of Justice, 1988). Yet, based on trends of imprisonment, the crime control act of 1994 mandating the increase of jail and prison beds to 100,000 by the year 2000 will not resolve the problem of overcrowding. At an estimated average annual cost of $25,000 to $30,000 per bed, this mandate translates to approximately $3 billion. Implementation of the Crime Act will also increase the number of state and local police officers by 100,000. Specific drug provisions in the 1994 Crime Act will also provide funds to establish state and local drug courts to administer community-based treatment and diversion programs. The Crime Act, which amends the Omnibus Crime Control and Safe Streets Act of 1968, also includes a variety of other drug-crime-related legislation (see Violent Crime Control and Law Enforcement Act of 1994).

In an address to the National Press Club shortly after congressional passage of the crime bill, Attorney General Janet Reno outlined several of the Act's provisions. She included a brief description of the mandated functions of community policing. The articulation of those mandated functions are reminiscent of prevention and organizational activities commonly performed by social workers prior to and during the War on Poverty and Model Cities efforts of the 1960s and 1970s. Although some improvement resulted from these programs, for example, access to higher education, Head Start, community-based treatment, and diversion, a basic shift of emphasis in professional practice was also developing. The 1960s and 1970s were an era of ferment and discord within the ranks of professional social workers. Demands for social justice and social welfare policy reform gave rise to a recommitment to community-based practice and social action. It was a period in which trained social workers were actively involved at the "grass roots" level (Ehrenreich, 1985; Katz, 1993; Specht & Courtney, 1994). Here they were able to more effectively work with chemically dependent individuals and engage the problems of drugs and drug-connected crimes. At this level, micro and macro methods combined to re-emphasize traditional social work practice.

In his Crime Prevention Model, Lab (1992) discusses three models of crime prevention. These models—*primary, secondary,* and *tertiary*—are applicable to social work practice with the problems of drug addiction and the environmental conditions commonly associated with drugs and crime. Within the context of this model, primary prevention "identifies conditions of the physical and social environment that foster criminal activity" (Lab, 1992, p. 13). During the Senate debate on the Crime Bill, Senator Joseph Biden, chair of the Senate Judiciary Committee, described the tasks of identifying such conditions as functions of community policing (Conference Report, 1994). Biden asserted that illicit drug activities usually do not occur where there is a police presence, and when they do there is usually an arrest. He also asserted that the average drug addict commits approximately 154 "street crimes" each year. In a supporting study of New York heroin users, it was found that the ratio of crimes committed was 225 per known addict per year. These crimes are described as offenses against person and property (Cole, 1992). Street crimes include robbery, burglary, shoplifting, and systemic violence. Systemic violence frequently results from "competition between drug dealers, retaliation for poor drug quality or high prices, robbery of drug dealers or users" (Lab, 1992, p. 13) and illicit drug market control. "Drive by" shootings and "gangster style" assassinations are indicative of systemic violence. As a consequence, current societal concern about street crime, particularly when drugs are involved, has prompted a major portion of drug control resources to be channeled into deterrence and incapacitation.

But as previously suggested, while formal law enforcement mechanisms are necessary, the most effective drug control and prevention requires active community involvement. The implications for social work are clear. If social workers are to play a role in primary drug prevention, they must go beyond the disease concept of chemical dependence and refocus on community as client. Law enforcement officials, in cooperation with neighborhood citizens, local businesses, and community institutions, must be coordinated to undertake macro activities such as monitoring day-to-day community interactions, safe street initiatives, and social planning. Community development is a prerequisite component to a successful drug prevention strategy. The goal of this strategy is to inhibit crime before it occurs by eliminating environmental factors commonly associated with drug use and drug law offenders.

Based on Lab's (1992) crime model, secondary crime prevention "is concerned with intervening in those situations and with those persons who are displaying a tendency for criminal behavior" (p. 17). Although the relationship between chemical abuse and criminal behavior involves a complex set of factors, targeting individuals who may potentially engage in street-level drug activities can serve to alleviate drug-related crime. In profile studies of drug addicts (Cohen, 1981; Milkman, 1985; Satinder, 1980; Schober & Schade, 1991; and Vetter & Silverman, 1978), the addict is typically a member of a minority group, comes from an impoverished background, lacks education, has few marketable skills, and has had some encounter with the law.

Secondary crime prevention from a Generalist Method approach means regular interaction by social workers with the day-to-day social environment of the addicted offender. It means visiting crowded, chaotic apartments in low income, often hostile, communities. It involves direct intervention into the lives of crack cocaine addicted women who share two-bedroom apartments with their drug addicted children and grandchildren, that is, three generational addicted families (Dash, 1994). This level of practice requires comprehensive foundation knowledge about individual, family, and group behavior, in addition to community and organizational development skills. At this level of practice, the generalist is able to utilize knowledge and skills in working collaboratively with law enforcement, health, and welfare systems. Guided by informed knowledge, skills, and values, the goals of practice are to divert the chemically dependent offender from the criminal justice system and from correctional institutions. The impact of diversion and community-based drug treatment, for example, methadone maintenance therapeutic communities and other outpatient programs, have proven to be of limited success (Walker, 1994; *National Drug Control Strategy,* 1994; Cohen, 1981; Shaffer & Neuhaus, 1989; Susman, 1972). But much of the work involved in secondary drug prevention targets social conditions, for example, poverty, racism, lack of education, under/unemployment, and other social problems. Generalist practice focuses on helping individuals, families, and groups to identify and utilize the resources necessary to enhance quality of life.

In developing the tertiary level for the crime prevention model, Lab (1992) maintains that practice methods used in working directly with drug offenders are "tertiary in nature" (p. 13). Accordingly, tertiary prevention attempts to eliminate recidivistic behavior by drug offenders. Also at the tertiary level of prevention, emphasis shifts from potential drug offenders to individuals who have actually committed crimes for which they have been prosecuted, tried, and convicted. Usually these offenders are those who have been convicted of (1) drug-defined crimes such as possession and sales; (2) crimes in which the interactional effects of drug addiction and socioeconomic living styles are manifested in criminal behavior; and (3) drug-related crimes committed by addicts to satisfy their addiction (Walker, 1994). Tertiary prevention focuses on drug addicts as individuals, chiefly the offenders who are at the incarceration end of the criminal justice system. For these drug offenders, incapacitation has been imposed to deter their drug-taking and criminal activity. They have been labeled criminals and for a variety of reasons fail to meet criteria for admission and participation in either diversion or community-based correctional programs.

As noted above, incarceration is no guarantee against future drug use or abuse. Illegal drugs are regularly smuggled into jails and prisons. As a result, drug abuse and chemical dependence exists among incarcerated populations. One of the assumptions underlying incarceration is the necessity to deprive individuals of the capacity to commit additional crimes. Historically, incarceration has been viewed as an opportunity to rehabilitate offenders by treating those behaviors believed to be the source of their criminality. In the case of drug-abusing offenders, most correctional systems offer psychological, behavioral, and social services to deal with those behaviors. Within the correctional setting, these programs vary from "incarceration without specialized services through services that specifically target drug abuse problems" (Brown, 1992, p. 14). These institutionally based programs are within the area of tertiary prevention, despite the fact that the target of intervention is the individual already in the correctional setting. At this level of Lab's prevention model, the goal is to reduce recidivism rates.

The levels of prevention discussed in this crime-model approach are neither mutually exclusive nor represent separate practice domains. The idea of primary–secondary–tertiary drug prevention is consistent with the holistic practice approach of the Generalist Method. This approach moves the worker outside of the agency into the environment of the addict. Frans (1994) asserts that "social work must encompass an ecological view of chemical dependence that incorporates consideration of a range of factors, both individual and environmental, in making intervention decisions" (p. 35). He further asserts that the profession must look beyond the disease model of treatment which has tended to focus on the individual and blame the addict. While the well-being of the individual is germane to practice, overemphasizing the disease concept of addiction overlooks the need for structural changes in society. Amelioration of the environmental conditions in which drug taking is perpetuated can be more effectively dealt with by holistic interventions. Development, implementation, and evaluation of broad-based comprehensive drug deterrence programs also requires cooperation of law enforcement, health, and social service agencies. These coordinated efforts are within the perspective of the Generalist Method.

References

Allen, H. & Simonsen, C. E. (1986). *Corrections in America*. New York: Macmillan.

Andre, P. (1987). *Drug addiction*. Pompano Beach, FL: Health Communications.

Bakalar, J. B. & Grinspoon, L. (1987). Medical uses of illegal drugs. In A. Freedman & R. Hamonway (Eds.), *Dealing with drugs* (pp. 183–219). San Francisco, CA: Pacific Research Institute for Public Policy.

Brown, B. S. (1992). Program models. (Monograph). In *National institute of drug abuse research series*. (DHHS Publication No. ADM 92-1884, pp. 31–37). Washington, DC: U.S. Government Printing Office.

Bureau of Justice Statistics. (1988). *Prisoners in 1988.* (NCJ 116315, April 1988, p. 7). Washington, DC: U.S. Dept. of Justice.

Bureau of Justice Statistics. (1993). *Correctional populations in the United States, 1991.* (NCJ 142729, Aug. 1993). Washington, DC: U.S. Dept. of Justice.

Callison, H. G. (1983). *Introduction to community-based corrections.* New York: McGraw-Hill.

Cohen, S. (1981). *The substance abuse problems.* New York: Hawthorne Press.

Cole, G. F. (1992). *The American system of criminal justice.* Pacific Grove, CA: Brooks/Cole.

Conference Report. (1994). *Violent Crime Control and Law Enforcement Act of 1994.* Washington, DC: U.S. Government Printing Office.

Connaway, R. S. & Gentry, M.E. (1988). *Social work practice.* Englewood Cliffs, NJ: Prentice Hall.

Dash, L. (1994). Rosa Lee's story. *The Washington Post,* Sept. 18, pp. A1, A32.

Doweiko, H. E. (1993). *Concepts of chemical dependency.* Pacific Grove, CA: Brooks/Cole.

Ehrenreich, J. H. (1985). *The altruistic imagination.* Ithaca, NY: Cornell University Press.

Frans, D. (1994). Social work, social science and the disease model: New directions for addictions treatment. *Journal of Sociology and Social Welfare, 21,* (2), 32–37.

Hamowy, R. (Ed.). (1991). *Dealing with drugs.* San Francisco, CA: Pacific Research Institute for Public Policy.

Hunter, A. M. & Pudim, R. A. (1989). Addictive behavior and the justice system. In H. B. Milkman & H. J. Shaffer (Eds.), *The addictions* (pp. 75–84). Lexington, MA: Lexington Books.

Jenike, E. M. (1989). Drug abuse. In E. Rubinstein & D. D. Federman (Eds.), *Scientific American medicine.* New York: Scientific American Press.

Johnson, E. H. (1978). *Crime, correction and society.* Homewood, IL: Dorsey Press.

Johnson, G. L. (1993). Socioeconomic correlates of violent behavior. Unpublished data.

Katz, B. M. (1993). *The underclass debate: Views from history.* Princeton, NJ: N.p.

Lab, S. B. (1992). *Crime prevention approaches, practices and evaluations.* Cincinnati, OH: Anderson.

Lipton, D. S., Falkin, G. P., & Wexler, H. K. (1992). Correctional drug abuse treatment in the United States: An overview. In C. G. Leukefeld & F. M. Tims (Eds.), *Drug abuse treatment in prisons and jails* (pp. 8–30). Rockville, MD: N.p.

Little, C. B. (1989). *Deviance and control, theory, research, and social policy.* Itasca, IL: Peacock.

Matthews, W. G. (1988). Pretrial diversion: Promises we can't keep. *Journal of Offender Counseling, Services and Rehabilitation* 12 (2).

McMahon, M. O. (1989). *The General Method of social work practice* (2nd ed.) Englewood Cliffs, NJ: Prentice Hall.

McNeece, C. & DiVitto, D. (1994). *Chemical dependency: A systems approach.* Englewood Cliffs, NJ: Prentice Hall.

Meyer, R. G. (1992). *Abnormal behavior and the criminal justice system.* New York: Lexington Books.

National Drug Control Strategy, Executive Summary. (1994). Washington, DC: U.S. Executive Office of the President, Office of National Drug Control Policy.

National Institute on Drug Abuse. (1992). Drug treatment in state prisons. *Drug Abuse Services Research Series* (DHHS Pub. No. ADM 92-1898). Washington, DC: U.S. Government Printing Office.

Satinder, P. K. (1980). *Drug use: Criminal, sick or cultural?* Roslyn Heights, NY: Libra.

Schober, S. & Schade, C. (1991). Edipemiology of cocaine use and abuse. (NCJ No. 135854). Rockville, MD: U.S. Dept. of Health and Human Services and National Institute on Drug Abuse.

Schwartz, R. H. (1987). Marijuana: An overview. *The pediatric clinics of North America, 34* (2), 305–317.

Shaffer, H. J. & Neuhaus, C. Jr. (1989). Testing hypotheses: An approach for the assessment of addictive behavior. In H. B. Milkman & H. J. Shaffer (Eds.), *The addictions* (pp. 87–103). Lexington, MA: Lexington Books.

Siegel, R. K. (1982). Cocaine smoking disorders: Diagnosis and treatment. *Psychiatric annuals, 14,* 728–732.

Specht, H. (1972). The deprofessionalization of social work. *Social Work, 17,* 3–15.

Specht, H. (1988). *New directions for social work.* Englewood Cliffs, NJ: Prentice Hall.

Specht, H. & Courtney, M. E. (1994). *Unfaithful angels: How social work has abandoned its mission.* New York: Free Press.

Susman, J. (1972). *Drug use and social policy.* New York: AMS Press.

Toch, H. & Adams, K. (1988). Punishment, treatment and prison infractions. *Journal of Offender Counseling, Services and Rehabilitation, 12* (2), 5–18.

U.S. Congress, Office of Technology Assessment. (1993). *Biological components of substance abuse and addiction.* (OTA-BP-BBS-117). Washington, DC: U.S. Government Printing Office.

U.S. Dept. of Health and Human Services. (1992). *Drug use among American high school seniors, college students and young adults.* (U.S. Dept. of H.H.S. publication, Vol. 1-2). Washington, DC: U.S. Government Printing Office.

U.S. Dept. of Justice. (1988). *Report to the nation on crime and justice* (NCJ-105506). Washington, DC: U.S. Government Printing Office.

U.S. Dept. of Justice. (1992). *Drugs, crime, and the justice system* (NCJ-133652). Washington, DC: U.S. Government Printing Office.

U.S. Dept. of Justice (1993). *International narcotics control strategy report* (Dept. of State Pub. No. 10047). Washington, DC: U.S. Government Printing Office.

Vetter, H. J. & Silverman, I. J. (1978). *The nature of crime.* Philadelphia, PA: W. B. Saunders.

Waldorf, D. (1972). *Drug use and social policy.* New York: AMA Press.

Walker, S. (1983). *The Police in America: An introduction.* New York: McGraw-Hill.

Walker, S. (1994). *Sense and nonsense about crime and drugs.* Belmont, CA: Wadsworth.

Weisheit, R. (Ed.). (1990). *Drugs, crime and the criminal justice system.* Cincinnati, OH: Anderson.

White, H. R. (1990). *The drug use–delinquency connection in adolescence.* In R. Weisheit (Ed.), *Drugs, crime, and the criminal justice system* (pp. 215–256). Cincinnati, OH: Anderson.

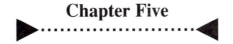

Chapter Five

Treatment and Intervention with Chemically Involved Adult Offenders

C. Aaron McNeece and Charles M. Daly

George Johnson has explained and graphically described the impact of chemical dependency on both society and the individual in the preceding chapter. He leaves no doubt that chemical dependency remains one of the most serious social and political issues of the twentieth century. Our task in this chapter is to examine in greater detail the extent of substance abuse among those individuals who are "clients" of the criminal justice system, the treatment approaches and resources available to use with chemically dependent offenders, the effectiveness of such interventions, and the roles of social workers in dealing with these clients.

Offender Use of Illegal Drugs

A critical step in the exploration of issues surrounding drug-abuse treatment for adult offenders is a basic understanding of the incidence of illegal drug use within this unique subculture. We have little definitive data on which to base a reliable profile of individuals who are both illegal-drug-dependent and involved in the criminal justice system. The most commonly used baseline for estimating drug usage among offenders is the Drug Use Forecasting (DUF) program of the National Institute of Justice (National Institute of Justice, 1990–1993). This effort, initiated in 1987, annually samples the drug-use behavior of arrestees in twenty-three major U.S. cities. The DUF program is an indicator of offender drug use based upon self-reporting and voluntary urine screenings.

Table 5.1 shows 1992 DUF data for a subsample of five major urban areas. These data break down the percentage of male and female arrestees testing positive for any drug (excluding alcohol). Here we see a clear and consistent pattern of illegal substance use by the arrestees. During 1992, the percentage of arrestees testing positive for at least one illegal drug ranged for racial groups from a low of 33 percent for Hispanic females in Houston to a high of 87 percent for African-American females in Manhattan. Females were more likely than males to test positive for drugs, and African-American arrestees tended to test positive slightly more often than do caucasians. Overall, Hispanics were significantly less likely to test positive than were their African-American or caucasian counterparts.

Table 5.1 also reflects the age ranges of arrestees testing positive. Here we see that age is a significant factor in drug use among offenders. The fifteen to twenty age group was consistently less likely to test positive for drugs. Drug use among arrestees peaks between the ages of twenty-one and thirty-five and then begins to decline. Females aged fifteen to twenty years are significantly less likely to test positive than are young males, but the gap closes in the twenty-one to twenty-five age group. The percentage of females testing positive for any drug equals or exceeds that of males after age twenty-six.

Table 5.2 shows the five-year arrestee drug-use trend in a subsample of five major urban areas. These data reflect few substantive changes in overall drug use despite greatly expanded treatment-intervention funding in the criminal justice system. Some sustained declines, especially among male offenders, are evident in Los Angeles and Manhattan between 1988 and 1990, but the 1992 data suggest a new upward trend.

Table 5.3 reflects the trends specific to cocaine use among arrestees from 1988 through 1992. Here we see that, of those testing positive for at least one drug, cocaine was the drug of choice for as many as 75 percent of female arrestees in Manhattan but for only 41 percent among male arrestees in Houston. Overall, females tended to test positive for cocaine more often than did males. With the possible exception of Atlanta, the data on females did not reflect a sustained downward trend in cocaine use in any of the urban areas in our subsample, while males in Manhattan had sustained a decline since 1988. Until 1992, males in Los Angeles had also shown a steady decline in cocaine use.

The heavy use of illegal drugs by both male and female arrestees, reflected in our subsample of major U.S. urban areas, leaves little doubt that such drugs play a major role in the criminal-justice-offender subculture. Despite a great deal of research, there is still much uncertainty about the nature of the drugs-crime relationship. While there is convincing documentation that

Table 5.1: Percentage of Arrestees Testing Positive for Any Drug, 1992

	Atlanta		Ft. Lauderdale		Houston		Los Angeles		Manhattan	
	Male	Female	Male	Female	Male	Female	Male	Female	Male	Female
Racial Groups										
African American	69	62	69	57	66	59	80	84	82	87
Caucasian	66	79	62	65	59	54	73	78	75	77
Hispanic	**	**	44	**	46	33	56	46	70	84
Other	**	**	**	**	**	**	67	**	**	**
Age Groups										
15-20	53	28	64	44	40	26	52	39	54	41
21-25	69	57	67	55	55	45	57	69	72	69
26-30	77	80	66	70	70	65	70	74	86	87
31-35	77	78	68	70	70	63	81	82	87	80
36+	65	66	59	58	57	59	72	76	80	76

**Fewer than 20 cases

Table 5.2: Trends in Percentage of Offenders Testing Positive for Any Drug, 1988–1992

	1988		1989		1990		1991		1992	
	Male	Female	Male	Female	Male	Female	Male	Female	Male	Female
Atlanta	NA	NA	NA	NA	62	71	63	70	69	65
Ft. Lauderdale	62	NA	66	63	60	66	61	64	64	62
Houston	65	NA	65	58	64	59	65	59	59	54
Los Angeles	75	76	70	78	65	71	62	75	67	72
Manhattan	83	80	79	76	76	71	73	77	77	85

NA=data not available

Table 5.3: Trends in Percentage of Offenders Testing Positive for Cocaine, 1988–1992

	1988		1989		1990		1991		1992	
	Male	Female	Male	Female	Male	Female	Male	Female	Male	Female
Atlanta	NA	NA	NA	NA	59	68	57	66	58	58
Ft. Lauderdale	42	NA	50	53	46	55	44	55	46	47
Houston	49	NA	52	48	53	49	56	52	41	44
Los Angeles	60	61	52	65	45	55	44	62	52	58
Manhattan	74	75	72	67	65	64	62	66	62	72

NA=data not available

heroin addicts frequently turn to crime as a way of financing their addiction (Inciardi & McElrath, 1995, p. 238), the same cannot be said of cocaine and marijuana abuse (Rasmussen, Benson, & Mast, 1994). Subculture theories describe most drug use by criminals as a process by which persons become acculturated to a deviant subculture. Smoking "dope," snorting cocaine, or injecting heroin are simply what many members of this subculture do. Proper socialization to the subculture requires a certain expectation regarding drug use (Estes & Heineman, 1986).

The Target Population for Treatment

While ongoing drug education programs for drug-abusing criminal offenders are clearly indicated, not all drug-involved offenders require treatment intervention. Indeed, diagnosis of drug addiction or dependency represents one of the more complex obstacles to achieving a better understanding of how best to design and target treatment resources for offenders. According to Peele (1985, p. 18) "we cannot define the state called 'addiction' apart from a subjective interpretation: In general, we believe a person is addicted when he says he is." Abadinsky (1993, p. 9) suggests that drug dependency is best defined in functional terms: "A preoccupation with drug acquisition-compulsive use despite adverse consequences." Criteria established by the American Psychiatric Association in its *Diagnostic and Statistical Manual, DSM-IV,* are commonly used by treatment providers receiving third-party (e.g., Blue Cross, Medicaid) reimbursements for drug treatment services. These criteria require that the insured meet any three of these general criteria:

- Unsuccessful attempts to cut down on drug use
- Using drugs in progressively larger amounts and/or over longer periods of time
- Spending large amounts of time obtaining or recovering from the use of drugs
- Frequent failure to meet responsibilities to their job, finances, school, and family/home
- Withdrawal from important social, occupational, or recreational activities
- Persistent drug use despite knowledge of the problems and dangers it presents
- Use of drugs to relieve or avoid withdrawal symptoms
- Recurrent drug use in situations likely to be physically dangerous (e.g., driving)

Drug-abuse assessment and treatment providers typically utilize one or more screening instruments, related to some degree on the *DSM-IV* criteria, in the assessment of individual offenders. The Drug Abuse Screening Test (DAST), Substance Abuse Subtle Screening Inventory (SASSI), and Addiction Severity Index (ASI) are among the more commonly used standard instruments.

Unfortunately, no one really knows what proportion of drug-involved offenders exhibit the symptomatic behaviors of substance abuse at any given time. Estimates by the Institute of Medicine (Gerstein & Harwood, 1990, p. 84) suggest that approximately 43 percent of the individuals under the jurisdiction of the criminal justice system at any given time meet the *DSM-IV* criteria for substance dependence (including alcohol). Our own research with substance-involved offenders in Florida indicates that approximately half the offenders in treatment report substances other than alcohol as their drugs of choice (McNeece, 1991; 1992). These estimates, taken together, suggest that perhaps 20 percent of the offenders in the criminal justice system may need treatment for illegal substance dependency.

Assessment and Treatment of Drug Involved Offenders

Until the mid-1960s, drug dependency was largely viewed as incidental to an offender's criminal behavior. Once an arrest was made for a drug-related offense, the criminal justice system focused on establishing the individual's guilt or innocence and on administering sanctions accordingly. Regardless of the outcome (freedom, probation, jail, or prison), the drug dependency issue was considered to be outside the court's jurisdiction. At the same time, publicly supported drug-abuse-treatment resources were almost nonexistent.

By the mid- to late 1960s there was a growing realization in the criminal justice system that prosecution and incarceration of drug-dependent offenders did little to deter future drug abuse or other anti-social behaviors. Indeed, research suggested that the labeling of drug abusers as felons and ex-convicts often had the unintended consequence of creating career criminals (Inciardi & McBride, 1991, p. 10). The federal Comprehensive Drug Abuse Prevention and Control Act of 1970 stimulated this growing recognition by sanctioning the diversion of some drug-involved offenders from the criminal justice system to the drug abuse treatment system. Similar state legislation soon followed, with the primary focus on diversion of nonviolent first offenders. It was also during the mid- to late 1960s that the still fledgling Community Mental Health system began to improve offender access to publicly supported substance abuse treatment programs.

Today, the drug-dependent offender typically accesses treatment in one of three ways. He or she can (1) avoid the sanctions of the criminal justice system by voluntarily seeking treatment for an addiction before an arrest for the use of illicit drugs; (2) avoid criminal sanctions by voluntarily accepting treatment in lieu of prosecution following an arrest; or (3) voluntarily or involuntarily enter treatment as part of a criminal justice sanction following an adjudication of guilt.

The substance-dependent individual who voluntarily seeks help—and has sufficient insurance or personal resources—can readily access the full spectrum of residential and outpatient treatment resources. Those without sufficient insurance or personal resources must depend upon publicly funded treatment programs with their severely strained resources and long waiting lists. Our focus here is on the drug-dependent offenders entering the justice system. There are two commonly used vehicles for facilitating offender access to treatment following an arrest on drug charges: pretrial interventions and postadjudication intervention.

Pretrial Intervention

Pretrial intervention programs vary greatly from one jurisdiction to another, but their basic purpose is to offer substance-involved, nonviolent, first offenders an opportunity to avoid a criminal record by voluntarily agreeing to participate in a prescribed treatment program. In some pretrial intervention programs, the states attorney and presiding judge will agree to withhold adjudication of the individual's drug charges pending successful completion of a treatment plan, after which the charges are dropped. In other jurisdictions the offender may plead guilty with the understanding that the court record will be either sealed or expunged if the offender successfully completes treatment and has no subsequent arrests within a fixed time period, usually one year.

Pretrial Release

Perhaps the simplest type of pretrial intervention program simply screens criminal offenders for a drug abuse problem. Eligibility generally requires that the offender have no previous felony convictions, no history of violent behavior or mental illness, and a demonstrated need for treatment. The need for treatment may be demonstrated by the arrest record, a diagnostic interview, or urine testing. Typically the client will be released, maintained under court supervision, and referred for treatment. Regardless of any possible benefits to the offenders, pretrial release programs are becoming increasingly popular because of the tremendous potential for financial savings to county and city government. Such a program saved Brevard County, Florida, approximately $2.5 million in 1991 (McNeece, 1992).

Drug Court

In areas with a high volume of drug possession cases, the trend has been for some jurisdictions to establish a "drug court" system in which one or more judges are assigned to hear all such cases and track their progress over time. Most formal drug court programs are designed either to provide or purchase drug education, drug treatment, and case management/offender tracking services. Many drug court programs have emulated a service model first developed in New York City. Its approach is unique in that, once the offender enters the program, the judge, prosecutor, and public defender work as a team instead of operating in traditional adversarial roles. Typically, the drug court judge plays a very active and relatively informal role, including regular verbal exchanges with each drug court client. Another unique feature borrowed from the original New York model is the use of acupuncture as a regular part of the initial drug treatment regimen. Although there is no logical reason why drug courts must operate in tandem with acupuncture clinics, this seems to have become a common practice.

A key element of all pretrial intervention programs is the availability of a formal mechanism for tracking the treatment progress of the offender and providing prompt feedback to the court. In most cases, periodic urine screening is an integral part of the treatment plan. In many instances the designated substance abuse treatment provider is called upon to periodically report progress directly to the court. Other jurisdictions utilize specialized case managers to perform this function, and still others depend upon existing local probation program officers/counselors to track progress and report to the court.

Postadjudication Intervention

When a jurisdiction has no pretrial intervention program or the substance-involved offender has a criminal history that makes him or her ineligible for such programs, the criminal justice system has other options for dealing with the substance abuse problem. Once an adjudication of guilt has been entered, the court either places the offender on probation or orders incarceration. Depending upon the seriousness of the offense and the length of the sentence, the incarcerated individual will serve the time in a local jail, a prison, or perhaps a less restrictive alternative.

Boot Camp

A relatively recent variation on the incarceration option is "boot camp." Boot camp programs commonly operate as separate jail or prison facilities and target younger (late teens to early twenties), substance-involved offenders. Combining military-like discipline with more traditional substance abuse education and treatment interventions, boot camps are becoming increasingly popular around the country. Unfortunately, initial research on them indicates that they are no more effective than other, more traditional forms of intervention (Parent, 1989).

Probation and Incarceration

When sentencing a substance-involved offender to probation, the judge typically makes participation in a prescribed treatment program a condition of that probation, and the offender's progress in treatment is tracked by an assigned probation officer/counselor. If the court's sentence involves a period of incarceration, an increasing number of jail and prison facilities now offer drug abuse education and treatment programs, usually on a voluntary basis.

Regardless of the vehicle through which the substance-involved offender accesses the treatment system, the basic categories of service usually available remain essentially the same—assessment, case management, treatment, and aftercare.

Assessment and Case Management Services

During the late 1960s, problems with offender assessment methods, doubts about court and law enforcement, the efficacy of alternatives to incarceration, and frequent communication breakdowns between the local criminal justice and treatment systems brought about experimentation with a variety of service delivery models.

The Treatment Alternative to Street Crime (TASC) program is the best known and most widely used national model. TASC was initially funded in 1972 through grants from the Law Enforcement Assistance Administration (LEAA) and the National Institute of Mental Health (NIMH). Representing a major new field of opportunity for trained social workers, the TASC model was designed to establish, within the criminal justice system, a formalized system of drug-involved offender identification, assessment, treatment referral, and follow-up. Early TASC programs were often administratively independent of both the courts and the treatment system. They were charged with responsibility for working with offenders, judges, defense attorneys, prosecutors, and substance abuse treatment providers to plan, implement, and supervise community-based alternatives to prosecution and/or incarceration. The TASC counselor serves as the offender's case manager, facilitating treatment access, helping with access to other needed services, and providing feedback to the court on the offender's progress.

Direct federal funding for TASC ended in 1980 with the inception of criminal-justice block grants to the states, but the basic TASC model has remained viable and has continued to evolve. While often no longer referred to as TASC, and frequently aligned administratively with either the court or a substance abuse treatment provider, some variation of the basic TASC linkage model has been adopted by most criminal justice jurisdictions in the country. This model relies heavily on the unique skills of the trained social worker to carry out its assessment and case management functions. In recent years, many TASC and TASC-like programs have added their own education and treatment components that also rely heavily on the skills of trained social workers.

Substance Abuse Treatment and Aftercare Services

Once offender identification and assessment are complete and the criminal justice system has determined the disposition of any criminal charges, the offender may enter a prescribed treatment program. Depending upon the individual's legal status, he or she may receive treatment services in the home community, in jail, or in prison. Local communities and correctional facilities vary greatly in the range of treatment services offered and in the availability of treatment slots. Social workers commonly perform central roles in working with offenders in all three settings, either as employees of the jail or prison or as employees of treatment-provider agencies under contract to the facility.

Modalities of Treatment

Categorizing and describing the various approaches to substance abuse treatment for offenders is complicated by the lack of standardization in terminology, as well as a considerable overlap among various treatment interventions. Peters (1993) suggests a useful taxonomy that divides common treatment approaches into four basic categories: (1) Chemical Dependency/Self-help; (2) Pharmacological; (3) Psychoeducational; and (4) Therapeutic Communities.

Chemical Dependency/Self-help Approach

Treatment interventions based on the chemical dependency/self-help approach are found in most offender treatment programs operating today. They are often referred to as "12-step" or "28-day" programs. Stemming from what is sometimes referred to as the "Chronic Disease Model," they are designed around the basic belief that substance addictions are an "illness" resulting from a combination of physiological, psychological, and social factors that can be ameliorated through treatment but never "cured." The goal of treatment is total abstinence. During abstinence the addiction "disease" is viewed as being in remission. Relapse is considered to be part of the treatment process, and continuous peer and professional support are seen as critical to preventing relapse.

Alcoholics Anonymous (AA) and Narcotics Anonymous (NA) groups are most frequently associated with this model of treatment, but the basic philosophy is commonly incorporated into the programs of private and public sector treatment providers. For the treatment of more serious addictions some programs employ a three to six week residential "drying out" period during which the "twelve steps" (see Doweiko, 1993, p. 358) to addiction recovery are emphasized. The addict is counseled in understanding his or her dependency and in planning relapse prevention efforts following release from the residential program. Other programs handle this counseling entirely on an outpatient basis, both individual and group. Ongoing participation in AA or NA groups is seen as essential to treatment and relapse prevention.

It is not uncommon for courts to divert first offenders or to grant pretrial release or probation for drug offenders who agree to follow a prescribed treatment regime utilizing some variation of this treatment model. Frequently, case managers or probation officers assume responsibility for tracking the offender's progress in treatment and periodically reporting that progress to the court.

Some variation of the chemical dependency/self-help approach is found in many jail and prison substance-abuse-treatment programs as well as in community-based programs. In some cases the treatment is limited to allowing AA or NA meetings on the jail or prison grounds. In other facilities the treatment program may include a residential component operated entirely by social workers and other trained professionals employed by the facility. The more common practice is for jails and prisons to contract with public or private treatment providers to bring an array of services into the facility. Participation in treatment is usually voluntary for incarcerated offenders, but if the offender has a history of substance abuse, participation in a treatment program is often ordered as a condition of parole.

Treatment Effectiveness

Most offenders participating in these chemical-dependency-model treatment programs are alcohol addicted and, according to Gerstein and Harwood (1990, p. 190), research on their effectiveness in treating other types of addiction is inadequate. The few follow-up studies that have been conducted suggest that ". . . primary drug clients have poorer outcomes than primary alcohol clients."

Pharmacological Approach

Treating addictive "diseases" with pharmacological, or biochemical, intervention stems logically from the medical model of treatment. Pharmacological intervention is most commonly employed in cases of severe and chronic addiction when other treatment methods have repeatedly failed. Typically, the treatment involves the short- or long-term use of a drug that reduces the addict's craving for illegal drugs. The two most commonly used pharmacological interventions involve either naltrexone hydrochloride or methadone.

Naltrexone Hydrochloride

Naltrexone hydrochloride has recently been found to block the euphoric effects of injected opiates (Doweiko, 1993, p. 351). Use of this chemical is ordinarily limited to a short-term period after detoxification (Holloway, 1993). A physically dependent heroin user undergoes a severe and abrupt withdrawal when placed on an antagonist drug such as naltrexone (Crabtree, 1984). This treatment assumes that the addict is less likely to use the illegal drug if it no longer produces the desired euphoric effect. One problem with naltrexone is that the binding and blocking of opioid receptors is not permanent. By taking a greater-than-usual dose of heroin, an addict taking naltrexone can still "get high" (Leccese, 1991). According to Doweiko (1993), the effectiveness of naltrexone for long-term treatment of narcotics addiction remains unproven. One study found that only 5 percent of heroin users complied with treatment programs involving naltrexone (Greenstein, Evans, & McLellan, 1983). There is some evidence that naltrexone may be somewhat more effective for opiate addiction when given in combination with other drugs such as clonidine. Unlike naltrexone alone, this combination may be used to induce a much quicker withdrawal in opioid-dependent individuals (Charney, Heninger, & Klever, 1986).

Methadone

Methadone is a synthetic narcotic utilized for the treatment of opiate addiction. Typically, the drug is used as a short-term vehicle to lessen the side effects of withdrawal from heroin. In more serious cases of chronic addiction, a "methadone maintenance" approach may be employed as a long-term substitute for the illegal drug. The use of methadone, while not uncommon, is highly controversial. According to Doweiko (1993), there is little indication that the physical discomfort associated with opiate detoxification warrants the use of a substitute narcotic when readily available nonnarcotic drugs can be just as effective.

Research on methadone maintenance programs (Mirin, Weiss, & Greenfield, 1991) indicates that many addicts, while in these programs, frequently use nonopiate illegal substances such as cocaine. However, Gerstein and Harwood (1990) concluded that methadone maintenance programs more than pay for themselves by reducing the criminal activity of the participants.

Pharmacological approaches to the treatment of nonopiate addictions are currently being tried, but with mixed success. Antidepressants, for example, have been found to have some limited utility in the treatment of cocaine addiction (Doweiko, 1993).

Pharmacological treatment is rarely used in jail or prison programs because of security considerations, but it is often available to parolees or probationers who have long treatment histories and chronic opiate addiction.

Acupuncture

While not strictly a pharmacological intervention, the use of acupuncture to reduce a patient's craving for alcohol, opiates, and cocaine has been increasing in popularity in recent years. In theory, acupuncture needles applied to selected points on the patient's ear can promote the production of beta-endorphins or other naturally occurring substances in the body. These substances, in turn, are said to reduce the individual's craving for drugs or alcohol.

Acupuncture treatment has potential advantages over ingesting synthetic chemicals such as naltrexone or methadone, but few controlled studies of the effectiveness of acupuncture have been conducted and those that have tend to produce conflicting results (Brumbaugh, 1993).

Psychoeducational Approach

Psychoeducational treatment models vary greatly, but they typically introduce substance abuse and "life skills" education materials in a highly structured group setting. Some models are commercially marketed with a series of instructional video tapes, workbooks, and instructor discussion guides. Psychoeducational techniques are frequently used as an integral part of outpatient and residential group treatment programs. The commercially available "packages" are ideally suited for jail programs where the offender's sentence is three months or less.

Psychoeducational programs are designed around the assumption that addiction is caused by multiple biopsychosocial factors, and that to abstain from drugs the substance abuser must understand the physical, social, and economic forces that contribute to his or her compelling need for them. Using educational materials, homework, modeling, role playing, and group dynamics, the treatment is intended to help the offender understand the role that drugs have played in his or her life and to prepare the offender to deal more effectively with the contributing physical, social, and economic forces in the future.

These programs frequently include AIDS awareness components and place considerable emphasis on practicing techniques for improving interpersonal relationships at home and in the workplace. Many of the programs also encourage the individual to explore his or her educational or vocational needs and aspirations following release. When used in the jail setting or as part of a prerelease planning program in prisons, psychoeducational programs often emphasize introducing the offender to treatment resources available in the community and preparing him or her to take maximum advantage of those resources. (Christiansen, 1988; Peters & Dolente, 1990; Peters, 1993).

Therapeutic Communities Approach

As is true for all of the treatment methodologies examined in this chapter, therapeutic community (TC) models share certain common elements but vary greatly in their actual operation. Typically, a therapeutic community is a highly structured nine to twelve month residential treatment program. It is not uncommon for clients to remain in a TC for three to four years. Such long-term programs are costly and usually serve individuals who have had a long history of drug abuse and several failed drug abuse treatment experiences. The basic treatment philosophy is that the addiction lies with the person, not with the drug, and that it is merely a symptom of a larger problem (Pan et al., 1993, p. 35).

The treatment goal of the therapeutic community is to help the drug abuser achieve and maintain a responsible, drug-free life-style. Psychoeducational techniques are commonly used as part of the treatment regimen. The treatment relies heavily on mutual self-help and self-governance among members of the community. Rules of the community are usually very specific and are strictly enforced by the residents themselves. Violation of rules results in sanctions imposed on the resident, and repeated offenses result in expulsion from the community.

The treatment-staff members are often former substance abusers who themselves have successfully completed treatment in a therapeutic community. Individual and group counseling is employed to help the individual recognize and change negative attitudes, behaviors, and feelings that lead to the need for illegal substance use, but "peer encounter" is viewed as the cornerstone of the treatment process. This treatment method is typically highly confrontational, and it is common for residents to leave within the first three months of treatment (Goldapple, 1990).

In recent years the therapeutic community model has become increasingly popular as part of prerelease programming for incarcerated offenders who have histories of serious substance abuse. These programs usually isolate the therapeutic community from the rest of the jail or prison population. When properly designed and administered, these programs offer an opportunity to "re-socialize" the inmate by offering a nonpunative, supportive environment that contrasts greatly with "normal" prison life (Pan, et al., 1993).

Most research into the postrelease drug and crime experiences of offenders leaving prison-based therapeutic community programs has not shown them to be significantly more successful than with offenders who did not participate in treatment. However, other research has shown that therapeutic community programs, when closely linked to community-based supervision and treatment programs, can significantly reduce rearrest rates (Gerstein & Harwood, 1990, p. 191).

Social Work Roles

Social workers are involved in a number of different roles in working with drug-involved offenders. Among those services we have observed, the most common roles seem to be program planning, advocating, referring, educating, counseling, and monitoring and supervision.

Social workers, especially those with experience working directly with drug-involved clients, can provide valuable input and leadership in the planning, development, and implementation of programs. Although the program planning role is significantly different from direct service work, the latter experience is invaluable for anyone with programming responsibility. In our view, management skills combined with clinical experience is the best possible combination in a planner's background.

Advocacy can occur at many different levels: providing testimony to legislative committees, interceding with service providers, and running interference for the client with the legal system. Each of these is a relatively specialized activity, and few social worker advocates are likely to be equally active or skilled in both.

Referral is perhaps the most common function of social workers for drug-involved offenders. Contrary to popular myth, there is a plethora of services available for these clients in most communities. Knowing how to access those services is sometimes the weak link. Federal Anti-Drug Abuse Act appropriations alone provided more than $580 million for programs related to drug-involved criminal offenders in federal fiscal year 1994–95, and these funds have been matched with millions more at the state and local levels.

Educating drug-involved offenders is a critical service. Most offenders do not seem to be aware of the specific physiological impact of drugs on the body, the psychological impact of drugs on their moods, feelings, and behavior, or the devastating effect that drug abuse can have on family members. Many other important educational services are provided by social workers, including AIDS education and the relationship between drug-use and AIDS, training in job-seeking skills, interpersonal relationship building, and other personal coping skills.

Counseling is provided to drug-involved clients by a number of different professionals, as well as far too great a number of nonprofessionals. (In our research we have found many counselors with no specific credentials to qualify them to work with drug-involved offenders other than their own recovery from drugs or, in some cases, ordination to the ministry!) Most social workers who counsel drug-involved offenders appear to be employed by not-for-profit organizations that contract with a public agency for those services.

Monitoring and supervision of drug-involved offenders are also crucial functions of social workers. Periodic urinalysis has become almost universal for drug-involved offenders, and social workers are generally expected to monitor urine screening records and report any positive tests to the appropriate justice system agency. Social workers employed as probation officers do this as well as supervise many other aspects of a client's behavior.

It is unfortunate that most social workers who perform any of these functions for drug-involved offenders have to acquire most of the appropriate skills through on-the-job training, since only a few professional programs in social work provide them. Those who do offer courses in drug abuse/chemical dependency rarely provide any specific training regarding drug-involved offenders. Even fewer professional programs offer courses with relevant skills for planning or advocacy in the criminal justice system (McNeece & DiNitto, 1994).

References

Abadinsky, H. (Ed.). (1993). *Drug abuse: An introduction.* Chicago: Nelson-Hall.

Brumbaugh, A. (1993). Acupuncture: New perspectives in chemcial dependency treatment. *Journal of Substance Abuse Treatment, 10*(1).

Charney, D., Heninger, G., & Klever, H. (1986). The combined use of clonidine and naltrexone as a rapid, safe and effective treatment of abrupt withdrawal from methadone. *American Journal of Psychiatry, 143,* 831–837.

Christiansen, P. (1988). Contra Costa County, California jail school program. *American Jails, 21,* 30–35.

Crabtree, B. (1984). Review of naltrexone, a long-acting opiate antagonist. *Clinical Pharmacy, 3,* 273–280.

Doweiko, H. (1993). *Concepts of Chemical Dependency.* Pacific Grove, CA: Brooks-Cole.

Estes, N. J. & Heinemann, M. E. (Eds.). (1986). *Alcoholism: Development, consequences, and interventions.* St. Louis, MO: Mosby.

Gerstein, D. & Harwood, H. (Eds.). (1990). *Treating drug problems, vol. 1: A study of the evolution, effectiveness, and financing of public and private drug treatment systems.* Washington, DC: National Academy Press.

Goldapple, G. (1990). Enhancing retention: A skills-training program for drug dependent therapeutic community clients. Ph.D. diss., Florida State University.

Greenstein, R., Evans, B., & McLellan, A. (1983). Predictors of favorable outcome follwing naltrexone treatment. *Drug and Alcohol Dependence, 12,* 173–180.

Holloway, M. (1993). Rx for addiction. *Scientific American, 264*(3), 94–103.

Inciardi, James A. (Ed.). (1993). *Drug treatment and criminal justice.* Newbury Park, CA: Sage.

Inciardi, J. (1995). Heroin use and street crime. In J. Inciardi & K. McElrath (Eds.), *The American drug scene: An anthology.* Los Angeles, CA: Roxbury.

Inciardi, J. & McBride, D. (1991). *Treatment alternatives to street crime (TASC): History, experiences, and issues.* Rockville, MD: National Institute on Drug Abuse.

Leccese, A. (1991). *Drugs and society.* Englewood Cliffs, NJ: Prentice Hall.

MacKenzie, Doris L. & Uchida, Craig D. (Eds.). (1994). *Drugs and crime: Evaluating public policy initiatives.* Thousand Oaks, CA: Sage.

McNeece, C. A. (1991). Substance abuse treatment evaluation project: Overview of the evaluation findings. Tallahassee: Florida State University, Institute for Health and Human Services Research.

McNeece, C. A. (1992a). An evaluation of Anti-drug Abuse Act grant funded substance abuse treatment programs in Florida. Tallahassee: Florida State University, Institute for Health and Human Services Research.

McNeece, C. A. (1992b). An evaluation of the Brevard County drug addiction and prevention treatment program. Tallahassee: Florida State University, Institute for Health and Human Services Research.

McNeece, C. A. & DiNitto, D. (1994). *Chemical dependency: A systems approach.* Englewood Cliffs, NJ: Prentice Hall.

Mirin, S., Weiss, R., & Greenfield, S. (1991). Psychoactive substance use disorders. In A. Galenberg, E. Bassuk, & S. Schoonover (Eds.). *The practitioners guide to psychoactive drugs.* New York: Plenum Medical Book Co.

Pan, H., Scarpitti, F., Inciardi, J., & Lockwood, D. (1993). Some considerations on therapeutic communities in corrections. In J. Inciardi (Ed.), *Drug treatment and criminal justice* (pp. 31–43). Newbury Park, CA: Sage.

Parent, D. (1989). Shock Incarceration: An overview of existing programs. Washington, DC: National Institute of Justice, U.S. Dept. of Justice.

Peele, S. (1985). *The meaning of addiction: Compulsion experience and its interpretation.* Lexington, MA: Heath.

Peters, R. (1993). Drug treatment in jails. In J. Inciardi (Ed.), *Drug treatment and criminal justice.* Newbury Park, CA: Sage.

Peters, R. & Dolente, A. (1990). Relapse prevention for drug-dependent inmates in the Hillsborough County jail. *American Jails, 3,* 107–110.

Rassmussen, D., Benson, B., & Mast, B. (1994). Entrepreneurial police and drug enforcement. Working paper, Florida State University, Department of Economics.

U.S. Dept. of Justice, National Institute of Justice. (1989). *Drug use forecasting: 1988 annual report.* Washington, DC: U.S. Government Printing Office.

U.S. Dept. of Justice, National Institute of Justice. (1990). *Drug use forecasting: 1989 annual report.* Washington, DC:U.S. Government Printing Office.

U.S. Dept. of Justice, National Institute of Justice. (1991). *Drug use forecasting: 1990 annual report.* Washington, DC: U.S. Government Printing Office.

U.S. Dept. of Justice, National Institute of Justice. (1992). *Drug use forecasting: 1991 annual report.* Washington, DC: U.S. Government Printing Office.

U.S. Dept. of Justice, National Institute of Justice. (1993). *Drug use forecasting: 1992 annual report.* Washington, DC: U.S. Government Printing Office.

Weisheit, R. (Ed.). (1990). *Drugs, crime and the criminal justice system.* Cincinnati, OH: Anderson.

Chapter Six

Using the Criminal Justice System to Prevent Adolescent Drug Abuse

John G. Robertson

This chapter begins with a brief historical review of social work with at-risk youth. It then reviews the scope of the problem of substance abuse both at the societal and personal level and discusses prevention activities. It focuses next on prevention and prevention programs, followed by an overview of the role of the police, the courts, and corrections. Three actual prevention programs are then presented and the chapter closes with a discussion of ethical issues and future roles for social workers.

Adolescent Drug Abuse

The increasing level of drug and alcohol abuse among adolescents is a cause of continuing concern to the public and among professionals. Violent crime, suicide, school drop-outs, teen pregnancy, petty crime, and vandalism are all strongly related to the use of substances that alter the user's mood. Young people's involvement with drugs and alcohol can bring them into contact with the criminal justice system. The criminal justice system (i.e., the police, the courts, probation, corrections, and other programs such as diversionary prevention efforts) is designed both to enforce the law and to maintain social order for people of every age and walk of life. The system is, however, sorely taxed with the number of adolescents who commit drug-related crimes.

The basic question is "What is the system's role with these young people?" Is it simply to sort out guilt or innocence, to punish, or to intervene in order to help the young person? Unfortunately, these various roles are frequently in conflict. For example, releasing a young person because of lack of evidence may mean that the individual does not get the help he or she really needs. Some would argue that placing a young person in a community drug program instead of prison may lead the individual to believe there are no serious consequences for criminal actions. On the other hand, sentencing an offender to time in a youth correction facility may mean that a more angry and destructive drug abuser is released six months later only to continue in an escalated life of crime. The following three scenarios could take place in almost any city and town in the United States. They provide a focus for the rest of the chapter.

> *Colin.* Colin, a seventeen-year-old white male, is picked up by the police in a suburban town for speeding. He was clocked driving 85 miles an hour down a city street at 3:30 in the morning. His breath smells of alcohol and the pupils of his eyes are dilated. He is taken to the police station and his mother is called.

> *Maria.* Maria, a fifteen-year-old female, is arrested for shoplifting in a mall. She has a vial of amphetamines in her purse. She is hostile to the police and swears at them all the way to the station. The police call her mother, who speaks no English but comes down to the station with Maria's older brother who translates for her.

> *Ramel.* Ramel, a fourteen-year-old African American male, is arrested on a street corner in a big city with ten bags of marijuana and a vial of crack in his possession. He also has $250 in cash. He is charged with selling cocaine and placed in the juvenile detention center to await trial.

The criminal justice system struggles to cope with the problems of adolescents who are involved with mood-altering substances, twenty four hours a day, seven days a week, year in and year out. In order to work effectively within the criminal justice system as it responds to young people such as Colin, Maria, and Ramel, social workers need an understanding of how the juvenile criminal justice system developed. In addition, social workers need to be clear on the differing roles the criminal justice system has played and continues to play with children and adolescents.

A Brief History of Practice with At-Risk Adolescents

A comprehensive history of interventions with at-risk youth has yet to be written. However, there are events and trends that can be examined here. Without a doubt the most important response to at-risk children in America has been and remains free public education. The decision made in the middle of the nineteenth century to provide education to every child was based on a concern that poor children, at that time the overwhelming majority of all children, would become useful working members of society only if they were taught to read and given a basic education (Heidenheimer & Layson, 1982). Today, public education remains the second largest area of public social welfare expenditures in the United States (Bixley, 1994).

A very early movement to intervene with at-risk youth was the "child saving movement." Charles Loring Brace, Secretary of the Children's Aid Society in New York from 1853 to 1890, found the city awash with indigent boys working as newsboys, stable boys, shoeshine boys, and so on. Many begged for a meal or the price of a night's lodging. He called them "dangerous classes" because he believed their future would be "pauperism, crime, and political villainy." The Children's Aid Society established lodging houses for these boys, the precursor of group homes and large children's institutions. They also sent many of the children to farmers in the midwest who were asked to serve as foster parents in return for the labor that the boys performed on the farms. This program was an early version of foster care except that child labor was an integral component. It was only later that similar programs were established for girls (Katz, 1986; Lieby, 1978).

At the turn of the century, the family court became another major movement to address at-risk children. In 1899 in Chicago and then in 1901 in Denver, juvenile courts were established. Until this time, the courts had made no distinction between children and adults, with both children and adults being placed in the same jails and prisons. The social forces of the "progressive era" at the turn of the century created the juvenile court in order to shift the focus from punishment to rehabilitation. The juvenile court was given broader powers than criminal courts to investigate the environment of the child, the family situation, housing, schools, etc. The court employed special workers to explore the needs of these youth and to supervise the juvenile offenders. These workers were called probation officers (Katz, 1986; Polier, 1989).

Also, just after the turn of the century, settlement houses worked to improve the quality of life in poor urban neighborhoods with public health activities, home economics programs, and other educational and cultural activities. The settlement house movement was very concerned about the needs of children, but children in the context of their nuclear families, extended families, and neighborhoods. Throughout this century, the history of community interventions designed to assist at-risk youth is rooted in the settlement house model of cooperation and outreach. The model seeks to broaden the horizons of poor children in order to give the children viable choices for their lives (Trattner, 1989). A much more recent and very important manifestation of this approach was "Mobilization for Youth," the prototype program of the 1960s

"Great Society." Mobilization for Youth focused on the street gang culture of the late fifties. Gang leaders were recruited to join and lead organizations of neighborhood youth. The focus of these organizations was community building, increased participation in legal employment, and direct action to push the government towards improving the situation of the poor (Patterson, 1986).

Also at the turn of the twentieth century, the Progressive Era (1900–1920) focused on public health, with major concerns on sanitation and healthy food. The public health concerns merged with the temperance movement and became part of the drive that led to America's second prohibition period from 1919 to 1932 (the first prohibition period occurred just prior to the Civil War) (Goshen, 1973; Kobler, 1973). Public health activities involved teaching individuals about health and activities that could harm their health. The need to educate people about self-protective health practices led to a major drive to include information about the dangers of illegal drugs in the school curriculum. From 1915 to 1930 American school curriculum had required units on drug prevention. These were removed during the 1930s, but they reappeared in the 1980s (Musto, 1987).

It is clear that prevention programs for working with at-risk juveniles have existed for the last one hundred fifty years. Although this is only a brief summary of relevant programs, one can see the early roots of group homes, court-based interventions, neighborhood-based interventions, and public health activities. While such programs have not just been aimed at adolescents who are abusing drugs, they do represent major responses to drug abusers and others at risk. In reality, the only genuinely new intervention strategy in recent times has been the use of the media. Reviewing some of these attempts in more detail could help us to (1) avoid repeating past mistakes and (2) learn which interventions have led to successful outcomes.

Scope of the Problem

In 1992 there were 74,981 drug arrests of individuals under the age of eighteen and 248,015 age twenty-one and younger in the United States. There were 125, 513 arrests related to alcohol use for individuals under the age of eighteen and 552,020 age twenty-one and younger (Federal Bureau of Investigation, 1993).[1] The arrest rate does not, however, reflect the true extent of the problem, since

1. Alcohol arrests include driving while intoxicated, breaking the liquor laws, and public drunkenness. Drug abuse violations are defined as the unlawful sale/manufacture or the possession/use of such narcotics and drugs as opium and cocaine and their derivatives (e.g., marijuana and hashish), synthetic narcotics (e.g., demerol and methadone), and other dangerous nonnarcotic drugs (e.g., barbiturates, amphetamines, and hallucinogens) (Uniform Crime Reports, State of New Jersey, 1990).

robberies, burglaries, and aggravated assaults that are committed in order to support drug use are not counted.

The 1991 National Survey of High School Seniors (NSHSS) found that drug use is on the rise in American high schools. For most of the 1980s, the overall rate of drug use had actually been declining. It is a matter of some concern that the trend of drug use is moving in the wrong direction again (Johnston, O'Malley & Bachman, 1994). The survey reported that in 1991, 85 percent of high school seniors had already consumed alcohol for recreational purposes and that 51 percent had drunk within the last month—almost all illegally, since they were under age. Additionally, 33 percent had used marijuana, with 5 percent reporting use within the last month; and 12 percent had used cocaine, 1 percent within the last month.

Drug and alcohol use seriously affects the lives of young people. Some 59,469 young adults (twenty-one and under) went to hospital emergency rooms due to recreational substance use in 1991. An additional 80,032 went to emergency rooms after attempting suicide with a drug overdose (Bureau of Justice Statistics, 1993, table 3.98). In 1991, 3,995 sixteen-to-twenty-year-olds were killed in car accidents in which the driver was impaired by drug or alcohol (Bureau of Justice Statistics, 1993, Table 3.120). In 1989, 51,485 adolescents were treated for alcoholism and 76,203 for drug addiction (O'Brien, Cohen, Evans, & Fine, 1992). Dawkins and Dawkins (1983) found that drinking and drug use by adolescents is positively correlated with both serious and minor crimes. The picture painted here is one of widespread abuse of drugs and alcohol that is having very serious consequences for young people.

E. D. Wish (1991) examined the data from the National Household Survey Drug Abuse (NHSDA) and NSHSS and compared the results with the National Institute of Justice's Drug Use Forecasting (DUF) program. DUF measures the self-reported use of drug and the urinalysis results of arrestees in the country's twenty-two largest cities. Wish found that there are more weekly, regular drug users among those arrested in the country's twenty-two largest cities than found in the entire country by NHSDA. The discrepancy can be explained by examining the samples used at that time by the NHSDA and NSHSS.[2] The NHSDA did not gather data on people living in group homes, the military, dormitories, hotels, hospitals, jails, or from transients, including the homeless—all at high risk of drug abuse. The NSHSS counted only students in school, not drop-outs, who are more likely to be substance abusers. Since drug use is increasingly a phenomenon among those who live in a drug-using culture—those in poor inner-city communities and among the so-called under-class of America—there are more regular drug users in the criminal

2. Recent work has been done to extend the sampling frame of both surveys to include those who have been systematically missed. However, as yet there are no results reported from these modifications.

justice system than can be found in the entire mainstream culture (Wish, 1991).

The Effect of Substance Abuse on the User

The term "substance abuse" as defined in this chapter is the use of mood-altering drugs, including alcohol, narcotics (heroin, morphine, opium, and others), amphetamines, cocaine, LSD, PCP, marijuana, tranquilizers, nicotine, and caffeine. Each of these substances has specific effects on the body. However, they have this common effect: as their use continues, addiction becomes more probable. Addiction occurs when the individual is no longer in control of his or her use (i.e., use of the drug becomes compulsive). The individual must use the substance whether or not in more rational moments he or she wants to, and must use it whether or not that use causes physical harm to the user. A common example of this phenomenon is a cigarette smoker on the first day of a cold who fights between satisfying the craving for nicotine and drawing smoke into already congested lungs (Wood, 1993).

Addiction or compulsive use is associated with a constellation of other problems, precisely because the user is driven to use regardless of the consequences. For example, he or she may experience problems on the job or in school due to lateness or poor performance. Use reduces concern for personal safety and accidents become more likely. Use causes health problems, and compulsive use leads to reduced attention to one's health. Family and other personal relationships become strained as the use becomes increasingly inappropriate and destructive. Users lose self-respect because they become aware of an inability to control their behavior. Use leads to negative encounters with the law, perhaps not only because of the consumption of the illegal drugs but also because the individual's behavior becomes more and more irresponsible (e.g., driving while intoxicated).

Many addicts die as a result of substance abuse. Medical complications include liver disease, heart attacks, and HIV/AIDS infection through the sharing of contaminated needles or having sex with an infected person. Drug- and alcohol-related accidents are a common cause of death. Due to lack of control, family disagreements often escalate into violent confrontations. While seeking drugs, addicts enter the criminal underworld and can become homicide victims. Criminal involvement also increases the likelihood of incarceration. Reduced self-respect and depression (a side effect of the use of many substances, including alcohol and cocaine) lead to higher rates of suicide.

Compulsive use of mood-altering drugs constitutes a painful and destructive syndrome that captures many people who naively believe they can stop anytime they wish. Addictions develop in different patterns, sometimes quickly as in crack/cocaine use, where one or two experiences may be sufficient to establish addiction, or over the years as in some forms of alcoholism.

What separates the addict from the user is the compulsive nature of the use. Not all users, however, become addicts. Unfortunately, the process of addiction is still not well understood. When does a person cross the line between use and addiction? Why does one casual user become addicted while another user is apparently unaffected? Although medical and social research continue in the attempt to understand the addictive process, these questions have not yet been satisfactorily answered. At the moment, the best answer seems to be that some individuals may be predisposed to developing compulsive use. Some of these predispositions appear to be physical. Some people's bodies react to alcohol in such a way that addictive behavior starts immediately after first use. Other predisposing elements may be social. Some individuals are strongly influenced by factors in their environment. For example, living in poor neighborhoods, in areas of chronic unemployment, or in areas where drug use is high may influence many individuals who otherwise would not be vulnerable. Coming from a family with a history of addiction also increases the likelihood that an individual will become addicted. Addiction is influenced by the existence of both genetic and social factors. Individual characteristics such as failure in school, learning difficulties, deafness, or certain types of mental or emotional problems also can increase the likelihood of compulsive use of substances (Wood, 1993; Kinney & Leaton, 1991).

Each of the three young people introduced earlier—Colin, Maria, and Ramel—are at significant risk of addiction. The very fact that their drug and alcohol involvement has brought them into contact with law enforcement agencies is an indicator of their vulnerability. The question is, "What can be done to intervene in the addictive process?"

Prevention

Levels of Prevention

Preventing drug abuse among adolescents is divided into three levels—primary, secondary, and tertiary. Primary prevention is the most comprehensive. It includes any and all activities that inform the public about the dangers of drug use and ways to avoid becoming involved. Primary prevention includes education in the public schools which seeks to change attitudes about drugs, to provide information about the effects and dangers of drug use, and to educate individuals about alternative recreation and problem-solving techniques. Media campaigns that deliver a message of "Say No to Drugs" or that educate the public about the effects of drugs are also primary prevention activities.

Secondary prevention involves somewhat similar activities but is targeted at more specific populations (e.g., those at high risk of becoming involved with or addicted to drugs and alcohol). People at risk include those whose parents or grandparents were drug abusers, those who are failing in school or have dropped out, those who have already become involved in illegal activities, those who live in neighborhoods with high levels of drug use, and those who have been physically or sexually abused. The high-risk category also includes those who have had initial experiences in using or selling drugs. Secondary prevention includes education about the effects of drugs and drug abuse, family counseling and intervention with drug-using family members, and attitude-changing activities (e.g., group discussion or games). Individual and group counseling is a part of the intervention to help resolve conflicts within the family or in schools and to develop healthy life choices and alternative future plans that do not include drug and or alcohol use but do increase self esteem.

The "at-risk model" has been criticized for being too comprehensive—by including just about everything as an at-risk behavior. Brown and Horowitz (1993) argue that the list of at-risk factors is sometimes so broad that it covers almost every child in school. However, in some inner cities that may well be the case. The at-risk model has also been criticized because it stresses the deficits of individuals rather than their strengths. Begun (1993), among others, has argued that an alternative resiliency model should be promoted, in which the prevention program probes the factors that help some adolescents to avoid drug use and how such strengths can be passed on to other adolescents.

Tertiary prevention is actually treatment for drug abuse or addiction. It normally involves education, support and self-help groups such as Narcotics and Alcoholics Anonymous, group and individual counseling, vocational counseling and planning, and family counseling. It can be inpatient with out-patient aftercare or entirely outpatient. It normally lasts for eighteen–twenty-four months, including aftercare.

These levels of prevention are hierarchical, with the tertiary level including all the components of the lower levels. While at-risk adolescents can benefit from all three levels, secondary prevention is the major one.

Prevention programs have used a variety of models and theories in the attempt to change behavior: problem behavior theory, social learning theory, cognitive and social inoculation, stage theory, and biopsychosocial theory. Norman and Turner (1993) evaluated many of these programs and concluded that changing norms and expectations about substance use, building and enhancing social skills and skills of resisting peer pressure toward use, and interventions that attempt to change community norms are most effective in changing behavior and preventing further involvement with drugs. Other research indicates that effective prevention programs focus on providing coping and decision-making skills as well as developing positive alternatives to substance abuse while still incorporating credible and accurate information (LoSciuto & Ausetts, 1988). Being able to resist peer pressures, make informed decisions, and cope with crises in ways that avoid the use of drugs and alcohol is critical to developing a positive life style. Unfortunately, some programs for which there were positive expectations (e.g., the strictly cognitive approaches) seem to have had no effect (Dryfoos, 1993).

Teenagers Colin, Maria, and Ramel each are beyond the primary prevention level. Their use of mood-altering substances and their involvement with the law indicate that they are at risk of continued involvement. Careful assessment is required to determine whether or not they are already addicted.

The Role of Coercion in Confronting Substance Abuse

External pressure or even coercion play an important role in the intervention process with drug abusers and those at risk. Court diversion programs are an example of strong legal pressure. Since society has defined drug abuse as a deviant activity, it constantly seeks to prevent addiction and to protect the public from the negligent or criminal activities of abusers. Reasons for laws prohibiting drugs and controlling who can or cannot use alcohol include that concern for public safety as well as concern for the physical and mental health of the individual user, the reduced productivity of drug abusers, and the effects of drug users on the family. More recently, however, to some of these more humanistic concerns have been added a desire for reducing the financial drain on the health and criminal justice systems. In addition, many have argued that the puritan tradition in the United States is offended by such pleasure-seeking activities. Those who use or sell drugs, however, usually do not share society's concerns. Frequently, they view drug use as a free choice and a personal right, as a form of recreation, as a way of expanding their experience, and in the case of drug sellers as a way of making a living. A significant component in interventions with those at risk for drug and alcohol abuse is to induce each individual to recognize and conform to society's expectations. This strategy is, of course, not unique to drug use. Speeding laws, laws requiring that children be sent to school, and tax laws are all ways that the broader society requires individuals to conform to common rules and norms. In order to accomplish its goal, drug abuse prevention programs often employ an iron fist in a velvet glove. While the central prevention message is cloaked in the language of concern for the individual, it also includes a second theme that serious consequences face the individual who does not conform. Indeed, in the United States in the last twenty years the threat has been relentlessly carried out. Drug offenders comprise a significant proportion of all those arrested and imprisoned in this country.

De Leon (1988) has compared the impact on individuals who are court mandated to drug treatment with the impact on those who volunteer for treatment. He found no significant difference in outcomes (i.e., those who were forced to accept treatment were just as likely to recover as those who voluntarily entered treatment). While De Leon's study is of a particular treatment modality (therapeutic community) and does not necessarily generalize to all treatment approaches, it does provide hope for the future of criminal-justice-mandated interventions with resistant at-risk clients. Colin, Maria, and Ramel, by virtue of their encounters with the law, would thus be eligible for an effective intervention program.

One reason why coercion is useful in confronting those at risk is that drug and alcohol abuse involve the psychological defenses of denial and minimization. It is very common for a family member of a drug abuser to deny that the abuse even exists. Not only has the family member become co-dependent, but also over time the drug and alcohol use has become the normal situation, the "scenery," of the person's life. In addition to denial by family members, substance abusers themselves are very defensive of their habits. They fear that if the true amount and effect of their abuse was recognized, they would have to admit there actually was a problem. Such recognition would inevitably lead to the imperative that they stop the abuse or at least reduce the amount used. Addicts are dependent on their substances and cannot face day-to-day life without them. Hence, in each case, denial sets in early and the individual and his or her family can no longer see what is happening.

Minimization is a different form of the same response. The family or user admits that the abuse is happening but "forgets" some of its most serious consequences. The ticket for driving while intoxicated is ignored. The family celebration that was disrupted by the abuser is overlooked or is blamed on someone or something else. Those caught in the cycle of abuse and denial lose the ability to see what is happening both to themselves and to their family. When a family member is forced into treatment due to breaking the law, however, the cycle of denial can be broken and the family can reexamine the true consequences of the involvement with drugs. For example, Colin's father thinks that it is normal for a boy to "sow his wild oats." He cannot understand that his son's drinking has passed beyond mere social use. Colin's mother defends him by saying that he drinks heavily only on weekends. When Colin is asked about his drinking, he becomes abusive and attacks the motives of the person who asks. Similarly, Maria's mother does not believe that her daughter is using drugs. Maria claims the drugs were given to her by a friend just to hold. Ramel sees himself as a businessman earning a living. His mother has no idea that he has been selling drugs. He has hidden it from her. She is horrified when she learns the truth, since five years earlier her sister had died of a drug overdose and Ramel's father is in jail for crimes relating to supporting his drug habit.

Roles for Part of the Criminal Justice System

The focus of this chapter is on the role of criminal justice in preventing substance abuse among at-risk adolescents. Most of the material to this point has been more general, looking at the broader issues of addiction and prevention.

In this section, we will begin to address the specific issues for adolescents in the criminal justice system.

The first criminal-justice professionals to deal with the substance-abuse problem are the police. They encounter teenagers in the mall hanging out with groups of friends, smoking marijuana or drinking. They stop a car for speeding and discover six teenagers who have been drinking. They are called to a street fight and find a group of young people who have been drinking. They are called to a family confrontation and find a drunk father waving a gun at his wife and teenage son or daughter. Police officers pick up many more adolescents than they arrest. They release some to their families without booking them, hoping that the mere act of "taking the kid in" will deter further criminal activity. They book others but release them to adult guardians; while still others are actually made to spend time in juvenile detention. These events are often frustrating encounters for the police. They do not want to overreact to adolescents who are making a mistake; they do not want to give a teenager a mark on his or her record. However, each of these encounters is an opportunity to intervene with an at-risk youth. As previously discussed, societal coercion is a major motivator in changing drug-related behavior. In many cases, the police officer taking the adolescent to the police station and calling his or her parents precipitates a crisis that can lead to a reexamination of behavior by the young person. Indeed, the negative consequences of substance abuse can be one of the central factors in causing the user to change his or her behavior.

The criminal justice system can also be caught in a denial and minimization cycle. Very often the system does not intervene at an early stage when change is relatively easy, but seems oblivious to or ignores behavior that should be addressed. Later, when the use has escalated to a more severe stage, the justice system is required to deal with a much more serious problem.

Overall, when addressing the prevention of drug abuse, law enforcement activity should be tough, making sure that the drug abuse leads to swift and fair consequences. Police activity should be consistent, sending a message that such behavior is unacceptable. But most of all, it should focus on the good qualities of the adolescent. Consequences should be strong enough to warn, but it should also be delivered so that the message is one of concern for the young person's well being.

The courts, the second major component in the criminal justice system, handle drug cases in several ways. The court can divert cases to treatment programs prior to the assessment of guilt or innocence, thus protecting the juvenile from having a permanent record. The court can hear the case and sentence the adolescent to a treatment or prevention program possibly with probation as well. The court can order probation or can incarcerate the young person. In addition, the juvenile court has the power to order a complete assessment of the offender's home, school, and community life. The judge can ask the intake unit of the court, the investigations unit, probation, or a private program to assess the adolescent and recommend which program would be most effective for the particular individual. Roberts and Camasso (1991), in reviewing the literature, have found that programs for juvenile offenders are cost effective. In the long run, the cost of these programs is cheaper than not having a program because they save in future law enforcement expenses.

During the typical assessment interview, the adolescent's level of drinking and drug use is evaluated. Since there is a normal tendency to minimize or deny substances use, the agency representative doing the assessment often seeks collateral information from the family, school authorities, or other sources. Assessments require a skilled counselor experienced with the population being evaluated. Because of the denial, minimization, and defensiveness of substance abusers, it is important that the counselor be able both to establish rapport with the client and to probe the client's background for signs of substance abuse. These signs include changes in friendship patterns, repeated negative interactions with authority, health problems (especially trips to the emergency room), conflicts with family members, and sleeplessness, combined, of course, with a pattern of drug and alcohol use.

If regular use is established, the adolescent is normally ordered to a treatment program for a period of time. For an adolescent who is not in control of his or her use of drugs and alcohol, residential treatment is usually required. There are two common types: the medical model and the therapeutic community (Robertson & Waters, 1994; Breschner & Friedman, 1985). If the adolescent does not show signs of addiction but is involved with selling drugs and is out of school, he or she may be ordered to a day treatment program that includes education, group therapy, and work or recreation. If there are manifestations of emotional or psychological distress, or if the parents exhibit sufficient distress, the adolescent may be referred to a mental health clinic. If the client is still in school, he or she may be mandated to participate in a neighborhood recreational program. In addition, the judge can intervene in a family situation, ordering the family into counseling instead of incarceration for the youth.

Judges find it difficult to respond effectively to teenage drug sellers. Frequently, these juveniles do not need drug treatment since many are not addicted. There are few alternatives. Youth detention centers are seen as schools for criminal behavior rather than for rehabilitation. Probation case loads are so large that very little supervision is possible. The courts are constantly in search of programs designed to prevent future criminal activity and addiction. Polsky and Fast (1993) have studied the "boot camp" model, based on military basic training, and now being widely used for drug offenders. Their findings question how much the changes seen in the young people in the artificial environment of this program are sustainable after the person is released back to his or her original environment.

Adolescents are at a stage of life where fairness is very important to them; they see the world in "black or white." In addition, they also have a very strong need to feel that adults are actually listening to them. Juvenile courts are overburdened. The court tends to put most of its resources into very serious cases or into cases where the guilt or innocence of the defendant is in question. Consequently, the adolescent court has a system of plea bargaining where the prosecuting attorney and the defense attorney negotiate a sentence. Usually in these cases, the juvenile does not even see the judge. He or she is left with the impression that the court system functions as a marketplace where everything can be traded. The court needs to understand the importance of using visible power. The adolescent needs his or her day in court in order to accept the fairness of the judgments. Plea bargaining leads to a misunderstanding of law. For many individuals, it is not until they encounter the adult court with its much stiffer sentences that they comprehend the real consequences of selling drugs.

In Colin's case, the police officers may release him to his mother. However, this decision would only reenforce the denial of the family. Here, the police officer would do well to use available diversion opportunities. Colin could be required to have a complete assessment of his drinking. He would benefit from being required to participate in a secondary prevention program. In many states, a driving while intoxicated (DWI) conviction leads to a substance-abuse assessment and a short-term course that educate the offender about addiction.

Maria also could be released to her mother with no consequences other than being picked up. This decision could give her the message that her behavior was not serious. First, however, the police themselves should provide an interpreter for the mother other than the brother so they can be certain the entire message is communicated correctly. Maria would also benefit from a short-term intervention that would reenforce the message that her behavior is not acceptable and that would help her sort out what led to her drug involvement. The possible causes could be anything from school failure to negative peer pressure to family conflicts to unreported sexual abuse or any combination of them. Once these causes are determined, appropriate intervention can be planned.

Ramel will almost certainly be referred to court. The court needs to have an assessment performed of his involvement with illegal substances. In addition, his school performance and his family situation should be evaluated. Utilizing his mother's strong aversion to his drug involvement, a short-term intervention should be planned. It would involve close supervision for a period of time, the requirement that he attend school regularly, the requirement that he find a job, (even a job in fast food), and the expectation that he develop positive recreational activities. In addition, the assessment would address his father's incarceration, and through group and individual counseling help him sort out his family's substance-abuse history and its effect on him. A judge's authority could have a significant impact on Ramel's life.

Examples of Effective Prevention Programs

Over the last ten years, prevention has become a major focus in the national war on drugs. Congress created the Office of Substance Abuse Prevention (OSAP) within the National Institutes of Health in 1986. OSAP was reorganized in 1993 and became the Center for Substance Abuse Prevention (CSAP). OSAP and then CSAP developed a series of program-based differential approaches to prevention. These approaches are based on the school, the community and the criminal justice system (Dryfoos, 1993). Programs to address teenage drug involvement range from short-term minimal interventions to long-term residential treatment. The three programs described below are among many that were funded by OSAP.

In Denver, Colorado, a multiagency residential program, founded in 1989, includes the state juvenile correction agency, the state division of alcohol and drug abuse, a residential facility run by a hospital, "Partners" (a group providing adult volunteers), a community college, and a research group serving court-adjudicated adolescents. Using a model that strengthens prosocial bonding and unlearned delinquent bonds while developing skills during a period of residential treatment, the program attempts to integrate the adolescent into society and improve his or her commitment to a drug-free life. The program also includes a fifteen-day wilderness experience and vocational and academic education. No specific time length for the residential program is specified. In the first two years, forty-four youths were served. Fifty-five percent of the participants completed the program, and 33 percent received their General Education Diploma (GED) (Stein et al., 1992).

In Philadelphia, another multiservice agency serving court-adjudicated youth in a residential setting provided additional services to address their risk of drug use. Two models were tested. The first was a life-skills model including techniques in problem-solving designed to increase self control, relieve stress, and develop relaxation and assertiveness skills. The second was a values-clarification, antiviolence model. The values-clarification approach was designed to help the individual choose freely, consider alternatives and consequences, and act consistently. The antiviolence approach taught the individual to understand the course and the effect of violence, identify the risks of violence, handle anger, and seek alternative responses to anger. The values-clarification and anti-violence programs served eighty-four adolescents in two years. While knowledge and attitudes changed positively over the two years, behavior as measured by continued smoking and having trouble at home did not change. The values clarification, anti-violence model produced more change in knowledge and attitude than did the life-skills model (Friedman & Utada, 1992).

In Essex County, New Jersey, the Prevention Intervention and Education Program (PIE), started in 1986, is a court-diversion program for young people arrested for drug and alcohol involvement. Most of the adolescents referred to PIE begin their drug involvement by selling rather than using illegal substances. Selling is considered a gateway to later addiction, to other criminal activities, and to violence. The PIE staff works with the young people and their parents to prevent the adolescents from becoming drug or alcohol users and to prevent further arrests. Some who have already become drug or alcohol users are referred to treatment programs. Others are referred to support services for the families. All are educated about the dangers of the use and abuse of drugs and alcohol and are instructed in the addiction and recovery process.

Adolescents (ages twelve to eighteen) and their parents attend an assessment appointment with a trained addictions counselor. The youth and their parents are then scheduled for four group sessions, which are held in the county court house in order to reinforce the fact that the adolescent's activities are illegal. The first session actually focuses on the adolescent's illegal activity. After presenting the program goals and rules and a movie about the effects of drug use on America, the counselors lead a discussion in which each teenager is expected to describe his or her illegal involvement with drugs. Those adolescents who continue to maintain their innocence are encouraged to return to the court to seek justice since the program is targeted at those who have a problem with drug/alcohol involvement. The parents are encouraged to discuss the feelings they have about being required to attend a program due to their children's illegal activities. During the session, parents often hear for the first time the children's account of the arrests and the activities that led to those arrests. These revelations reestablish honest communication between adolescents and parents and lay a foundation for restoring trust. Parents are challenged to think about the power they have to change their children's behavior and they are encouraged to create realistic consequences for their children's behavior during the session.

The second session focuses on the major issues of addiction (e.g., how use becomes dependency and how families are affected by addiction). A counselor who is a recovering addict gives his or her addiction experience. In addition to the problem of the adolescent's involvement, it has been noted that almost all of the families have another immediate member who is addicted. The subject of parents who are themselves drug abusers is introduced. Often, over half of the adolescents in the sessions have lost at least one parent to addiction.

The third session focuses on feelings and choices. The discussion covers alternative ways of feeling good, such as working and earning money, engaging in sports, getting an education, and gaining family respect, and why the adolescent might choose one of these ways over another. The fourth session begins with a presentation on HIV/AIDS and its prevention. A video is followed by a talk by an HIV prevention counselor. The rest of the session, which returns to the criminal involvement issue, is a discussion with each of the families concerning the consequences if the adolescent is rearrested and what positive plans the family has made to change the adolescent's environment in order to help prevent further drug and alcohol involvement. Alternative consequences such as taking away the adolescent's driver's license and television, stereo, and phone privileges, and tightening curfews are discussed.

PIE has received 650 referrals each year, most of whom were inner-city residents (60%), African American (84%), and males (80%). Intervention costs less than $100 per client when working with adolescents who are beginning their involvement with drugs and/or alcohol. Data indicate that the clients and parents who participated in the program are well satisfied. The program was evaluated by studying the rearrest records of PIE clients at least nine months after they completed the program. The results were encouraging, with 47 percent of the program completers being rearrested as opposed to 71 percent of dropouts (Robertson, Waters, & D'Amico, 1991). However, before we become overly enthusiastic about PIE's outcomes, longitudinal studies that follow the participants over time will need to be completed (De Jong, 1987a, 1987b). Although nine months is a very short follow-up period, utilizing a longer period would mean that many of the PIE participants would have become adults. At the time of this writing, it was not possible to match adolescent and adult arrest records.

Issues and Constraints

Ethical Issues

When anyone is working with adolescents in the criminal justice system, issues of confidentiality arise. Juveniles have the right to have their identities protected. Federal law also protects the confidentiality of those in substance abuse treatment (*Federal Register,* 1987). Therefore, clinicians, administrators, researchers, law enforcement officers, and others who are working in prevention programs must be very careful to maintain confidentiality and to understand their agency's policies. Frequently in social work, we have to address problems without the full information needed. Social work is a profession in which individuals are helped to sort out their person–environment fit. Social workers have to assist a person to address his or her problems by using the existing state of knowledge. Although there is much for society and science to learn about substance abuse and addiction, those who suffer from these problems cannot wait until all the research questions are answered. We must use our limited knowledge and attempt to address as many of the issues as possible now. At-risk-of-addiction categories are very broad and certainly include many people who will never become addicts. However, it is much better to take action to reduce risk among these entire categories than do nothing and wait for new knowledge to clarify the problem. Moreover, our limited knowledge should motivate us to continue the search for new and better understanding of the problem. We should also keep a proper perspective about our own limited abilities. While trying our best to help clients, we certainly do not want to take undue risks with people's lives or futures when our knowledge is so incomplete.

When one is working with clients who have been mandated to a program by the criminal justice system, it is important to attend to the social work ethic that seeks to give the client personal control over his or her treatment. Since institutions have only limited ability to control behavior, it is necessary that the individual client become convinced of the need to change. It is not possible to bring about real change against the will of the client. The social work technique of contracting with the client to work on obtainable goals that he or she can support is very valuable in resolving this conflict (Hepworth & Larsen, 1993, ch. 12; Rooney, 1992).

The Public Will

The United States is spending a larger and larger portion of the federal budget on law enforcement and incarceration. But increases in such funding do not necessarily lead to greater allocations for prevention activities. "Get tough on crime" approaches do not focus on trying to intervene to change the at-risk individual's behavior. Rather they seek to deter the behavior strictly based on the consequences of punishment. In order to fully address the prevention needs of adolescents who are at risk of substance abuse, significant new investments must be made in intervention programs for them. For example, society must invest in their neighborhoods, in vocational and educational programs to prepare them for employment, and in assuring that there are employment opportunities. Social workers concerned about at-risk adolescents must also invest some of their energies in creating a public climate for more investment in these young people.

Conclusions

There are at present and are likely to continue to be many social-work employment opportunities for those interested in working with at-risk adolescents. Courts hire social workers to do assessments and to plan appropriate interventions. Social workers serve as parole officers and work in correctional institutions. Social workers manage and work in many of the prevention programs that receive the young people referred by the courts. It is certainly a challenging and constantly developing career. Social workers in these programs need to acquire more knowledge about what works and what does not. Better models delineating the influences that lead to involvement with drugs and alcohol need to be developed and alternative interventions tested. Social workers should continue to serve as advocates for programs that assist the individual to change rather than support responses that are essentially punitive—if young people such as Ramel, Colin, and Maria are to receive the help they need.

References

Begun, A. L. (1993). Human behavior and the social environment: The vulnerability, risk and resilience model. *Journal of Social Work Education, 29*(1), 26–35.

Bixley, A. K. (1994). Public social welfare expenditures, Fiscal year 1991. *Social Security Bulletin, 57*(1), 96–104.

Breschner, G. M. & Friedman, A. S. (1985). Treatment of adolescent drug abusers. *The International Journal of the Addictions, 20*(6&7), 971–993.

Brown, J. H. & Horowitz, J. E. (1993). Deviance and deviants:Why adolescent substance use prevention programs do not work. *Evaluation Review, 17*(5), 529–555.

Bureau of Justice Statistics. (1993). *Source book of criminal justice statistics, 1992.* Washington, DC: U.S. Dept. of Justice.

Dawkins, R. L. & Dawkins, M. P. (1983). Alcohol use and delinquency among black, white and Hispanic adolescent offenders. *Adolescence, 18*(72), 799–809.

De Jong, W. (1987a). A short-term evaluation of Project DARE (Drug Abuse Resistance Education): Preliminary indications of effectiveness. *Journal of Drug Issues, 17,* 279–294.

De Jong, W. (1987b). *Arresting the demand for drugs: Police and school partnerships to prevent drug abuse.* Washington, DC: National Institute of Justice.

De Leon, G. (1988). Legal pressure in therapeutic communities. *Journal of Drug Issues, 18*(4), 625–640.

Dryfoos, J. G. (1993). Preventing substance use: Rethinking strategies. *American Journal of Public Health, 83*(6), 793–795.

Federal Bureau of Investigation, U.S. Dept. of Justice. (1993). *Crime in the United States: The Uniform Crime Report 1992.* Washington, DC: U.S. Government Printing Office.

Federal Register. (1987). Confidentiality of alcohol and drug abuse patient records; Final rule. Tuesday, June 9. Washington, DC: U.S. Government Printing Office.

Friedman, A. S. & Utada, A. T. (1992). Effects of two group interaction models on substance-using adjudicated adolescent males. *Journal of Community Psychology,* OSAP Special Issue, 106–117.

Gerstein, D. & Harwood, H. (1990). *Treating drug problems, Vol. 1: A study of the evolution, effectiveness, and financing of public and private drug treatment systems.* Washington, DC: National Academy Press.

Goshen, C. E. (1973). *Drinks, drugs, and do-gooders.* New York: Free Press.

Heidenheimer, A. J. & Layson, J. (1982). Social policy development in Europe and America: A longer view on selectivity and income testing. In I. Garfinkel (Ed.), *Income tested transfer programs: The Case for and against.* New York: Academic Press.

Hepworth, D. H. & Larsen, J. A. (1993). *Direct social work practice: Theory and skills.* Chicago: Dorsey Press.

Johnston, L. D., O'Malley, P. M., & Bachman, J. G. (1994). *Drug use among American high school seniors, college students, young adults, 1975–1993.* Rockville, MD: National Institute on Drug Abuse.

Katz, M. B. (1986). *In the shadow of the poor house: A social history of welfare in America.* New York: Basic Books.

Kinney, J. & Leaton, G. (1991). *Loosening the grip: A handbook of alcohol information.* St. Louis: Mosley Year Book.

Kobler, J. (1973). *Ardent spirits: the Rise and fall of prohibition.* New York: Putnam's.

Leiby, J. (1978). *A history of social welfare and social work in the United States.* New York: Columbia University Press.

LoSciuto, L. & Ausetts, M. A. (1988). Evaluation of drug abuse prevention programs: A field experiment. *Addictive Behaviors, 13*(4), 337–351.

Musto, D. (1987). *The American disease: Origins of narcotic control.* New York: Oxford University Press.

Norman, E. & Turner, S. (1993). Adolescent substance abuse prevention programs: Theories, models and research in the encouraging 80's. *Journal of Primary Prevention, 14*(1), 3–20.

Office of the Attorney General (1991). *Uniform Crime Reports, State of New Jersey, 1990.* Trenton: Office of the Attorney General, State of New Jersey.

O'Brien, R., Cohen, S., Evans, G. & Fine, J. (1992). *The encyclopedia of drug abuse.* New York: Facts on File.

Patterson, J. T. (1986). *America struggle against poverty, 1900–1985.* Cambridge, MA: Harvard University Press.

Polier, J. W. (1989). *Juvenile justice in double jeopardy: The distant and vengeful community.* Hillside, NJ: Erlbaum.

Polsky, H. W. & Fast, J. (1993). Boot camps, juvenile offenders and culture shock. *Child and Youth Care Form, 22*(6), 403–415.

Roberts, A. R. & Camasso, M. J. (1991) Juvenile offender treatment programs and cost-benefit analysis. *Juvenile & Family Court Journal, 42,* 37–45.

Robertson, J. G. & Waters, J. E. (1994). Inner-city adolescents and drug abuse. In A. R. Roberts (ed.), *Critical Issues in Criminal Justice.* Thousand Oaks, CA: Sage.

Robertson, J. G., Waters, J., & D'Amico, M. (1991). *PIE program evaluation.* Newark, NJ: Integrity.

Rooney, R. H. (1992). *Strategies for work with involuntary clients.* New York: Columbia University Press.

Stein, S. L., Garcia, F., Marler, B., Embree-Bever, J., Garret, C. J., Unrein, D., Burdic, M. A., & Fishburn, S. Y. (1992). A study of multiagency collaboration strategies: Did juvenile delinquents change? *Journal of Community Psychology,* OSAP Special Issue, 88–105.

Trattner, W. I. (1989). *From Poor Law to Welfare State.* New York: Free Press.

Wish, E. D. (1991). U. S. Drug Policy in the 1990's: Insights from new data from arrestees. *International Journal of the Addictions, 25*(3A), 377–409.

Wood, G. (1993). *Drug abuse in society: A reference handbook.* Santa Barbara, CA: ABC-CLIO.

Chapter Seven

Juvenile Delinquency and Drug Abuse: Implications for Social Work Practice in the Justice System

Jeffrey M. Jenson

Frequent use of alcohol and illicit drugs is common among delinquent youth (Dembo, et al., 1988; Jenson, 1993). Studies indicate many of the same factors that predict the onset of delinquent behavior are related to the initiation of drug use among adolescents (Hawkins, Catalano, & Miller, 1992; Hawkins et al., 1988). The evidence suggests that drug-abuse intervention and treatment programs are needed in the juvenile justice system. Unfortunately, juvenile justice systems across the United States often lack the resources to effectively treat youthful offenders who have drug and alcohol problems. In many states, juvenile justice personnel do not even possess the assessment tools needed to determine the severity of drug use among the youth they serve (National Council of Family and Juvenile Court Judges, 1987; Stone, 1990).

Treatment of adolescent substance abusers in the justice system poses difficult challenges to practitioners. Effective intervention requires familiarity with the legal system, awareness of assessment and treatment approaches, and knowledge of community, individual, peer, and family factors that contribute to delinquency and drug use. Social work's emphasis on contextual factors in the etiology and mainte-nance of delinquency and drug use is an important contribution to rehabilitation efforts in the justice system. Practitioners in the juvenile justice system are in an excellent position to implement interventions addressing multiple causes of delin-quency and drug abuse. This chapter discusses the relationship between drug use and delinquency and identifies current trends in offending and in drug use among adolescents. Promising approaches to treating adjudicated delinquents with sub-stance-use problems are noted. Implications for social work practice are delineated.

Prevalence of Delinquency and Adolescent Drug Use

Prevalence of Delinquency

Criminologists and social work practitioners have three sources for measuring and interpreting delinquent behavior: (1) official records maintained by law enforcement and correctional agencies; (2) reports from victims; and (3) self-reported offending. Each of these sources indicates that the overall juvenile crime rate has remained relatively stable since the late 1980s (Office of Juvenile Justice and Delinquency Prevention, 1993). However, each source reveals that rates of serious and violent crimes among juveniles have increased.

Self-reported delinquent behavior for serious offenses, including aggravated assault, robbery, and rape, have risen sharply in the past decade (Elliott, 1994; Osgood et al., 1989). Data from the National Youth Survey, a longitudinal study of a national probability sample of 1,725 youths begun in 1976, reveal that 36 per-cent of African American and 25 percent of caucasian males commit a serious vio-lent offense, including aggravated assault, robbery, and rape, at the peak age of seventeen. In an annual study of drug use and delinquency among the nation's high school seniors, Osgood et al. (1989) found significant increases in violent acts such as aggravated assault and robbery between 1979 and 1985.

Increases in serious and violent juvenile offenses are also reported in official record data. According to law enforcement statistics, juvenile arrests for violent crimes increased 41 percent from 1982 to 1991 (Office of Juvenile Justice and Delinquency Prevention, 1993). Arrests for murder increased by 93 percent and arrests for aggravated assault increased by 72 percent between 1982 and 1991 (Snyder, 1993). Admissions to juvenile detention facilities and correctional facil-ities increased from 638,000 in 1981 to 760,644 in 1990 (Krisberg, 1992).

Juvenile gang activity has grown across the United States since the late 1980s. In a national study of gangs, Spergel and Chance (1991) estimated there were 1,439 gangs and 120,636 gang members in thirty-five American cities. Self-report studies of delinquency, gang involvement, and drug use indi-cate gang members are more active in drug sales and drug use than are non-gang members (Esbensen & Huizinga, 1993; Jenson, 1994). Gang members with arrest records are also responsible for a disproportionate amount of all violent and drug-related crimes committed by juveniles (Snyder, 1993).

Prevalence of Adolescent Alcohol and Drug Use

The major source of data concerning the prevalence of drug use among American youth is the High School Seniors Survey (HSSS) (Johnston,

O'Malley & Bachman, 1991), sponsored by the National Institute on Drug Abuse and the University of Michigan. The HSSS is an annual assessment of drug use in a random sample of the nation's seniors. Approximately 17,000 students are surveyed each year.[1]

Results of the HSSS indicate that the use of most drugs has been declining since the early 1980s. With the exception of cocaine, most drug use peaked around 1980. In 1990, the three most common substances ever used by seniors were alcohol (89.5%), cigarettes (64.4%), and marijuana (40.7%). In terms of regular use, 57.1 percent of students reported drinking alcohol, 29.4 percent smoking cigarettes, and 14 percent using marijuana in the past month. Fewer than 1 percent of high school seniors report *daily* use of any illicit drug other than marijuana; 2.2 percent of seniors used marijuana daily in 1990.

Recent findings from the PRIDE national survey of adolescent drug use indicated that marijuana and hallucinogen use among junior and senior high school students increased significantly between 1992 and 1993 (Hall, 1993). Whether drug-related emergency room visits among adolescents have increased correspondingly, as was the case with adolescent cocaine use during the 1980s (Blanken, 1993), has not yet been determined. Anecdotal reports indicating an increase in drug-related emergency room episodes have surfaced in the past year. However, reliable national statistics for the number of emergency room visits are not currently available.

Drug Use by Gender and Ethnicity

Earlier studies of drug use among adolescents indicated that substance use was more prevalent among males than among females (Johnston, O'Malley, & Bachman, 1985). But recent results from the HSSS show a decrease in gender differences. Female high school seniors are more likely than males to smoke cigarettes and use amphetamines, and they use alcohol and marijuana at nearly the same rates as male seniors. Males continue to be more involved in heavy drinking and drunk driving than are females (Johnston et al., 1991).

HSSS results indicate that alcohol and drug use are more prevalent among Native Americans and Caucasians than among African Americans, Hispanics, or Asian Americans (Johnston et al., 1991). In 1990, annual prevalence of marijuana use was highest among Native Americans (42.0%) and Caucasians (40.2%) and lowest among Asian Americans (19.6%). Marijuana use among

---

1. The HSSS may underestimate the magnitude of drug use among adolescents in the United States because it does not include school dropouts (an estimated 15% to 20% of students in this age group), a group at high risk for drug use and involvement in the juvenile justice system. Estimates of drug and alcohol use among minority groups may be particularly affected because more Native Americans and Hispanics drop out of school than do African Americans, Asian Americans, or Caucasians (Wallace & Bachman, 1991).

African Americans (29.8%) and Hispanics (37.3%) lay between Caucasians and Asian Americans. Native Americans and Caucasians had the highest annual prevalence rates for cigarette and alcohol use among all ethnic groups. Asian American and African American seniors had the lowest annual rates of cigarette and alcohol use and Hispanics were in the intermediate range (Johnston et al., 1991).

Prevalence of Alcohol and Drug Use among Delinquent Youth

Several studies have examined the drug and alcohol use of adjudicated youth. Dembo et al. (1988) assessed the drug use of 145 youths placed in a detention center in the southern United States and found that 90 percent of them used alcohol prior to being detained. Sixty-two percent of detainees used alcohol in the month prior to the survey. Forty-one percent used marijuana more than one hundred times in their lives. Twenty-four percent used cocaine and 22 percent used stimulants prior to the survey. These rates are considerably higher than rates reported by seniors in the HSSS annual survey.

Jenson (1993) examined the drug and alcohol use among 475 youths placed on probation in Utah. Marijuana, alcohol, and tobacco were the three most commonly used drugs among probationers; seventy percent of subjects used marijuana, 90 percent used alcohol, and 92 percent used tobacco prior to the survey. Figure 7.1 compares lifetime prevalence of drug and alcohol use among probationers and a random sample of school-aged youths in Utah. Youth in the school-aged sample were between twelve and eighteen years old and were attending public schools at the time of the survey (Bahr, 1989).

Probationers report higher lifetime prevalence of all drugs when compared with the Utah schools sample. For example, 70 percent of probationers used marijuana in their lifetime, compared with only 16 percent of youths in the Utah schools sample. Similarly, 43 percent of probationers used LSD in their lifetime, compared with only 5 percent of Utah school-aged youth. The difference in amphetamine use is also great: 49 percent of adolescents on probation used amphetamines while only 10 percent of youths in the Utah schools sample ever tried these drugs.

Huizinga, Loeber, and Thornberry (1994) examined the relationship between delinquency and drug use in three separate cohorts of youth between seven and fifteen years of age in Denver, Pittsburgh, and Rochester, NY. The investigators found that serious involvement in drug use was related to serious or chronic delinquency among the youth in each cohort. Interestingly, drug use stimulated more changes and had a larger impact on subsequent delinquency than the reverse (Huizinga et al., 1994). Risk factors and correlates of delinquency and drug use are discussed in the following section.

Figure 7.1:   Lifetime Prevalence of Drug Use among Delinquent and Nondelinquent Youth in Utah

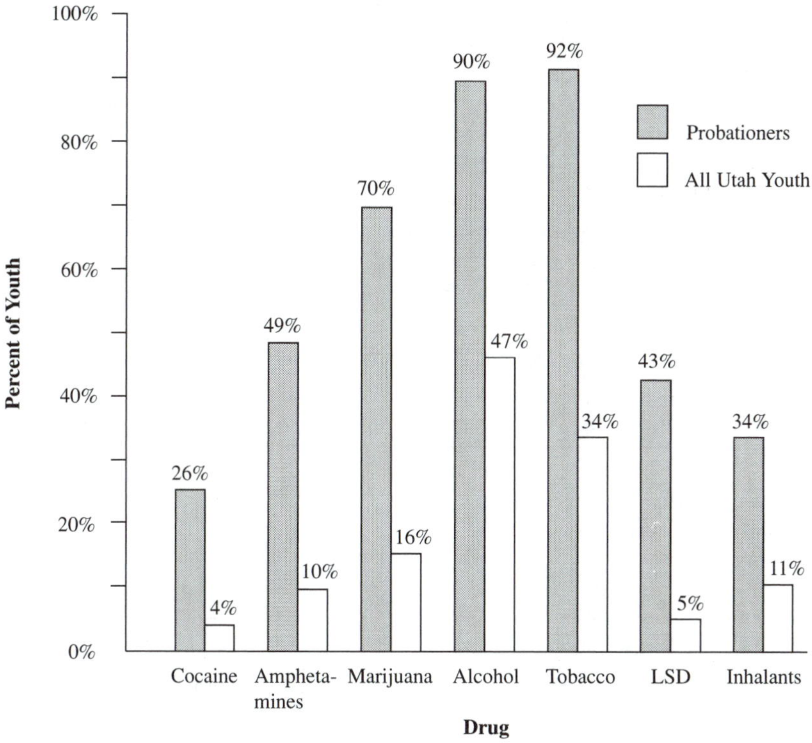

Source: Bahr, S. J. (1989). Data are from classroom surveys with 26,731 youth between grades 7 and 12 across Utah.

Risk Factors and Correlates of Delinquency and Drug Use

The study and treatment of adolescent problems traditionally has been divided into distinct areas such as delinquency, school dropout, teenage pregnancy, and substance abuse. This division has been supported by research agencies and academic institutions that separate adolescent problems according to funding priorities and government divisions (Elliott, Huizinga & Menard, 1989). Based on research indicating that adolescent problems have a common etiology and involve concomitant forms of behavior, there is reason to question this division.

Research and clinical experience indicate that many individual, social, and environmental factors correlate with both delinquency and drug use during adolescence. Among these risk factors are child abuse and neglect, ineffective parental discipline, conduct disorder and hyperactivity in children, school failure, learning disabilities, negative peer influences, inadequate housing, and residence in high-crime neighborhoods (Hawkins et al., 1992; Huizinga et al., 1994).

Risk factors or correlates of delinquency and drug use cannot be equated with causal factors. However, risk factors do provide knowledge of the characteristics of young people who are most likely to become delinquent or to develop problem drug use. While every child or youth who experiences a risk factor does not become a delinquent or a drug abuser, the presence of multiple risk factors in a young person's life does increase the likelihood of developing problems in adolescence (Newcomb et al., 1987).

Risk factors for delinquency and drug abuse are present in the context of a youth's community, family, school, and peer environments. As shown in table 7.1, there are many common risk factors for delinquency and drug use.

Social work practitioners in the juvenile justice system are likely to be familiar with these risk factors. Environmental factors such as poverty, fre-

Table 7.1:   Risk Factors for Delinquency and Drug Abuse*

Community Risk Factors
Availability of drugs
Community laws and norms favorable toward drug use and delinquency
Transitions and mobility
Low neighborhood attachment
Community disorganization
Poverty

Family Risk Factors
Family history of high risk behavior
Family management problems
Parental involvement in crime and drugs

School Risk Factors
Early anti-social behavior in school
Academic failure in elementary school
Lack of commitment to school

Individual and Peer Risk Factors
Rebelliousness
Lack of bonding to society
Friends who use drugs or commit delinquent acts
Favorable attitude towards crime or drug use
Early initiation of delinquency or drug use

*For a complete review see Hawkins, Catalano, & Miller (1992) and Jenson & Howard (1991).

quent mobility, and low neighborhood attachment are common among young offenders. Children who live in deteriorating neighborhoods that offer little hope for the future are at increased risk for involvement in delinquency and drug use (Farrington et al., 1990). Similarly, communities that have norms favorable to drug use and delinquent behavior send messages to young people that increase their likelihood of involvement in these behaviors (Robins, 1984).

Poor family management practices increase the risk of delinquency and drug use (Brook et al., 1990). A lack of expectations for good behavior, failure of parents to monitor their children's behavior, and inconsistent discipline are examples of family management practices that increase the risk for delinquency and drug use.

Academic failure and lack of commitment to school in the later elementary grades increase the risk that a child will develop problems with drug use or delinquency during adolescence (Gottfredson, 1988). Many youth in the juvenile justice system have dropped-out of school or are behind one or more grade levels.

Youth who experience early rebellious and antisocial behavior are at risk for delinquency and drug use (Kellam & Brown, 1992). Antisocial behavior includes activities such as fighting and skipping school at an early age. Associations with friends who engage in delinquency or drug use is among the strongest predictors of subsequent involvement in illegal behavior. Even children who come from well-managed families and do not experience other risk factors are susceptible to peer influence. Finally, early initiation of drug use or delinquency increases the risk of serious involvement at a later age. Evidence suggests that many youth in the juvenile justice system initiate drug use and delinquent behaviors at a young age (Jenson, 1993).

Viewing delinquency and drug use as interrelated behaviors characterized by common risk factors has important implications for intervention in the juvenile justice system. An understanding that behaviors such as delinquency and drug abuse overlap among young offenders suggests that intervention should focus more on the predictors of the behaviors than on the behaviors themselves (Dryfoos, 1990, Elliott, Huizinga & Menard, 1989). Juvenile justice responses to treating delinquents who have drug and alcohol problems and to promising treatment approaches are reviewed below.

Treating Juvenile Delinquents with Drug or Alcohol Problems

Juvenile Justice Responses

Knowledge of the factors that place youth at risk for involvement in delinquency or drug use has been used to design school- and family-based prevention programs for high-risk youth (Jenson & Howard, 1991). Risk-focused prevention programs have successfully delayed initiation of drug use and increased children's interests in school and prosocial activities (Hawkins, Catalano, & Miller, 1992). Knowledge of risk factors has also been incorporated into drug treatment programs as evidenced by the inclusion of parent training, family therapy, and skills training components in many programs for juveniles. Unfortunately, knowledge of risk factors for delinquency and drug use has not been systematically applied to all treatment efforts in the juvenile justice system.

Juvenile justice programs for treating alcohol abuse and illicit drug abuse are similar. Treatments generally include individual or group counseling, family involvement, recreation, school support, and attendance in a self-help group (e.g., Alcoholics Anonymous). Most programs acknowledge that adolescent treatment must address not only substance abuse and delinquency (Schinke, Botvin & Orlandi, 1991) but also their underlying causes (e.g., family tensions, school failure, peer associations).

Promising Approaches to Treating Delinquency and Drug Abuse

There are several promising approaches to incorporating knowledge of risk factors for delinquency and drug abuse when treating delinquent youth with drug problems: social-skills training, family therapy, case management systems, and post-treatment supports.

1. Social-skills training is widely used in juvenile justice programs to treat adolescent substance abuse. Implemented in institutional and community placements, skills training has had some, albeit limited, success in reducing drug use and delinquency (Jenson & Howard, 1990). Social-skills training is based on findings indicating that adolescents who abuse drugs or commit delinquent acts display more skills deficits than do adolescents who do not abuse drugs or commit crimes (Hollin, 1990; Jenson & Howard, 1990). Interventions teach assertiveness, communication, anger management, and relapse prevention skills. Outcome studies indicate that training programs successfully teach skills to adolescents (Hawkins et al., 1991); however, few studies demonstrate long-term effects of acquired skills on reduction in alcohol and drug use (Jenson et al., 1993).

Jenson et al. (1993) explored the relationship between self-efficacy, skills, and later drug use among treated and untreated institutionalized juvenile delinquents in Washington State. Adolescents who were confident in their ability to refrain from substance use at posttest had lower intentions to use alcohol or drugs following treatment. Decreased intentions, in turn, were related to lower rates of alcohol and drug use at six- and twelve-month follow-ups. These results suggest that skills training interventions should incorporate motivational components for adolescent substance abusers. The implementation and effectiveness of such programs should be monitored and evaluated.

2. Family therapy with juvenile offenders is based on the assumption that family behaviors, criminal behaviors, and drug use patterns contribute to a youth's decision to use alcohol or drugs or to engage in delinquency. Effective alcohol and drug treatments have been linked to four different types of family therapy: (1) structural (Minuchin, Rosman, & Baker, 1978); (2) strategic (Stanton & Todd, 1982); (3) functional (Alexander et al., 1978); and (4) behavioral (Patterson, 1982; Patterson, Reid, & Dishion, 1992). Programs based on the integration of these four types have also been successful in reducing adolescent alcohol, cocaine, and marijuana use (Lewis et al., 1990).

Engaging parents and other family members in treatment programs is challenging. Attrition, lack of family cooperation, and limited resources pose barriers to the successful implementation of family treatment. However, because delinquent youth who use drugs or alcohol frequently have family histories of drug abuse, parental involvement is a necessary component of treatment efforts in the justice system.

3. Case management systems that coordinate treatment services for adolescent offenders and other family members appear promising. In the Utah and Hawaii youth corrections systems, case managers are assigned to monitor an adolescent's treatment progress and to provide support to, and communication between, providers and family members. A recent study of ninety-three delinquent youth receiving case management services in the Utah system indicated that coordination of substance abuse treatment services was the most common activity of case managers (Jenson et al., 1994). Case managers rated drug treatment services to be effective for 60 percent of youth released from a state correctional program. Scant empirical evidence exists to support case management as an effective interventive component (Babor et al., 1991); however, its potential utility has important implications for the coordination of juvenile justice services.

4. Posttreatment supports such as self-help groups, relapse prevention, and aftercare are necessary for juvenile offenders with drug problems. Juvenile justice programs pay little attention to aftercare programming (Greenwood, Piper Deschenes & Adams, 1993), yet posttreatment factors (e.g., family support, self-help group attendance, school enrollment) are the strongest predictors of outcome among youth involved in court or corrections programs (Catalano et al., 1989). (See chapter 3 for a full discussion of aftercare.)

The Chemical Abuse/Addiction Treatment Outcome Registry (CATOR) is currently the most extensive longitudinal data base on adolescent drug treatment outcomes (Harrison & Hoffmann, 1989). Results, derived from interviews with 493 youths at six- and twelve-month follow-ups, indicate that adolescents who remained in self-help groups (e.g., Alcoholics Anonymous) for one year following treatment fared better than youths who attended only occasionally or not at all. Alford, Koehler, and Leonard (1991) found that adolescents who participated in Alcoholics Anonymous or Narcotics Anonymous groups following inpatient treatment had significantly higher abstinence rates than adolescents who completed inpatient treatment only. These findings underscore the importance of posttreatment support as a predictor of outcome; however, neither study randomly assigned subjects to alternative treatments, and it is possible that adolescents attending self-help groups following treatment were particularly motivated.

Self-help is the single most widely used treatment approach in the country; it is also the least evaluated. Results of the CATOR (Harrison & Hoffmann, 1989) and Alford, Koehler, and Leonard's studies (1991) provide limited support for the effectiveness of self-help modalities. Unfortunately, evidence supporting the efficacy of self-help groups such as Alcoholics Anonymous is largely based on anecdotal reports (Miller & Hester, 1986). In addition, many self-help programs are designed to meet the needs of adult offenders or drug abusers. Caution should be exercised in referring young offenders to adult self-help groups that may prematurely label youth as drug addicted.

Several models of relapse prevention are effective with adult drug and alcohol abusers (Gorski & Miller, 1979; Marlatt & Gordon, 1985). Relapse prevention training helps offenders identify high-risk situations for alcohol or drug relapse and develop coping skills to avoid relapse. Evaluations of relapse prevention programs for adolescents in the juvenile justice system should be conducted.

Aftercare programs in the juvenile justice system are particularly important for youth with drug or alcohol problems. Studies show that many youth in juvenile justice programs improve their attitudes, self-efficacy, skills, and behaviors during the course of treatment (Catalano et al., 1989). However, because most incarcerated youth are returned to the environment that supported their antisocial behavior, they often fail to maintain such changes in the community (Greenwood, Piper Deschenes, & Adams, 1993). Despite this evidence, the percentage of juvenile-justice funding directed to aftercare programming is relatively low in most states (Altschuler & Armstrong, 1991). Inadequate funding for aftercare is likely due to perceived public pressure by policymakers and elected officials to invest the majority of resources in other parts of the juvenile justice system.

Several aftercare programs for juvenile offenders have been developed and tested in recent years. Altschuler and Armstrong (1991) developed a comprehensive aftercare intervention model based on social control, strain, and social-learning theories. The model includes five principles designed to guide the selection of specific program components: (1) preparing youth for increased responsibility and freedom in the community; (2) facilitating youth–community interaction and involvement; (3) working with offender and community support systems; (4) developing new resources and supports; and (5) monitoring and testing (Altschuler & Armstrong, 1991). Tests of this model's ability to reduce recidivism are currently underway.

Aftercare services must be intensive. Several recent evaluations of after-care programs for serious delinquents using traditional casework approaches produced no significant differences in recidivism between treated and untreated subjects (Greenwood, Piper Deschenes, & Adams, 1993; Jenson et al., 1993). It may be that case-work strategies are inadequate to deal with the difficult situations confronting young people following incarceration or residential placement in the juvenile justice system.

Implications for Social Work Practice in the Juvenile Justice System

Developing a Continuum of Services

Most evaluation research in drug treatment and juvenile justice systems describes or examines the effects of specific clinical interventions or program models (e.g., a particular group home or day treatment model). While important, such evaluations do not always contribute to the development of comprehensive systems of care for juvenile delinquents with drug problems. Because responsibility for adolescent care is not centralized, collaboration between schools and substance abuse, mental health, child welfare, and juvenile justice agencies is needed to better match client needs to programs (Jenson, Howard, & Yaffe, in press; Tracy & Farkas, 1994).

A number of factors contribute to the importance of systems collaboration. Organization factors were discussed in chapter 1. There also have been considerable advances in community-based drug treatment in the past decade. Adolescents who receive intensive, individualized, and family-based treatment in the community attain outcomes at least as positive as adolescents placed in traditional training school or other residential programs (Friedman, 1992). Developing a continuum of community-based programs is a critical component of any comprehensive juvenile justice or drug abuse treatment system.

Approaches to treating adolescent offenders with alcohol and drug problems should be viewed on a continuum that includes: (1) brief intervention; (2) outpatient treatment; (3) day treatment; (4) residential treatment; and (5) inpatient treatment. Figure 7.2 identifies common program components by treatment type. For the delinquent, as for the adult offender with an alcohol or drug problem, there must be a wide array of alternatives. Included in this continuum are education, individual therapy, family therapy, social skills training, case management, therapeutic community, self-help, medical, and relapse prevention approaches.

Developing continuity of care that meets the diverse needs of delinquent youth is an important aspect of improving treatment outcome and reducing recidivism. Because no single drug or delinquency treatment approach is supe-

Figure 7.2: Continuum of Alcohol and Drug Treatment for Adolescent Offenders

Severity of Alcohol and Drug Abuse ➝

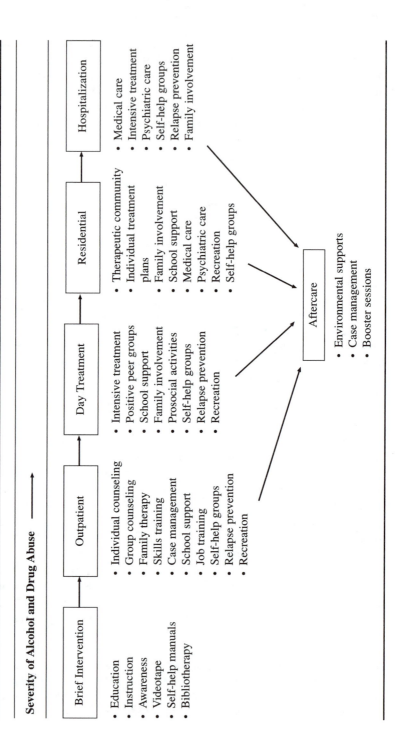

rior to all others for all adolescents, a range of services is needed to increase the likelihood of appropriate treatment matching and successful outcomes. Additional research and practice innovations are needed in the following areas: (1) screening and early identification of drug abuse; (2) diagnostic evaluation procedures, including examination of social and psychological factors; (3) criteria for matching individual offenders to appropriate treatments; (4) effectiveness of different interventions; and (5) efficacy of coordination, case management, and monitoring of treatment services.

Programs for Special Populations

Delinquents who are HIV positive or who have AIDS, and who abuse alcohol and drugs, are vulnerable to medical and emotional problems. Because HIV has a long incubation period, the number of adolescents who currently have AIDS does not accurately reflect the magnitude of the problem. Juvenile justice programs treating adolescent substance abusers who are HIV positive, or who have AIDS, need to be expanded. Promising approaches for adults appear to be street outreach programs, storefront education centers, and methadone maintenance and comprehensive addiction programs (Kravis, Weiss, & Perry, 1991). Specialized foster homes for youth who are HIV positive or who have AIDS have been established in some states (Dryfoos, 1990). Unfortunately, rigorous evaluations of such programs have not been conducted. While intravenous drug use accounts for a small percentage of adolescent drug users nationally, the risks associated with such use are high. Alcohol and drug treatment can play an important role in reducing the spread of AIDS among intravenous and other high-risk drug users.

Few programs are designed to meet the needs of female or minority adolescent substance abusers in the juvenile justice system (Jenson, Howard, & Yaffe, in press; Yaffe, Jenson, & Howard, in press). The special needs of female delinquents include comprehensive medical attention and child care. Adolescent females who abuse alcohol and drugs are at higher risk for early and unwanted pregnancies (Dryfoos, 1990). Promising approaches for preventing pregnancy and reducing alcohol and drug use among female offenders include skills training and interventions providing case management and in-home services (Freeman, 1992). To date, comparative evaluations of culturally sensitive treatment have not been reported (Gilbert & Cervantes, 1988). At a minimum, programs serving minorities in the juvenile justice system should offer bilingual counseling and family involvement (Panitz et al., 1983).

Conclusion

Intervention programs in the juvenile justice system should simultaneously treat delinquency and concomitant problem behaviors such as drug abuse.

Delinquency, drug abuse, and other adolescent problems share many risk factors. Interventions in the juvenile justice system must target these factors and provide a continuum of comprehensive treatment services for young offenders.

Social work practitioners routinely treat adolescent substance abusers in community-based services and residential programs administered by the juvenile justice system. Yet many practitioners spend little time studying the etiology and treatment of substance abuse and delinquency during graduate education (Kagle, 1987). To ensure competent juvenile justice personnel, comprehensive training in the addictions, in juvenile delinquency, and in the application of social work interventions (e.g., case management, family therapy, and social support) to adolescent problems should be encouraged by the profession. Inadequate training in delinquency and substance abuse treatment is likely to have an adverse impact on the effectiveness of intervention. Social work, with its emphasis on the role of environmental, social, and psychological factors in the etiology and maintenance of problem behaviors such as substance abuse and delinquency, has much to contribute to the understanding and treatment of substance abusing adolescents in the juvenile justice system.

The author acknowledges the support of the University of Utah Lowell Bennion Community Service Center, the Utah State Division of Youth Corrections, and the Utah Commission on Criminal and Juvenile Justice in the preparation of this manuscript.

References

Alexander, J. F., Barton, C., Schiavo, R. S., & Parsons, B. V. (1978). Systems-behavioral intervention with families of delinquents: Therapist characteristics, family behavior, and outcome. *Journal of Consulting and Clinical Psychology, 44,* 656–664.

Alford, G. S., Koehler, R. A., & Leonard, J. (1991). Alcoholics Anonymous–Narcotics Anonymous model inpatient treatment of chemically dependent adolescents: A two-year outcome study. *Journal of Studies on Alcohol, 52,*(2), 118–126.

Altschuler, D. M., & Armstrong, T. L. (1991). Intensive aftercare for the high-risk juvenile parolee: Issues and approaches in reintegration and community supervision. In T. L. Armstrong (Ed.), *Intensive interventions with high-risk youths: Promising approaches in juvenile probation and parole.* Monsey, NY: Criminal Justice Press.

Babor, T. F., Del Boca, F. K., McLaney, M. A., Jacobi, B., Higgins-Biddle, J., & Hass, W. (1991). Just say Y.E.S.: Matching adolescents to appropriate interventions for alcohol and other drug-related problems. *Alcohol Health and Research World, 15,* (1), 77–86.

Bahr, S. (1989). Drug use among Utah students, 1989. Unpublished manuscript. Utah State Division of Family Services, Salt Lake City, Utah.

Blanken, A. J. (1993). Measuring use of alcohol and other drugs among adolescents. *Public Health Reports, 108,* 25–30.

Brook, J. S., Brook, D. W., Gordon, A. S., Whiteman, M., & Cohen, P. (1990). The psychosocial etiology of adolescent drug use: A family interactional approach. *Genetic, Social, and General Psychology Monographs* (Whole No. 2).

Catalano, R. F., Wells, E. A., Jenson, J. M., & Hawkins, J. D. (1989). Aftercare services for drug-using institutionalized delinquents. *Social Service Review, 63,* (4), 553–557.

Dembo, R., Dertke, M., Borders, S., Washburn, M., & Schmeidler, J. (1988). The relationship between physical and sexual abuse and tobacco, alcohol, and illicit drug use in a juvenile detention center. *The International Journal of the Addictions, 23,* (4), 351–378.

Dryfoos, J. G. (1990). *Adolescents at risk: Prevalence and prevention.* New York: Oxford University Press.

Elliott, D. S. (1994). Serious violent offenders: Onset, developmental course, and termination. The American Society of Criminology 1993 Presidential Address. *Criminology, 32,* (1), 1–21.

Elliott, D. S., Huizinga, D., & Menard, S. (1989). *Multiple problem youth: Delinquency, substance abuse, and mental health problems.* New York: Springer-Verlag.

Esbensen, F. A. & Huizinga, D. (1993). Gangs, drugs, and delinquency in a survey of urban youth. *Criminology, 31,* (4), 565–590.

Farrington, D. P., Loeber, R., Elliott, D. S., Hawkins, J. D., Kandel, D. B., Klein, M. W., McCord, J., Rowe, D. C., & Tremblay, R. E. (1990). Advancing knowledge about the onset of delinquency and crime. In B. B. Lahey & A. E. Kazdin (Eds.), *Advances in clinical child psychology* (Vol. 13, pp. 283–342). New York: Plenum Press.

Freeman, E. M. (1992). Addictive behaviors: State-of-the-art issues in social work treatment. In E. M. Freeman (Ed.), *The addiction process: Effective social work process* (pp. 1–9). New York: Longman.

Friedman, R. M. (1992). Mental health and substance abuse services for adolescents: Clinical and service system issues. *Administration and Policy in Mental Health, 19,* (3), 159–178.

Gilbert, M. J. & Cervantes, R. C. (1988). Alcohol treatment for Mexican Americans: A review of utilization patterns and therapeutic approaches. In M. J. Gilbert (Ed.), *Alcohol consumption among Mexicans and Mexican Americans: A binational perspective* (pp. 199–231). Los Angeles: Spanish Speaking Mental Health Center, University of California.

Gorski, T. T. & Miller, M. (1979). *Counseling for relapse prevention.* Hazel Crest, IL: Alcoholism Systems Associates.

Gottfredson, G. D. (1988). Issues in adolescent drug use. Unpublished final report to the U.S. Dept. of Justice, Johns Hopkins University, Center for Research on Elementary and Middle Schools, Baltimore, MD.

Greenwood, P. W., Piper Deschenes, E., & Adams, J. (1993). *Chronic juvenile offenders: Final results from the Skillman aftercare experiment.* Santa Monica, CA: RAND.

Harrison, P. A., & Hoffmann, N. G. (1989). *CATOR report: Adolescent completers one year later.* St. Paul, MN: Chemical Abuse/Addiction Treatment Outcome Registry, Ramsey Clinic.

Hawkins, J. D., Catalano, R. F., & Miller, J. Y. (1992). Risk and protective factors for alcohol and other drug problems in adolescence and early adulthood: Implications for substance abuse prevention. *Psychological Bulletin, 112* (1), 64–105.

Hawkins, J. D., Jenson, J. M., Catalano, R. F., & Lishner, D. L. (1988). Delinquency and drug abuse: Implications for social services. *Social Service Review, 62,* 258–284.

Hawkins, J. D., Jenson, J. M., Catalano, R. F., & Wells, E. A. (1991). Effects of skills training intervention with juvenile delinquents. *Research on Social Work Practice, 1*(2), 107–121.

Hollin, C. R. (1990). Social skills training with delinquents: A look at the evidence and some recommendations for practice. *British Journal of Social Work, 20,* 483–493.

Huizinga, D., Loeber, R., & Thornberry, T. P. (1994). *Urban delinquency and substance abuse: Initial findings.* Washington, DC: U.S. Dept. of Justice.

Jenson, J. M. (1993). Drug and alcohol use among juvenile probationers in Utah. Unpublished manuscript. Social Research Institute, Graduate School of Social Work, University of Utah. Salt Lake City.

Jenson, J. M. (1994). Factors related to gang membership among juvenile probationers. Unpublished manuscript. Social Research Institute, Graduate School of Social Work, University of Utah. Salt Lake City.

Jenson, J. M., DeWitt, J. R., Downing, R. H., Chang, R., & Riechmann, T. (1994). Factors associated with recidivism and placement in secure custody. Unpublished manuscript. Social Research Institute, Graduate School of Social Work, University of Utah. Salt Lake City.

Jenson, J. M. & Howard, M. O. (1990). Skills deficits, skills training, and delinquency. *Children and Youth Services Review, 12,* 213–238.

Jenson, J. M. & Howard, M. O. (1991). Risk-focused drug and alcohol prevention: Implications for school-based prevention programs. *Social Work in Education, 13* (4), 246–256.

Jenson, J. M., Howard, M. O., & Yaffe, J. (In press). Treatment of adolescent substance abusers: Issues for practice and research. *Social Work in Health Care.*

Jenson, J. M., Wells, E. A., Plotnick, R. D., Hawkins, J. D., & Catalano, R. F. (1993). The effects of skills and intentions to use drugs on posttreatment drug use of adolescents. *American Journal of Drug and Alcohol Abuse, 19* (1), 1–17.

Johnston, L. D., O'Malley, P. M., & Bachman, J. G. (1985). *Drug use among American high school seniors, college students, and young adults, 1975–1984.* Rockville, MD: National Institute on Drug Abuse.

Johnston, L. D., O'Malley, P. M., & Bachman, J. G. (1991). *Drug use among American high school seniors, college students, and young adults, 1975–1990.* Rockville, MD: National Institute on Drug Abuse.

Kagle, J. D. (1987). Women who drink: Changing images, changing realities. *Journal of Social Work Education, 23* (3), 21–28.

Kellam, S. G., & Brown, H. (1982). *Social, adaptational, and psychological antecedents of adolescent psychopathology ten years later.* Baltimore, MD: Johns Hopkins University Press.

Kravis, N. M., Weiss, C. J., & Perry, S. W. (1991). Drug and alcohol addiction in AIDS. In N. S. Miller (Ed.), *Comprehensive handbook of drug and alcohol addiction* (pp. 891–904). New York: Marcel-Dekker.

Krisberg, B. (1992). *National juvenile custody trends 1978–1989.* Washington, DC: U.S. Dept. of Justice.

Lewis, R. A., Piercy, F. P., Sprenkle, D. H., & Trepper, T. S. (1990). Family-based interventions for helping drug-abusing adolescents. *Journal of Adolescent Research, 5,* (1), 82–95.

Marlatt, G. A., & Gordon, J. R. (1985). *Relapse prevention: Maintenance strategies in the treatment of addictive behaviors.* New York: Guilford Press.

Miller, W. R., & Hester, R. K. (1986). The effectiveness of alcoholism research: What research reveals. In W. R. Miller & N. Heather (Eds.), *Treating addictive behaviors: Processes of change* (pp. 175–204). New York: Plenum.

Minuchin, S., Rosman, B., & Baker, L. (1978). *Psychosomatic families: Anorexia nervosa in context.* Cambridge, MA: Harvard University Press.

National Council of Family Court Judges (1987). *Juvenile and family substance abuse: A judicial response.* Reno, NV: National Council of Family Court Judges.

Newcomb, M. D., Maddahian, E., Skager, R., & Bentler, P. M. (1987). Substance abuse and psychological risk factors among teenagers: Associations with sex, age, ethnicity, and type of school. *American Journal of Drug and Alcohol Abuse, 13,* 413–433.

Office of Juvenile Justice and Delinquency Prevention (1993). *Comprehensive strategy for serious, violent, and chronic juvenile offenders.* Washington, DC: U.S. Dept. of Justice.

Osgood, D. W., O'Malley, P. M., Bachman, J. G., & Johnston, L. D. (1989). Time trends and age trends in arrests and self-reported illegal behavior. *Criminology, 27,* (3), 389–418.

Panitz, D. R., McConchie, R. D., Sauber, S. R., & Fonseca, J. A. (1983). The role of machismo and the Hispanic family in the etiology and treatment of alcoholism in Hispanic American males. *The American Journal of Family Therapy, 11,* 31–42.

Patterson, G. R. (1982). *Coercive family process.* Eugene, OR: Castalia.

Patterson, G. R., Reid, J. B., & Dishion, T. J. (1992). *Antisocial boys.* Eugene, OR: Castalia.

Robins, L. N. (1984). The natural history of adolescent drug use. *American Journal of Public Health, 74,* 656–657.

Schinke, S. P., Botvin, G. J., & Orlandi, M. O. (1991). *Substance abuse in children and adolescents: Evaluation and intervention.* Newbury Park, CA: Sage.

Snyder, H. (1993). *Arrests of youth in 1993.* Washington, DC: U.S. Dept. of Justice.

Spergel, I. A., & Chance, R. L. (1991). National youth gang suppression and intervention program. *National Institute of Justice Reports, 224,* 21–24.

Stanton, M. D., & Todd, T. C. (1982). *The family therapy of drug addiction.* New York: Guilford.

Stone, K. (1990). Determining the primacy of substance use disorders among juvenile offenders. *Alcoholism Treatment Quarterly, 7,* (2), 81–93.

Tracy, E. M., & Farkas, K. J. (1994). Preparing practitioners for child welfare practice with substance-abusing families. *Child Welfare, 73,* (1), 57–68.

Wallace, J. M., & Bachman, J. G. (1991). Explaining racial/ethnic differences in adolescent drug use: The impact of background and lifestyle. *Social Problems, 38,* (3), 333–357.

Yaffe, J., Jenson, J. M., & Howard, M. O. (In press). Women and substance abuse: Implications for treatment. *Alcoholism Treatment Quarterly.*

PART III

Direct Practice, Advocacy, and Outreach

We begin this section with chapter 8, by Albert Roberts and Pamela Fisher, on victim/witness assistance programs, covering everything from direct service roles to policy and administration. Creasie Hairston's chapter 9 examines family programs in state prisons. She criticizes the minimal involvement of social workers and traditional social service organizations in prison programs, and calls for the profession to play a more active role. Susan Chandler and Gene Kassebaum (chapter 10) describe a number of programs that are designed specifically to meet the needs of female offenders, including those of probation or parole, or in jail or prison. In chapter 11 Rudolph Alexander explores the historical involvement of social workers in the justice system, rebuts the argument against noninvolvement, describes various justice system roles, and speculates about the future of practice in this area. Karen Knox and Allen Rubin (chapter 12) provide us with an insightful illustration of intervention with adolescent sex offenders, a group of clients at extremely high risk for recidivism. Finally, in chapter 13, Mary Jackson and David Springer discuss an important but extremely small area of practice, social work with African American juvenile gangs. Like previous authors, they also deal with the lack of interest and involvement by the profession in this area.

Chapter Eight

▶ •••••••••••••••••••••• ◀

Policy, Administration, and Direct Service Roles in Victim/Witness Assistance Programs

Albert R. Roberts and Pamela Fisher

Twenty years ago, victim rights advocates and victim service and victim/witness assistance programs were rarely available in communities throughout the United States. Now, in the mid-1990s, there are over 6,000 victim/witness assistance programs, battered women's shelters, rape crisis programs, and support groups for survivors of violent crimes nationwide. The victims' movement has grown remarkably during the past two decades. The proliferation of programs is a direct result of the federal Victims of Crime Act (VOCA) funding, state and county general revenue grants, and earmarking a percentage of state penalty assessments and fines levied on criminal offenders.

In cities and counties throughout the country, victims of crime are receiving help from victim service and witness assistance programs. Whether people are victimized in a small town with a population of 17,000 such as Black River Falls, Wisconsin, or in major metropolitan areas such as Atlanta, New York City, or San Francisco, services from a victim/witness assistance program are available to them (Roberts, 1995).

Scope of the Problem

There has been a growing awareness among social work leaders, police administrators, and prosecutors alike of the alarming prevalence of violent crimes and the need to address the rights of crime victims. Based on recent data from the National Crime Survey (NCS), the Uniform Crime Reports (UCR), and the Fatal Accident Reporting System (FARS), it is estimated that more than 800,000 individuals are seriously injured and more than 20,000 are killed each year by major crimes (Bureau of Justice Statistics, 1992). In 1987 the NCS indicated that a total of 140,900 attempted or completed rapes had occurred, of which 64,210 resulted in the victim receiving medical care. The NCS also estimated that close to 4.5 million assaults occurred in 1987, and that only 9 percent (390,562) of the victims received medical care following the assault.

Each year, millions of crime victims are physically, emotionally, or financially damaged by perpetrators of violent crime. In the aftermath of a violent crime, victims often have to cope with physical pain, psychological trauma, financial loss, and court proceedings, which all too frequently seem impersonal and confusing. Many victims and witnesses have their first contact with the criminal justice system as a result of being victimized. This first contact can be frightening and confusing. During the past fifteen years, a growing number of counties and cities have developed victim service and witness assistance programs, victim compensation programs, and specialized domestic violence programs to reduce the impact of violent crime on the lives of victims and witnesses.

Brief Historical Background

For decades the rights of victims and witnesses have been ignored by the courts. Until the mid-1970s, correctional reformers and noted authors were revered as founders and international experts in criminology and penology. Millions of dollars were spent in the 1950s and 1960s on rehabilitation programs aimed at changing convicted felons into law-abiding citizens. Millions of dollars were also spent by the courts on processing and protecting the rights of defendants. In sharp contrast to this, crime victims had to wait in the halls of dreary courtrooms where defendants sometimes threatened or intimidated them. Separate waiting rooms for witnesses and their children were practically non-existent. While extensive correctional treatment, educational, and social services programs were available to convicted offenders (Roberts, 1971, 1974), the victims and their families who were often shattered by the victimization, were given no services (McDonald, 1976).

By the mid 1970s, when the first victim/witness assistance and rape crisis programs were initiated, the pendulum began to shift from providing rehabilitation programs for convicted felons toward providing critically needed services for innocent crime victims (Roberts, 1992). The focus on the treatment of crime victims was changing from their initial contact with police officers or detectives to their testimony in court. Historically, too many crime victims had been victimized twice: once during the actual crime and then, again, when insensitive, unresponsive police and prosecutors ignored their calls for assistance or subjected them to harsh, repeated, and victim-blaming questions (McDonald, 1976).

The crime victims' movement has come a long way in the past twenty years. Between fiscal years 1973 and 1975 the Law Enforcement Assistance Administration (LEAA) spent several million dollars for victim/witness assistance demonstration projects. During the early 1970s a growing number of prosecutors' offices in cities and counties throughout the United States became computerized. For the first time, several systematic victim studies were conducted. These studies indicated that "after the victim had decided to report the crime but before the problem of continuances and delays had begun to operate, many crime cases were lost because witnesses did not want to cooperate" (McDonald, 1976, p. 29).

The research documenting witness noncooperation and the insensitive, apathetic treatment of victims and witnesses by court staff led to the federal LEAA funding of eighteen victim and victim/witness assistance programs. Ten of these programs were prosecutor-based witness assistance programs; four were victim assistance programs under the direction of a nonprofit social service agency, a county probation department, and a police department. The remaining four programs focused on providing advocacy and crisis intervention to victims of rape or child abuse.

In the early 1980s, with the demise of LEAA, federal grants to victim assistance programs declined. Existing programs tried to make up for the loss of LEAA seed grants by requesting county or city general revenue funding. At first, some local government sources were unwilling to allocate sufficient funds. However. between 1981 and 1985, twenty-eight states enacted legislation to fund both established and new programs to aid victims and witnesses. The trend among state legislators has been to raise the funds for these programs by earmarking a percentage of penalty assessments and fines on criminal offenders. Nineteen of the twenty-eight states fund victim/witness assistance programs through penalty assessments and fines, while the remaining nine states fund victim assistance through general state revenues (Roberts, 1990).

Since the passage of the landmark Victims of Crime Act (VOCA) of 1984, responsive federal, state, and county agencies have allocated over $650 million to aid crime victims. A large portion of these funds come from fines and penalty assessments on convicted felons. Unfortunately, several states are rapidly losing ground in the collection of restitution and penalty assessments. The author predicts that those states with responsive legislators and highly organized victim compensation and restitution or corrections boards will hire the necessary number of accountants, fiscal monitors, and computer-literate administrators necessary for maintaining 90 percent or higher collection of fees (Roberts, 1995).

Comparing Victim Service and Victim/Witness Assistance Programs

Victim/witness assistance programs are usually located either within the local county prosecutor's office, the county court house, or across the street from the court house. These programs are designed to encourage witness cooperation in the filing of criminal charges as well as testifying in court. In general, these programs include a witness notification and case monitoring system in which staff keep witnesses advised of indictments, continuances, and postponements; specific trial and hearing dates; negotiated pleas; and trial outcomes. In addition, many of these programs provide secure and comfortable reception rooms for witnesses waiting to testify in court, transportation services, and court escorts (both in accompanying the witness to court and remaining with the individual in order to explain and interpret the court proceedings). Typically these programs also prepare and distribute court orientation pamphlets about the adjudication process, on topics such as "Crime Victims' Bill of Rights," "Witness Guidelines for Courtroom Testimony," "What You Should Know about Your Criminal Court and the Court Process," and "Information Guide for Crime Victims" (Roberts, 1992).

According to the senior author's national organizational survey of victim service and witness assistance programs, slightly under one-third of these programs reported having some form of childcare for the children of victims and witnesses while the parents testify in court. Such provision of responsible and structured childcare is an important service (Roberts, 1990). Unfortunately, most criminal justice agencies are very different from social work agencies in that they do not usually realize that victims' and witnesses' children are affected by their parents' emotional reactions, losses, physical injuries, and disruptions due to being crime victims. Victim/witness assistance programs should be concerned with the special needs of children, not only because many parent witnesses are unable to testify if they cannot find childcare during a traumatizing court ordeal but also because it is the humane thing to do. An added benefit is that some children may have witnessed the crime and noticed additional identifying characteristics of the perpetrator (Roberts, 1995).

The overriding objectives of victim/witness assistance programs and units are to assist witnesses in overcoming the anxiety and trauma associated with testifying in court, while encouraging witness cooperation in the prosecution of criminal cases. The primary objectives of these programs are as follows:

1. Providing victims and witnesses with the message that their cooperation is essential to crime control efforts and successful criminal prosecution.

2. Informing victims and witnesses of their rights to receive dignified and compassionate treatment by criminal justice authorities.
3. Providing information to witnesses on the court process, the scheduling of the case, the trial, and the disposition.
4. Providing orientation to court proceedings and tips on how best to accurately recall the crime scene and to testify (Roberts, 1990).

Victim service or crisis intervention programs for crime victims do not seem to be as common as victim/witness assistance programs. Victim-service programs are usually lodged in a police department, sheriff's office, hospital, probation department, or not-for-profit social service agency. Typically, they attempt to intervene within the first twenty-four hours after the crime. They provide a comprehensive range of essential services for crime victims, including responding to the crime scene; crisis counseling; help in completing victim compensation applications; emergency financial assistance and food vouchers to local supermarkets; transportation to court, the local battered women's shelter, the hospital, or the victim assistance program office; repairing or replacing broken locks and windows; assistance in replacing lost documents (e.g., birth certificates, marriage licenses, wills); and referrals to community mental health centers and social service agencies for extended counseling and short-term psychotherapy.

The primary objectives of victim service or crisis intervention programs include providing early and timely intervention and aid to crime victims through twenty-four-hour mobile response teams; crisis intervention at the crime scene, the hospital or local battered women's shelter; emergency lock repairs; assistance in completing victim compensation award applications; helping the victim complete forms for replacing lost documents; and referral to the prosecutor's domestic violence and sexual assault intake unit as well as community mental health centers.

Legislation, Funding, and Stability

During the past two decades, the organizational stability as well as the number of victim/witness assistance centers and programs have varied. Most victim/witness assistance programs are developed by county and city prosecutors. Most of these prosecutor-based programs have received annual federal VOCA pass-through grants from their respective state Attorney General's Office or state VOCA Coordinator. The programs seem to be the most well-established and stable with regard to their funding. In sharp contrast, some of the police-based and hospital-based victim assistance programs go out of business in three to five years. These temporary victim assistance programs are initiated through federal or state start-up grants (seed money) and with either no monetary match or only a 10 percent match from the county or municipal budget. Unfortunately, without a sustained monetary commitment from the mayor, city council, hospital president or CEO, or police chief, these programs are bound to fail.

The largest growth in the number of programs came about during the period from 1984 to 1991. For example, in Massachusetts, annual revenues surged in the beginning from $137,000 in fiscal year 1984 to $2.3 million in fiscal year 1985. During the next seven fiscal years, victim witness revenues steadily increased from $2.2 million in fiscal year 1985 to $7.9 in fiscal year 1991. This represents a major increase of over 250 percent in the seven-year period. However, revenues to the victim fund dropped by 25 percent between fiscal years 1991 and 1993. On the federal level, the funding of victim services, domestic violence, and witness assistance programs has also steadily increased from an allocation of more than $68 million in fiscal year 1985 to $115 million in fiscal year 1991 (Roberts, 1995).

Staffing Patterns

Victim/witness assistance programs are located throughout the United States. They are similar in a number of ways, particularly in the size and responsibility of their staffs. According to the senior author's national organizational survey, three-fourths of the programs were staffed by five or fewer full-time employees. Approximately 10 percent indicated that they had medium-size staffs of eleven or more full-time employees. Only 3 percent were large programs with twenty-four or more full-time staff. The predominant staffing pattern consisted of a victim/witness program director/coordinator, two victim advocates/counselors, a secretary, and a data-entry person. The program coordinator reported directly to the county prosecutor, the chief counsel to the prosecutor, or a deputy prosecutor responsible for all sex crimes (e.g., sexual assault and domestic violence cases). The primary responsibility of the victim advocates/counselors is provision of services to witnesses, particularly witnesses to violent crimes where a person has been charged with one or more criminal offenses. Victim/witness advocates are responsible for accompanying the witness to the prefiling hearing, preliminary hearing, deposition hearing, and the trial in order to ensure that each witness is treated fairly and compassionately by the attorneys, court clerk, and magistrate. In addition, it is important for the coordinator or victim advocates to accompany the victim/witness to all official appointments related to the filing and processing of the criminal court cases. For example, if the victim/witness has been sexually assaulted, the victim advocate either accompanies or meets the victim at the hospital or medical facility to make sure that the victim's rights are protected.

Many programs rely on volunteer assistance to provide needed services. More than half (52%) of the respondents to Roberts (1990) national survey reported that they utilized volunteers. While approximately one-third of the programs used one to four volunteers, almost half of the programs had eleven or more volunteers. Programs with smaller paid staff had a tendency to rely heavily on volunteers. Participation of volunteers enabled programs to provide services to victims and witnesses in small communities such as Xenia, Ohio (population 130,000, four full-time staff, fourteen volunteers), and Greensboro, North Carolina (population 360,000, two full-time staff, twelve volunteers). The programs in large cities had a small number of volunteers relative to their paid staff. For example, Pittsburgh, Pennsylvania, with a population of almost 500,000, has a victim/witness assistance program with fourteen full-time paid staff and fifteen to eighteen volunteers.

With regard to the staff's educational background, over 90 percent of the employees of victim/witness assistance programs have a bachelor's degree; of that group only 28 percent have a graduate degree. Usually the graduate degree is a master's in social work (M.S.W.) or a master's in sociology, counseling, or criminal justice. The professional degrees earned by the coordinators/directors of victim/witness assistance programs varies. Most of them have master's degrees in counseling, education, criminal justice, psychology, or social work. One-third have M.S.W. degrees and most of these program coordinators have completed courses in social welfare policy, planning and management, administration, and crisis intervention and brief treatment (Roberts, 1990).

One of the best ways to prepare for a career in victim services and victim assistance is to complete a block field placement at a comprehensive victim/witness assistance program. Most graduate schools of social work offer opportunities for their M.S.W. students to bridge theory and practice by placing them in a prosecutor-based victim assistance program, a sexual assault intervention center, a battered women's shelter, or a crisis intervention unit. Graduate programs in social work are unique because of the emphasis on field work, regular supervision of beginning social workers, and weekly case consultations.

The Development of Prosecutor-Based Victim/Witness Assistance Programs in New Jersey

In New Jersey, a number of legislative initiatives have paved the way for improved treatment of crime victims by the criminal justice system. The Crime Victim's Bill of Rights was signed into law on July 31, 1985. In January of the following year, legislation created the Office of Victim–Witness Advocacy within the Division of Criminal Justice and a county Office of Victim–Witness Advocacy within each county prosecutor's office. This legislation, which became effective in April 1986, required the Attorney General, through the Office of Victim–Witness Advocacy and in consultation with the county prosecutors, to promulgate standards for law enforcement agencies to ensure that the rights of crime victims are enforced. Additional legislation created the Victim and Witness Advocacy Fund, which is supported by penalty assessments imposed on convicted offenders and is used to establish and enhance services to victims and witnesses statewide.

The following victims' rights and services are guaranteed by these laws: the right to be notified of the status of cases; the right to be given financial aid and social services; the right to have property returned in a timely fashion once it has been used as evidence; the right to secure waiting areas in the courthouse; the right to be protected from intimidation; and the right to submit a victim impact statement to the prosecutor prior to formal charging decisions and to make an in-person statement directly to the sentencing court.

The rights guaranteed under the Crime Victim's Bill of Rights, and the services provided by the New Jersey state and county Offices of Victim-Witness Advocacy, ensure that crime victims will not be forced to endure the impact of criminal victimization alone.

The mission of the Offices of Victim-Witness Advocacy is to support and expand victim-witness services across the state in coordination with the law enforcement community. The goal of these services is to help victims cope with the aftermath of victimization and help make their participation in the system less ominous and burdensome.

Pursuant to New Jersey statute and upon recommendation of the County Prosecutor, the chief of the Office of Victim-Witness Advocacy has appointed victim-witness coordinators in each of the twenty-one counties. Each has been sworn into office by the Attorney General. The coordinators are responsible for implementing victims' rights and services in their jurisdiction. The county victim-witness coordinators are located in the County Prosecutors' Office and are jointly supervised by the county prosecutors and the chief of the Office of Victim-Witness Advocacy.

Funding for the operation of the state Office of Victim-Witness Advocacy is completely derived from the Victim and Witness Advocacy Fund. Funding for the county Offices of Victim–Witness Advocacy is partially derived from the Victim and Witness Advocacy Fund. Other funding sources for county offices include federal VOCA funds and county appropriations.

The first chief of the Office of Victim-Witness Advocacy was sworn into office by the Attorney General on June 23, 1986. Pamela Fisher, author of this section of the chapter, served as chief from 1986 to 1995. Additional state office staff includes three professional assistants and a secretary.

The state Office of Victim-Witness Advocacy is responsible for developing and implementing procedures and standards for law enforcement and for the county Offices of Victim-Witness Advocacy throughout the state; evaluating the effectiveness of each county program; developing and conducting law enforcement training programs; providing services upon request to victims and witnesses; allocating and distributing monies from the Victims and Witness Advocacy Fund; and administering the Federal Victims of Crime Act (VOCA) grant for the state. The office also co-sponsors the Annual Crime Victims' Right Week Conference every April with the New Jersey Prosecutors Victim-Witness Association.

The Office collects statewide statistical data on the number and type of victims the program serves and tracks the type and number of services provided as well as the number of case status notifications made. These statistics are analyzed to evaluate the activity of the county offices and are provided to the county prosecutors in a quarterly statistical report. Annual reports are used for analyzing program trends and effectiveness.

Administered in each of the twenty-one county prosecutors' offices, these programs have the most direct contact with the thousands of victims and witnesses proceeding through the criminal justice system. The goal of the county Offices of Victim-Witness Advocacy is to improve the treatment of victims and witnesses and ensure their rights by providing the assistance and services necessary to speed their recovery from a criminal act and to support, aid, and advocate for them as they move through the criminal justice process.

Prior to enactment of *N.J.S.A.* 52:4b-43 et seq. in 1986, most county prosecutors provided victim-witness services, but these programs operated with limited staffing and funding and without statutory authority. The coordinators in place at that time typically did not thave college degrees or expertise in helping people in crisis. Most were secretaries, paralegals, or entry-level investigators who had been temporarily assigned to victim advocacy duties. Frequently their duties were ill defined. After enactment of the statute, a full-time county victim-witness coordinator was employed in each county prosecutor's office and services were standardized statewide. Monies from the Victim and Witness Advocacy Fund have helped improve several programs components such as case status notification, transportation, emergency assistance, counseling services, and safe waiting areas in county courthouses.

The county offices notify all victims of each case development and possible delays in proceedings. Several county offices have used allotments from the Victim and Witness Advocacy Fund to develop computerized tracking systems that improve upon and streamline the notification process. The (prosecutor/court) (Promis/Gaval) computerized management information system has also been modified to include the notification requirements of the victim-witness program. The notification system consists of a series of letters that correspond to the following significant phases of criminal prosecution:

1. Initial contact or introductory letter that informs the victim or witness that the case has been referred to the prosecutor's office and explains and offers the services available from the county Office of Victim–Witness

Advocacy. This initial contact letter also informs victims of their right to submit a victim impact statement prior to formal charging decisions.
2. Pre-grand jury remand
3. Administrative dismissal
4. Grand jury remand
5. Grand jury dismissal (no bill)
6. Indictment returns (true bill)
7. Acceptance into Pre-Trial Intervention Program (PTI)
8. Termination from or completion of Pre-Trial Intervention program
9. Negotiated plea on all charges
10. Release on bail/conditions of bail
11. Fugitive status
12. Court dismissal
13. Sentencing date/notification of the right to speak at sentencing or to submit a written statement about the impact of the crime
14. Sentence imposed on the defendant by the court
15. Defendant's filing of an appeal and subsequent status charges
16. Disposition on all charges
17. Mistrial/retrial
18. Mistrial/dismissal
19. Other unique or special occurrences

Victims in a criminal case are provided with transportation and a court escort when their appearance is required. Transportation assistance can be in the form of reimbursement for travel expenses incurred or the staff themselves provide transportation. Several county offices have used the Victim and Witness Advocacy Fund to purchase vehicles in order to transport victims and witnesses to investigative and court proceedings.

When victims or witnesses are threatened with financial hardship or loss of employment from creditors or employers as a result of their physical injuries or their cooperation with the criminal justice system, county victim-witness coordinators are responsible for interceding on their behalf. Employers and creditors are typically provided with verification letters explaining why a victim's or witness's participation is essential for the prosecution of a case. County victim-witness coordinators notify creditors and attempt to forestall punitive action should a victim be temporarily unable to continue payments. When necessary, coordinators personally meet with employers to secure their cooperation in limiting or curtailing any loss of pay or benefits that an employee would suffer as a direct result of the crime and their participation in the criminal justice process.

Under the Attorney General Standards to Ensure the Rights of Crime Victims, property retained for prosecution is to be returned as soon as possible but not later than forty-five days after the judgment of conviction unless evidentiary requirements pertaining to an appeal prohibit it. Property not retained for prosecution is to be returned within thirty days of recovery. In many cases, photographs can be presented at trial in place of the actual physical evidence. County victim-witness coordinators assist victims with the property retrieval process by providing information and advocating on their behalf with law enforcement officials.

By law, county victim-witness coordinators are required to provide separate waiting facilities for victims and witnesses, but the crowded conditions of many courthouses in the state has made this difficult. Some counties use the county victim-witness coordinator's office to accommodate victims and witnesses if the courthouse lacks facilities. Several counties have used the Victim and Witness Advocacy Fund to create and furnish separate secure waiting areas. Most counties report that adequate space for victims and witnesses is not available.

Victims and witnesses are provided with childcare services when their appearance is required throughout the duration of a criminal case. In most cases, county office staff provide care for children themselves, but some have negotiated agreements with local, state-approved day care centers to provide temporary service.

Crisis intervention and short-term counseling are provided by county office staff. Referrals are made to a variety of social service agencies for further care. Several county programs sponsor support groups for sexual assault victims, relocation to shelters, and necessary assistance in obtaining food and clothing.

County victim-witness coordinators and their staff are responsible for providing victims with information about compensation and monetary restitution from criminal defendants. All county coordinators are trained to assess the special needs of victims of crime and to determine their eligibility for financial awards. Claim forms for compensation are usually sent to victims with their initial contact letter or are distributed during the initial interview. In addition, coordinators and staff work with assistant prosecutors and investigators to identify those victims who might be eligible for assistance. Office staff also assist in documenting and verifying losses suffered by victims in order to expedite claims and to advocate for restitution.

The county victim-witness coordinator informs victims of their right to provide a victim impact statement to the court prior to charging decisions upon notification of sentencing. Pamphlets and other printed forms that explain the victim's right to have input at the time of charging and at sentencing have been prepared by several county offices. County offices staff often assist victims in preparing both oral and written statements.

County coordinators help with victim input into the parole process by notifying victims of this right. They also tell victims how to register with the state parole board so that they may provide a statement prior to the defendant's parole hearing.

Because victims are often confused and disoriented about their involvement in the criminal justice system, county coordinators routinely provide an explanation of proceedings that may occur during the prosecution phase. They also give victims an idea of what to expect (i.e., time frames, possible sentencing options, and so on). Coordinators frequently help to orient victims by providing a courtroom walk-through, preparing them for what will happen before the grand jury and giving them advice about testifying.

Program statistics indicate that statewide in 1992 the program assisted 8,122 victims, 692 witnesses, and 2,647 family member of victims. In sharp contrast, during 1988, the program's first year of data collection, 665 victims, 30 witnesses, and 135 family members received services. This dramatic upsurge represents the increased utilization of victim-witness services over the five-year period.

The most frequently provided services in 1992 included outreach (32,528), criminal justice system orientation (22,036), advocacy on case decisions (27,247), counseling (22,651), and needs assessment (16,977). In 1988, victims were most frequently provided with counseling and needs assessment, reassurance calls by counselors, criminal justice system orientation, waiting/reception room services, preparation for grand jury, assistance in filing for compensation, and assistance with problems relating to harassment and intimidation.

The need for criminal justice system information and counseling and needs assessment have remained in consistently high demand over the five-year period. The number and type of case status notifications to victims has likewise increased dramatically overall from 142,481 in 1988 to 340,092 in 1992. This increase represents the improved ability to keep victims informed of any changes in their cases brought about by the use of the PROMIS/GRAVEL computerized management information system. As was true in 1988, white women between the ages of twenty-one and thirty-nine continue to be the most frequent clients of the program.

During the program's eight and a half year history, it has been directed by a program chief who holds a bachelor's degree in psychology and an M.S.W. in social policy. The chief came to her position after working in victim services in New York City—for the Victim Services Agency (VSA) in Manhattan and Brooklyn. While there, the chief was schooled in the many facets of victim service delivery, including store-front community offices, court-, police-, and prosecutor-based programs, hotlines operations, and the different goals and objectives of each, which in turn determine the number and type of service rendered. The combination of a social work background and entering the victim services field early in its growth as a profession provided a unique opportunity for the chief to bridge the gap in New Jersey between advocating for and providing services to victims and the related direct practice skills of social workers. Thus, an emphasis on social work models and methods has been instilled in the development of the program over time.

Social work practice methods are uniquely appropriate for working with crime victims because major focus is on the interaction between victims and the criminal justice system and between other service delivery systems, that is, health and mental health. The intervention services performed by victim advocates reflect the characteristics of generalist social work practice. Social work is concerned with the interactions between people and their social environment that affect the ability of people to accomplish their life tasks, alleviate distress, and realize their values. In viewing victimization, the advocate's first concern is with the immediate situation confronting victims and the support systems that could facilitate their coping.

For example, consider the case of M., who was shot by her father at point blank range with a .357 magnum in her home. He had been stalking his twenty-one year old daughter for weeks, blaming her for his marital problems and his break-up with his wife. He had threatened to kill his daughter on numerous occasions. He had finally followed through on his threat. M. suffered massive internal injuries and also lost sensitivity in her right side as well as ability to raise her left arm. Her medical bills were astronomical, and her mother and brother feared for their lives. The defendant—their own husband and father—had been released on bail and continued to threaten and harass the family with telephone calls.

The case was referred to the county Office of Victim-Witness Advocacy by an assistant prosecutor in the grand jury unit. Later, M. herself contacted the office for assistance in relocating and finding affordable housing for her mother and brother in order to avoid the harassment. Her mother had been on welfare, but when she found employment her benefits were cut. The victim-witness office called Section 8 of the county welfare office, which provides rental assistance to eligible families. Although they had a current waiting list of over a thousand names, the welfare director conditionally accepted them as an emergency referral and rental assistance was soon granted.

The office also helped the victim complete application forms for the Violent Crime Compensation Board (VCCB). M———'s own insurance took care of much of her medical expenses, but she wasn't covered for initial consultations by her neurologist, urologist, and dental and plastic surgeons. The victim-witness offices and VCCB combined efforts so that she could seek this medical attention. M. was also compensated for lost wages and supplemental disability payments. In the meantime, the VCCB supplemented her present earning because she was only working part-time.

When M.'s father was indicted and the trial date set, the office prepared her and her family for the trial. The various steps of the trial were explained to them; they were shown the courtroom and told what to expect. M. and her family were provided with transportation to the courthouse and were accompanied throughout the actual trial. Notification, both written and by phone, helped them to keep abreast of every legal procedure in the trial. The defendant was found guilty on five of the six counts and was sentenced from fifteen to thirty years in a state prison—just seven months after the actual crime. But this is not the end of the story. The Office of Victim-Witness Advocacy continues to be in touch with M., and when a parole hearing is scheduled, M. and her family will be notified of their right to provide a statement to a senior hearing officer of the parole board.

Another example of the program's social work intervention services is the statewide Community Crisis Response Team (CCRT), established in February 1993 as a project of the state Office of Victim-Witness Advocacy. The CCRT consists of service professionals from all over the state, including victim advocates and members of law enforcement and other social service professionals who have received forty-hour certification in critical incident debriefing methods from the National Organization for Victim Assistance (NOVA). The team for each disaster is formed to consider the particular community's demographics. All team members are volunteers. The state Office of Victim-Witness Advocacy sends a crisis response team to any communty in crisis within twenty-four hours of a request.

There are three tasks the crisis-response team performs: (1) helping local decision-makers identify all the groups at risk of experiencing trauma; (2) providing training to the caregivers who are to reach out to those groups; and (3) leading one or more group "debriefings" to show how private meetings can help victims start to cope with their distress.

In 1993 and 1994 the CCRT responded to the following incidents:

- *City of Passaic*—May 22, 1993; kidnapping and murder of seven-year-old Davina Genao.
- *Montclair, New Jersey*—March 8, 1993; tragic accidental shooting death of seven-year-old Deidre Coleman.

Crisis response teams have been set up in many large cities and states throughout the United States. In almost all cases these statewide crisis response teams are coordinated by a victim/witness coordinator. Whether the crisis is a plane crash, a mass murder in the workplace, a terrorist bombing of a daycare center and federal building, a child abduction, a hurricane, a train crash, or a tornado, NOVA's crisis response teams rapidly respond to the scene of the disaster. Dr. Marlene Young, executive director of the National Organization for Victim Assistance, frequently flies to the disasters and provides anywhere from forty-eight hours to two weeks of training to victim advocates, crisis intervenors, social workers, and other mental health professionals. (For a detailed description of NOVA crisis response work nationwide during the past six years, see Dr. Young's chapter in A. R. Roberts (ed.), 1995, *Crisis Intervention and Time-limited Cognitive Treatment* [Thousand Oaks, CA: Sage]).

Conclusion

In some communities, victim services and witness assistance programs have expanded to meet the special needs of child, adult, and elderly crime victims and their families. In communities throughout the United States, victim services have been expanded to include crisis intervention, support groups, emergency food vouchers and financial aid, emergency shelter for battered women, lock repair and replacement, childcare for witnesses' children while the witnesses testify in court, victim advocacy in the courtroom, home visits, short-term psychotherapy, relocation assistance to transitional housing, and intervention with witnesses' employers. At the same time, there are a number of cities and towns without fully staffed and comprehensive victim service programs.

The future looks promising at least for the next five years. The Violence Against Women Act (VAWA) was signed into law by President Bill Clinton on September 13, 1994. This act appropriates $1.2 billion to improve and expand crisis services, criminal justice agency responses, housing, and community support programs for victims of domestic violence and sexual assault (Roberts, 1996). For training future victim advocates and crisis intervenors, the federal Office of Crime Victims of the U.S. Department of Justice established the National Victim Assistance Training Academy. The senior author of this chapter, along with several other prominent professors, has been appointed to the national advisory board to the new interdisciplinary training academy. This new training and educational endeavor offers much promise in setting high standards of excellence and certification requirements for victim advocates and victim assistance program administrators.

References

Bureau of Justice Statistics. (1992). *Criminal victimization in the United States, 1991*. Washington, DC: U.S. Government Printing Office.

Cronin, R. C. & Bourque, B. (1981). *National Evaluation Program Phase I Report: Assessment of victim witness assistance projects*. Washington, DC: U.S. Dept. of Justice.

Gandy, J. T. (1983). Social work and victim assistance programs. In A. R. Roberts (ed.), *Social work in juvenile and criminal justice settings*. Springfield, IL: Charles C. Thomas.

McDonald, W. F. (ed.). (1976). *Criminal justice and the victim*. Beverly Hills, CA: Sage.

Roberts, A. R. (1971). *Sourcebook on prison education: Past, present and future*. Springfield, IL: Charles C. Thomas.

_____. (1974). *Correctional treatment of the offender*. Springfield, IL: Charles C. Thomas.

_____. (1990). *Helping crime victims: Research, policy and practice.* Newbury Park, CA: Sage.

_____. (1992). Victim/witness programs: Questions and answers. *FBI Law Enforcement Bulletin 61*(12): 12–16.

_____. (1995). *Victim services and victim/witness assistance programs.* In R. L. Edwards and J. Hopps (eds.), *Encyclopedia of social work,* pp. 2440–44. Washington, DC: NASW.

_____. (1996). *Myths, realities and policy reforms for battered women.* In A. R. Roberts (ed.), *Helping battered women: New perspectives and remedies,* pp. 3–15. New York: Oxford University Press.

Smith, M. J. (1990). *Program evaluation in human services.* New York: Springer.

Chapter Nine

▶ • ◀

Family Programs in State Prisons

Creasie Finney Hairston

The preservation and strengthening of families is a major social services objective and a stated public policy priority. Social welfare policies and programs that help families protect, nurture, and care for their members are recognized as a social investment, and many formal and informal efforts are directed toward that end. The well-being of prisoners' families and the maintenance of family relationships during imprisonment, however, have not been at the forefront of this social policy agenda. Similarly, services and activities that involve and assist prisoners and their families in maintaining family ties and addressing family needs have seldom been included in the strategic or program plans of social services and corrections agencies. Nevertheless, there is a pronounced need for prisoners to maintain family bonds and for family-oriented programs to support the strengthening and empowerment of families separated by incarceration.

Family programs serve important social services and corrections objectives and can be justified for humane and pragmatic reasons. The maintenance of family ties during imprisonment enhances the well-being of individual family members, helps preserve families, and promotes public safety.

Imprisonment and other forms of correctional supervision and criminal justice intervention affect not only the person convicted of a crime but children and other family members as well. Prisoners are not just numbers or lone individuals whose social networks are limited to the institutions in which they are confined. Most prisoners resided with their families or intimate partners at the time of their arrest and helped meet the financial, physical, and emotional needs of the persons with whom they resided (Hairston, 1991). Most are parents of dependent children and, in the case of women, were the sole caretakers of their children (Bloom & Steinhart, 1993; Harlow, 1994). Their postrelease plans include reunification with their families and children and resumption of family roles and responsibilities.

Prisoners' family relationships are very important to their mental health and to their post-release success. Problems related to the maintenance of family and other extra-prison relationships have been identified as a principal deprivation for women and men in prisons. Prisoners describe their inability to be involved in the daily lives of their children and other loved ones as a source of great psychological stress and pain (Baunach, 1985; Flanagan, 1981; Hairston, 1991; Lanier, 1993). Common problems of everyday living—death of a parent, divorce, chronic illness—are exacerbated when natural support systems and family functioning are disrupted by incarceration. Losing custody or knowledge of the whereabout of one's children, being denied parole, and other factors related directly to imprisonment also bring grief and feelings of loss and helplessness not easily handled in a prison setting.

When a person is imprisoned or under any form of correctional supervision or criminal justice intervention, his or her children and other family members are also deeply affected (Bloom & Steinhart, 1993; Fishman, 1990; Gabel, 1992; Hairston, 1991; Swan, 1981). Imprisonment disrupts normal family functioning and parent-child relationships and creates emotional distress, financial difficulties, social stigma and isolation, legal problems, and a host of other difficulties. Given that poor people of color experience incarceration, as well as criminal victimization, at rates far greater than the rest of the U.S. population, those who are already discriminated against, oppressed, and at risk of many social ills find themselves with even more burdens to bear.

Family programs and services help reduce the stress and lessen the pain felt by individuals separated from their loved ones. They help families maintain emotional attachments and physical contacts crucial to family preservation and reunification, meet daily living needs, handle family problems in relation to correctional institutions, and take actions to make the best possible decisions for their present and future.

Family programs also support institutional order by providing prisoners with constructive outlets and ways to use time. In addition, studies of prisoners consistently show that those who maintain strong family and friendship ties during imprisonment and assume responsible marital and parental roles upon release have lower recidivism rates than those who function without family ties, expectations, and obligations (Curtis & Shulman, 1984; Hairston, 1988).

Descriptions of Programs and Services

Family-oriented programs in prisons are services and activities that help prisoners and their families maintain and strengthen family relationships and address problems and needs precipitated or exacerbated by having a family member under correctional supervision. They include programs that take place in prison as well as community-based programs that provide services for prisoners' families during the prisoner's incarceration and for prisoners and their families following release from prison. With the exception of prison visits, which have been permitted since the early 1900s, family-oriented programs are a rather new development in U.S. corrections. Although the idea that inmates need to maintain constructive relationships with persons outside the prison was stated as a formal corrections principle as far back as 1953 (Hopper, 1994), most programs have emerged since the 1980s. Contemporary programs view families not only as outside contacts for prisoners but also as persons who may need assistance themselves.

Though programs vary considerably from one place to another, there are discernible features that permit a description of program types. The more common family programs found in prisons are visiting arrangements and activities, parenting programs, and support groups.

Visiting Programs

Visits between prisoners and their families and friends are firmly established and are the most visible family-oriented activity in U.S. prisons. Visits allow prisoners and families and friends to see each other, spend time together, discuss personal concerns, and assure each that the other is all right. Visiting conditions are highly regulated by state policy, administrative procedures, and individual staff practices. They vary considerably from one institution to another; even among the same type of institution in the same state. Visits can last as little as one hour to five hours or more. They may be permitted only on weekends, as is the case in Tennessee prisons, or daily as in some New York prisons.

Regular visits are supervised and take place in a heavily guarded visiting room or designated outdoor area. With the exception of maximum security facilities, where visitors are separated from inmates by a glass partition, most prisons permit contact visits. Some visiting facilities are clean and nicely furnished with chairs and tables that allow families to sit together in informal groups. They have vending machines with drinks and snacks, and restrooms furnished with basic amenities such as running water and toilet tissue. Others, however, are dirty, poorly ventilated, have broken furniture, and are infested with flies and rodents. Almost all are noisy and crowded on weekends, the heaviest visiting days.

Though visiting is designed to facilitate prisoners' contacts with their families and is part of a treatment or rehabilitation program, treatment and program staff are visibly absent from visiting operations. Visitors are not likely to be able to speak with anyone who can provide information about services or assistance with a family problem. They will have contact during visits, however, with several security staff as their identifications are checked, as they are patted down or frisked and searched for contraband, and as they are observed throughout the visit.

Opportunities for families to spend time together in a more informal, relaxed manner than is usual under regular visits are provided by a few prisons. Private, overnight visits (sometimes called conjugal visits) and special family days are examples. Generally, family days are centered around Christmas or other holidays and include activities such as games, entertainment, and refreshments. Unlike regular visits where prisoners and families must remain in designated seats throughout the visit, these special events allow mingling among prisoners and visitors. They frequently include outside guests, such as church volunteers, and sometimes prison staff in roles other than guards.

Overnight visits take place on prison grounds in secured trailers or special housing units and usually last from twenty-four to thirty-six hours. Families eat, sleep, and spend time together in much the same manner as one would in an apartment or motel with cooking facilities. While the area for the trailers is within the secure perimeters of the prison, guards interact with and observe the families only during check-in and check-out times and during mandatory inmate count times. Although overnight visits have been in existence in U.S. prisons for more than twenty years, fewer than ten states permit them (Hopper, 1994). In California and New York, prisoners, spouses, children, and other family members are permitted to participate in overnight family visits. The Dwight Correctional Facility for Women in Illinois, in contrast, limits overnight visits to mothers and their children.

Hospitality or visitor centers located on or near prison grounds such as those run by Family Connections in Kansas and Centerforce in California are more recent family-oriented services. These centers are similar to rest areas on major interstate highways and provide places for visitors to wait until it is time to be processed for visits or to wait for transportation back to the nearest town. Centers usually have a rest room and waiting area and provide refreshments, such as coffee and juice, and clothing for visitors whose clothing may not be in compliance with prison rules. They are also usually able to provide information about visiting policies and practices and about overnight lodging, transportation, and restaurants. Hospitality centers run by community organizations in Nashville, Tennessee, and Alderson, West Virginia, also provide overnight lodging at low or no cost for prison visitors. In some communities the hospitality centers, churches, or other community organizations provide transportation from urban areas to prisons or from the closest source of public transportation to prisons.

Parenting Programs

Almost all prisons for women and a few prisons for men provide parent education courses. The courses are usually from four to six weeks duration and cover basic child development and parenting skills and techniques (Boudouris, 1985; Lillis, 1994). Occasionally, parenting courses provide information on child custody, permanency planning, and parents' legal rights and obligations. The courses sponsored by Chicago Legal Aid to Incarcerated Mothers (CLAIM) for women incarcerated in Illinois prisons are examples of the latter.

Since the late 1980s there has been growing recognition by some prison administrators of the issues related to parenting from prison. In accordance, a few have established special visiting areas with toys, books, and games for children visitors. Some child-oriented visiting facilities are a part of the regular visiting room and can be used by any parent and their children who visit. Others are open only at specific times and are available only to parents and children enrolled in the prison's parent education courses. A few children's visiting centers are staffed by professionals—though seldom by social workers—who help parents and children select age-appropriate toys, model parent-child interactions for parents, and show parents how to use play as an effective parenting strategy for disciplining children and teaching them appropriate behavior. Most play areas and centers, however, are staffed by prisoner or community volunteers and rely on contributions and donations for their supplies and equipment.

Maine's Project HIP (Helping Incarcerated Persons) is an example of one of the more comprehensive parent education programs. In this program, medium or minimum security prisoners who complete parenting courses may also participate in a support group for parents and a Saturday parent-child workshop. The workshop permits parents and children to participate in a one-on-one situation, absent the other parent or child's caretaker. The three-hour visit includes planned, structured activities for different age groups and takes place in a special visiting room with different kinds of play equipment. Leadership for Project HIP is provided by the University of Southern Maine.

Residential programs that permit children to live with their incarcerated parents also provide parenting supports. They are rare, however, in U.S. prisons. There are currently only three prison nurseries, all in New York state. These nurseries permit women who give birth while incarcerated to keep their infants with them until the child is about one year old.

Support Groups

Support or self-help groups that rely heavily on prisoner or family leadership constitute an important and significant family program. These groups meet regularly, usually monthly, and provide opportunities for participants to address common parenting, family, and personal concerns. Support group models vary widely and include short-term focused groups, for example, marital enrichment workshops; open-ended general support groups; and formal inmate organizations such as Parent Anonymous chapters. In-prison group membership usually includes only prisoners. Sometimes spouses or children are permitted to participate in the prison group or have similar support groups in the community. Among the different types of community-based groups are groups for children of incarcerated parents and their caretakers, groups for spouses and partners of incarcerated persons, and post-release support groups for couples.

Family-support and self-help groups engage in both advocacy and service efforts. Groups have organized to advocate for changes in visiting policies, changes in telephone rates, dissemination of visitor handbooks, and establishment of visitor centers. Usually started by a prisoner or prisoner's family member, a few have been very successful in terms of group maintenance and goal achievement. Most, however, have short lives. Those that have been sustained over a period of time usually receive monetary or staff support from a church or other community organization.

It is fairly common for prisoner support groups to be formal organizations with by-laws, officers, and volunteer community and prison staff sponsors. These organizational features are sometimes required by the prison administration so that the members can function as an official entity. In addition to providing self-help services for members, the prisoner groups engage in fundraising, sponsor family activities, and provide services for the prison population. Among the popular activities are distributing gifts to children visitors on Christmas, providing cards to prisoners for their use on Mother's Day, and taking and selling family photographs in the prison visiting room. Occasionally, these in-prison support groups provide opportunities for spouses to participate in marital enrichment workshops (usually one or two sessions) led by community professionals who volunteer their services. The Parents in Prison chapters that operate in Tennessee prisons provide one example of support groups that are official inmate organizations (Hairston & Lockett, 1987).

Individual Assistance

The provision of counseling, information, and assistance to families and to prisoners with family problems are important services but are seldom identified as a formal program or as part of anyone's job description. Notable exceptions are in states and institutions where family counselors or professional social workers are hired for treatment or program staff positions. The need for such services is extensive and the requests are numerous. Services provided include making arrangements for family members to visit a prisoner who is ill; accompanying children on visits when there is no other responsible adult willing to do so; providing information about community services; calling family members on behalf of a prisoner; preparing children for visits with a parent they have not seen for several months; and helping families deal with disappointments such as denial of parole or transfer to a prison in a remote location. In the absence of professional staff with defined responsibilities to provide information and counseling, requests for help are made and often responded to by almost anyone connected in any way with family programs.

Current Problems and Issues

Although some aspects of family programs have been an accepted, or at least tolerated, component of prisons for many years, family-oriented services are not an institutionalized aspect of corrections. Prisoners' families and children are not ordinarily relevant at any point in criminal justice decision making. Family responsibilities do not usually affect the length of sentence or the place where the sentence is to be served or the conditions of parole. Only recently has there been any significant official attention given to provisions for alternatives to incarceration that might better enable prisoners to be punished and still carry out family roles and commitments. Official prison policies acknowledge the importance of families, but administrative rules and regulations and day-to-day practices do not support a family orientation. Maintenance of family ties, particularly parent-child bonds, during imprisonment is undermined by the wide discretion on visiting hours, times, and procedures, without minimal standards, that states give to individual institutions; by restrictions on who can visit and can accompany children on visits; and by the adult-like behavior required of children visitors (Hairston & Hess, 1989). Day-to-day practices at prisons, such as failure to provide shelter for visitors who often wait in line for hours to see prisoners and rude and discourteous treatment of prison visitors also work to deter family contact. Communication is further discouraged by placing inordinately high surcharges and rates on the collect telephone calls that prisoners make to families and by marking prisoners' outgoing mail to families with a large visible stamp saying "from a prison inmate."

Family-oriented correctional programs are also not a fundamental component of policies and programs designed to promote family preservation. The needs of parents and children separated by incarceration are not addressed directly in family preservation and support legislation. They are also seldom considered in requests for proposals for demonstration projects and research, in conferences and seminars that discuss best practices in meeting needs, or in regular programming of traditional family service agencies.

A major obstacle to family program development and maintenance is the absence of any significant, stable source of funding. It is rare for prisons to have staff, social workers or otherwise, whose primary responsibility is to develop, obtain funds for, implement, or evaluate family programs and services. A notable exception is the New York State prison system where staff are hired to be responsible for administration of the family reunion or family visiting programs. Regular prison visits are the only family-oriented program consistently funded in correctional budgets. Funds for other programs depend primarily on fundraising by prisoner self-help organizations, donations from community agencies, or one-time grants for special projects. Occasionally, a program such as a visitor hospitality center receives funding from profits generated by monies obtained through the institution's provision of services to prisoners and their visitors. Profits from visiting-room vending machines and prison commissaries that sell toiletries and food to inmates fall in this category.

As a consequence of this pattern of funding—or nonfunding—most programs are run by grassroots community organizations who rely heavily on donations, have only one or no paid staff members, and spend a great deal of time fundraising. They are fairly successful in obtaining permission from prison administrators to provide services in prison, but are rarely successful in convincing them or legislators that their services should be an integral part of the prison program or treatment budgets. Most family programs and organizations have short lives, as could be noted by changes in the Directory of Family and Corrections Programs (1992). Those that have sustained themselves for more than a few years are usually connected with a church or other religious organization that provides financial resources.

The minimal involvement of social workers and traditional social service organizations in family programs in prisons and in important family advocacy efforts also serves as a barrier to the advancement of a profamily orientation in correctional institutions. Prisons, with their oppressive environment, emphasis on social control and security—which often conflicts with treatment and service delivery—and coercive program participation requirements for inmates are often viewed as inappropriate places for social work practice. Few schools of social work prepare students to work in criminal justice, and corrections and social work degrees are not required for those who provide social services in most prisons. Social workers who choose to provide family programs in state prisons do so in an environment of social control and coercion and without support from the social work profession.

This noninvolvement of social work in direct service delivery in institutions extends to abdication of any leadership responsibility for advocating profamily policies and designing family-oriented correctional services. Concerns about working with involuntary clients, the need for self determination, and working in an oppressive system of social control have overshadowed parallel needs for the social work profession to be engaged in the debate about criminal justice policies, programs, and services. This situation exists in spite of the profession's commitment to work with and on behalf of the poor and the oppressed and the knowledge that prisoners and their families are among the most oppressed, economically disadvantaged, and vulnerable populations. While the nation builds more prisons to house more of a population that is predominantly poor and nonwhite, the social work profession has remained remarkably silent.

Finally, many programs that serve prisoners and their families have developed without a sound conceptual and empirical knowledge base. In some cases, it is not clear why and how program planners expect the programs, as designed, to achieve stated goals. In most cases, program evaluation is not a feature of program operations and there is little or no information available to determine to what extent goals were achieved. As an example, in current prison parenting programs many parent education courses are being taught and support services designed without considering the unique factors of parenting in prison. Among these factors are coparenting with a disinterested custodial parent or caretaker; parenting from a distance; cultural differences in child rearing; and preprison parenting relationships (Lockett & Hairston, 1991). Yet, these factors have a major impact on how and under what conditions parents in prison can carry out parenting roles, obligations, and commitments. Failure to consider them may also explain why participants in some parent education courses show regression rather than progress (Browne, 1989). Along the same line, some programs and support groups are not based on fundamental knowledge of human growth and development, family dynamics, elements of program design, strategies for organizational change, and so on.

In the absence of tested, replicated models that deal with issues specific to maintaining family relationships when a family member is in prison, considerable effort goes into reinventing the wheel. The best uses of limited resources are not made, and the potential for addressing critical family needs is compromised needlessly.

Social Work Roles and Tasks

There is a strong need for social work involvement and leadership in this pressing area of social need. The many volunteer efforts that have mounted important service initiatives are commendable. Volunteers represent a tremendous resource but should be an extension of, rather than a substitute for, professionally trained social service providers. Since few social workers are currently involved in any aspect of family services in state prisons, identification of current roles and tasks would provide a rather narrow and limited description of professional responsibilities in a family-oriented correctional system. A much broader, and more helpful, picture is obtained by looking instead at the areas wherein social work knowledge and skills, used in a manner that considers the practical realities of the prison environment, could provide meaningful services to maintain family bonds and support positive family outcomes.

Services to Individuals

Social workers in prison, regardless of their official positions or specific responsibilities, can expect and should be prepared to provide direct services to individuals. Not unlike persons in the outside "free-world," prisoners often need individual, immediate help to deal with major family crises. The death of a parent, notice of a divorce, and a spouse's illness are all events wherein a social worker may be sought out to provide information or to actively search for resources or concrete help. Even on ostensibly happy occasions, such as a first-time visit or a child's graduation from high school, assistance may be sought about the best, inexpensive places of lodging in the area or about ideas for a gift that can be purchased with meager funds, and so on. Sometimes prisoners just need someone to talk to about feelings that, if revealed in a prison setting, might leave them very vulnerable to exploitation or ridicule.

Providing direct intervention services to individuals in prison is a major challenge, since social workers usually do not have the authority to take major actions or make changes that might be considered most desirable. Social workers are not able to reassign prisoners, for example, to a prison closer to their homes, or to authorize furloughs to visit an ailing parent, or to arrange a weekday visit for an incarcerated mother whose child can visit only when their caseworker is available. Social workers can, on the other hand, help prisoners and their families identify options, obtain information, clarify feelings, and engage in problem solving that enables them to make the best decisions they can, given their knowledge and understanding of the circumstances.

Group Services

Providing group services is an important aspect of family programming in a prison setting, and facilitating the formation and maintenance of groups and achieving group goals are important social work roles. While some tasks differ, depending on group goals and type, there are similar tasks across groups. Unlike drug therapy or sex offender treatment groups in which prisoners may be mandated by criminal justice officials to participate, family groups are voluntary. They, therefore, require active recruitment of members and constant attention to the elements of the prison environment that work against retention.

Typical social work tasks include defining criteria for group participation, recruiting group members via prison newsletters or bulletin board postings, identifying and contacting community speakers or volunteers, helping the group set goals and agree on working principles, and providing guidance to the group in addressing group problems. A significant amount of effort is directed toward the logistics of holding a group meeting in a physically secure environment. Social workers who sponsor or supervise family groups must obtain approval from the prison administration to hold group sessions; arrange meetingroom time and space with proper security; provide prisoners with the forms they need to obtain passes to the meetingroom on meeting days; see that the meetingroom is set up as needed; arrange for special equipment to be delivered and tested; keep records of group attendance; and maintain records required by prison rules and regulations.

If community volunteers or guest speakers are involved, the social worker must provide orientation for the volunteers or guests; inform them of prison rules regarding identification, proper clothing, and searches; and make arrangements for them to clear security to enter the prison.

Significant attention must also be given to ways to keep group members motivated and involved and to deter them from using the group for illegal behavior or other activities prohibited by the prison administration. Motivational activities may include providing refreshments for group meetings, which in itself sets up a whole new set of rules and regulations that must be adhered to; holding a recognition ceremony, which usually includes getting prison administrators or influential community leaders to attend; or providing certificates of completion and arranging for copies to become a part of prisoners' official records. All of the tasks normally carried out by a social worker in providing group services take on a different meaning in prison because many inmates can do few tasks for themselves. In addition, the prison's emphasis on security and control mandates attention to details that in a nonprison setting would not be needed or would be considered undesirable.

Program Development and Evaluation

Given the developmental stage of family programs in prisons, designing, testing, and evaluating programs are core areas of responsibility for social work practice. The dissemination of program results and products enhances the probability that successful programs and program components will be replicated in other settings. A project carried out by the Indiana University School of Social Work in collaboration with the Parents in Prison Program at the Tennessee State Prison illustrates this role. The Parents in Prison Program was initiated by a group of prisoners who, with the help of social workers from a community agency, taught parent education classes to male prisoners, established a support group for men in prison, and sponsored family events in the prison visiting room (Hairston & Lockett, 1987). Social work researchers from the university conducted a formative evaluation and documented ongoing program experiences and outcomes, and they provided consultation and technical assistance in refining program services and procedures. The university-based social work educators developed policy guidelines, program and training manuals, and educational materials to aid others in developing programs (Lockett & Hairston, 1991). Dissemination of these materials led to replication of the Parents in Prison model and approach in several other states, even after the closing of the Tennessee State Prison, site of the original program idea.

Volunteer Development

The strong involvement of volunteers in this area of correctional services and the need to maintain such involvement suggests a critical role for social workers in recruiting, screening, training, and managing volunteers. Volunteers are diverse and have different things to offer and different reasons for volunteering. Some volunteers are professionals who provide services related to their professional training. An example is a family-life educator who conducts a one-time series of workshops on child development and parenting. Others are members of churches, college fraternities/sororities, or service organizations that provide more general services as a group project. Typical projects are sponsoring a support group, transporting families to the prison, giving a Holiday party and gifts to families of prisoners, and staffing the children's visiting area. Still others may participate as individuals on either a one-time or a regular basis. They may participate out of curiosity, because they have a special skill, or because they want to be involved in making a difference. Some want to have direct contact with prisoners as tutors, friends, or mentors. Others are satisfied with handling clerical duties, arranging for events, or making small gifts.

Most volunteers have had little or no previous contact with prisons and have little understanding of how their particular service could be helpful or be best applied to services in a prison. Most need orientation to the rules and regulations of the particular prison where services are to be provided as well as more general training and orientation on role expectations and accountability, issues that prisoners are likely to raise, the reality of working and living in prisons, and safety and security precautions. They also need to be provided with supports to sustain their interest and to assess and monitor their work and contributions.

Liaison Activities

An important social work role in establishing and maintaining family programs is that of liaison between the prison administration and prisoners and families. This role is more than that of a "go-between," however, and requires creative thinking, good judgment, and the willingness and ability to advocate for change. One of the critical functions of this role is to help prison administrators see how family programs contribute to the maintenance of safety and order in the institution and, at the same time, serve as a constructive outlet for prisoners. Without attention to the institution's fundamental focus on security, it is not likely that family programs will be permitted and/or sustained.

An example of this role in action is informative. A social worker advocating for a kids corner in a prison visiting room received permission to do so by demonstrating not only the benefits of the program in making visits more pleasant for prison parents and their children, but also by showing how the program would make visiting room supervision easier for the guards and how it could be set up and run with minimal disruption to normal prison visitation routines. The social worker was able to build her case based largely on observation and documentation of a similar program in another institution and the identification of factors that addressed the needs and concerns of both the administration and the prisoners and families at that institution.

A second liaison role is between the prison and the "free-world" community. There is a need for traditional social service agencies, whose decisions directly affect the lives of prisoners and their families and children, to be more responsive to their needs. This is particularly the case with child welfare agencies. Prison-based social workers who know and understand the child welfare system and the prison system could enhance permanency planning and family reunification, facilitate contact between child welfare case workers and mothers and fathers in prison, help parents in prison meet goals in case plans, and identify and bring community resources into the prison.

Future Social Work Practice

Given the importance of family ties to social services and corrections goals, and the millions of families whose lives are affected by incarceration, family-oriented programs must be given a greater priority by social workers and by other social services staff and corrections administrators and practitioners.

Greater vision and more dedication at the highest levels of social work and corrections are needed to guide program development. The success of even ad hoc, uncoordinated program efforts depends on a family-oriented policy focus and an environment conducive to implementation. Such policies provide the context for staff practices and administrative procedures and guide the allocation of identification of resources. In addition, they directly promote the development of family programs in prisons and significantly shape the nature and level of services.

Social workers must take on a more visible role as active partners in addressing criminal justice problems and issues. Active partnership is not a task that can be relegated solely to individual social workers in individual prison settings but that also involves a concerted national effort. While many corrections practitioners and policymakers may question the role of social workers in running prisons and guarding inmates, the social work profession's knowledge and understanding of family relationships and dynamics and its ability to provide social services are on much firmer ground. Claiming responsibility for family services in corrections and carving out a meaningful, helpful role for family programs that also address corrections goals of public safety and rehabilitation can give social work credibility and an important niche in corrections and criminal justice.

The successful development of family programs in prisons specifically, and family support services in corrections generally, depends on a change to a more pro-family orientation in corrections. Social workers should actively promote the central role of support and preservation services component to families separated by incarceration. This promotion includes public education and awareness campaigns, development of minimal standards to guide policy and program implementation, and advocacy of legislation and funding to support program development and research, including alternatives to incarceration for persons who can safely serve their time in the community.

A national family and corrections research and resource center that works with state and federal corrections departments and community family support organizations and service agencies to build their capacity for responding to family issues in a correctional setting would provide one of the strongest supports for a family orientation in prisons. The center would conduct research; disseminate information about program models, research, and needs; provide consultation and technical assistance to agencies in policy and program development; conduct training for administrators and staff; and sponsor seminars and conferences that included corrections practitioners, social workers, and other human service providers.

In order to assume leadership and be integrally involved in shaping policies and programs, social workers must know and understand the criminal justice system, its major purposes and goals, the ways in which those goals are currently being pursued, and the ways in which efforts for change can be best directed. It is, therefore, imperative that social work educational programs prepare students for practice in criminal justice settings. Internships in corrections family programs, class visits to prisons, lectures in social work classes by family program service providers, and course work specific to criminal justice settings (taken in social work programs or other departments) are all ways to move social work education forward.

In conclusion, prisoners are not just convicts, but members of families too. Family preservation and support efforts should acknowledge the needs of their families, and family programs in prison provide one important strategy for addressing those needs. With close to one million persons in state and federal prisons and continuing unprecedented growth in prison populations, it seems irresponsible for social workers to continue neglecting this population.

References

Baunach, P. J. (1985). *Mothers in prison.* New Brunswick, NJ: Transaction Books.

Bloom, B., & Steinhart, D. (1993). *Why punish the children? A reappraisal of the children of incarcerated mothers in America.* San Francisco, CA: National Council on Crime and Delinquency.

Boudouris, J. (1985). *Prisons and kids.* Laurel, MD: American Corrections Association.

Browne, C. (1989). Incarcerated mothers and parenting. *Journal of Family Violence, 4*(2), 211–219.

Curtis, R., & Shulman, S. (1984). Ex-offenders' family relations and economic supports: The significant women study of the TARP project. *Crime and Delinquency, 30,* 507–528.

Family and Corrections Network. (1992). *Directory of programs serving families of adult offenders.* Batesville, VA: Author.

Fishman, L. (1990). *Women at the wall: A study of prisoners' wives doing time on the outside.* Albany: State University of New York Press.

Flanagan, T. J. (1981). "Dealing with long-term confinement: Adaptive strategies and perspectives among long-term prisoners." *Criminal Justice and Behavior, 8,* 2, 201–222.

Gabel, S. (1992). Children of incarcerated and criminal parents: Adjustment, behavior, and prognosis. *Bulletin American Academy Psychiatry Law, 20*(1), 33–45.

Hairston, C. F. (1988). Family ties during imprisonment: Do they influence future criminal activity? *Federal Probation, 52,* 48–52.

Hairston, C. F. (1991). *Families and children: A study of men in prison.* Indianapolis: Indiana University School of Social Work.

Hairston, C. F., & Hess, P. M. (1989). Family ties maintaining parent child bonds is important. *Corrections Today, 51* (2), 102–106.

Hairston, C. F., & Lockett, P. (1987). Parents in prison: New directions for social services. *Social Work, 32*(2), 162–164.

Harlow, C. (1994). *Comparing federal and state prison inmates, 1991.* Washington, DC: Bureau of Justice Statistics.

Hopper, C. B. (1994). The status of prison visitation. Paper presented at the annual meeting of the Academy of Criminal Justice Sciences, Chicago, IL.

Lanier, C. S. (1993). Affective states of fathers in prison. *Justice Quarterly, 10* (1), 49–65.

Lillis, J. (1994). Family service groups and programs. *Corrections Compendium, 19*(1), 1–3, 18.

Lockett, P., & Hairston, C. F. (1991). *Fathers in prison: Parent education resource manual.* Indianapolis: Indiana University School of Social Work.

Shaw, R. (ed.). (1992). *Prisoners' children.* London: Routledge.

Swan, A. (1981). *Families of black prisoners: Survival and progress.* Boston: G. K. Hall.

Chapter Ten

►•••••••••••••••••••••◄

Meeting the Needs of
Female Offenders

Susan Meyers Chandler and
Gene Kassebaum

This chapter examines the needs of women in the criminal justice system in the United States—women on probation, in jail, in prison, on furlough from prison, or on parole. In recent years, women have become the most rapidly growing group within the criminal justice system (BJS, 1993). The lives of 4.1 million adults are currently being controlled by correctional agencies in the United States—12 percent of these adults are women. The number of women in prison at the end of 1992 was 50,409, up from 40,556 in 1989, a dramatic increase from fewer than 14,000 in 1980 (Gilliard, 1993). Combining jailed and imprisoned populations, Austin, Bloom, and Donahue (1992) report that 75,000 women in the United States are incarcerated on any given day.

Until recently, women have been a forgotten population in the criminal justice system. Historically, women offenders have been neglected in research, and even mention of them has been excluded from most textbooks written by criminologists before the mid 1960s. Moyer (1992) suggests there was little literature before 1965 acknowledging that women experienced incarceration differently than men, citing Ward and Kassebaum (1965) who "opened the door of credibility" for criminologists to study women in prison. Today the problems and issues of women in the American correctional system are obvious and clearly require attention.

It is not too simple to say that prisons for women are like those for men except that gender issues, reflecting broad social values, changes, and conflicts, affect what problems women confront both inside the prison and after release. Absent gender issues, women's prisons would have the same features and problems as men's prisons, and although these may be of crucial importance gender remains the big issue in determining what is distinctive for women in prison.

The Feminization of Corrections

Men are the great majority of prisoners. The rate of imprisonment for men in the United States is 636 per 100,000 males, eighteen times the 35 per 100,000 rate for women (Gilliard, 1993). This is lower than female representation in other sectors of the criminal justice and corrections system, where females are a distinct minority. In 1990, women comprised 14 percent of all convictions for felonies in state courts; 7 percent of all convictions for violent felonies; 17 percent for property offenses; 17 percent for drug possession; and 15 percent for drug trafficking (Maguire, Pastore, & Flanagan, 1993). Women comprised 15 percent of felony probation cases surveyed in a representative sample of thirty-two counties between 1986 and 1989; and they comprised 9.3 percent of all jail inmates in 1991 (Maguire, Pastore, & Flanagan, 1993). Thus, although women comprise a little more than half the adult population, they are only about 15 percent of the felony convictions, 15 percent of the felons under community supervision, and 6 to 9 percent of prisoners. In the most populous states (California, New York, Texas, Florida, Pennsylvania, and Illinois), there are substantial numbers of female inmates. Moreover, they are living in overcrowded and under-resourced facilities.

Historically, women were confined with male prisoners. In early times, they were housed with children and families in boisterous, exploitative, bawdy, and unhealthy congregate prisons. When Auburn Penitentiary in New York opened in 1821, women were confined in one isolated, congregate section—an attic. The first separate institution for women opened in 1839 near the male prison at Sing Sing, New York. By 1870, the new American Correctional Association (ACA) stated its preference for gender classification and segregation:

> Prisons, as well as prisoners, should be classified or graded so that there shall be prisons for the untried, for the incorrigible and for other degrees of depraved character, as well as separate establishments for women and for criminals of the younger class. (Shover & Einstadter, 1988, p. 97)

Rafter (1985) notes that the movement to build separate women's reformatories was most pronounced in the Northeast and Midwest, where population density, income, and level of industrialization were the greatest.

The rate of increase for women prisoners exceeded that for men between 1981 and 1990, but since 1991 the number of male prisoners has increased at a faster rate (7.3 percent per year for men; 5.9 percent for women). Note that imprisonment for both men and women has been increasing to the current high levels at an unprecedented rate. The United States has the highest rate of incarceration in the world (300 inmates per 100,000 population). There were 883,593 people in prison at the end of 1992. At the annual rate of increase of the previous several years (7.4%), the number should have reached one million by the end of 1995. This enormous increase in prisoners since 1980 is a factor in understanding the role of social workers in corrections, and it is particularly important in understanding and meeting the needs of women offenders.

The relatively small percentage of women prisoners has several implications. One is less flexibility and fewer options in work training open to female prisoners. Another is the small number of prisons for women, making it more likely that an average female inmate is farther from home than is a male inmate. "Thus, women are at a disadvantage both within prisons, which offer unequal programs and services, and in planning their release." (Shover & Einstadter, 1988, p. 104).

Fowler (1993) sees a third implication from recent ACA surveys, that "programs available to female offenders still concentrate on low paying, traditional female jobs such as sewing, cleaning, food service, and cosmetology." A fourth implication is that, except in the most populous states, a single prison for women means that violent and nonviolent offenders, both high risk and low, are housed in one institution. Typically, classification instruments used to establish custody and supervision levels and eligibility for certain programs and mobility (especially furlough from the facility) are standardized on male inmates. An ACA survey estimated that only 24 percent of state prisons and 26 percent of local jails use specific classifications standardized on female samples (Fowler, 1993).

The situation for women offenders in the United States is similar to that in other countries. A researcher in Canada writes the following:

> The history of women's imprisonment has been remarkably similar in most countries. Small numbers of women have been housed in often unsuitable accommodations, under regimes stressing the domestic roles of women in society and providing little access to programs or training. (Shaw, 1994, p. 13)

Research on Prisons and Corrections

Prisons have been of interest to sociologists and historians for decades. Some studies are highly specific to corrections (Sykes, 1958; Glaser, 1964; Kassebaum,

Ward & Wilner, 1971), concentrating on the prison organization with emphasis on the informal inmate culture (except for Glaser). Studies in this period were heavily influenced by structural functionalist theory, which viewed the prison as a closed social system and the events and roles within it as the product of the influences of that structure on the people introduced to it. The preeminent expression of this deprivation model is seen in the works of Irving Goffman, particularly *Asylums* (1961).

Following this period there was a change of emphasis, beginning with John Irwin's *The Felon* (1970), which looked at the importance of social characteristics and the circulation of prisoners in and out of the prison. James Jacobs (1977) added the influence of outside gangs and social changes such as the civil rights movement in affecting what goes on in prisons. Most recently, interest has shifted to two other themes: management differences and the effect of federal court litigation from inmates (DiIulio, 1987, 1990). Thus there has been a movement from looking at the prison as the product of institutional forces upon the inmate to interpreting the prison as another setting for the expression of social processes common to society as a whole.

Research on prisons for women has followed a sequence of theoretical styles. The earlier books (Ward & Kassebaum, 1965; Gialombardo, 1966; Heffernan, 1972) were functionalist and stressed institutional deprivation. Rafter (1985) looked at prisons as part of developing gender role and the disciplining of deviant women. More recent studies (Chesney-Lind & Shelden, 1992) see prisons for women as expressing the same gender themes inside their walls as outside. A second element in recent studies of contemporary prisons is the changing significance of race, with the much greater mobilization of militancy and conflict between African Americans, Anglos, and Hispanics.

Who Are the Women in Prison?

Although 1992 figures are available, a finer analysis of the incarcerated female population must be based on the last major survey, done at the end of 1986 and released in 1991 (Greenfield & Minor-Harper, 1991). At that time, an estimated 41 percent of the women in prison were there for a violent offense, nearly half of them for homicide. Of the remainder, 17 percent were doing time for fraud, 15 percent for theft, 12 percent for drug law violations, and 5 percent for public-order offenses, with the remaining for "all other offenses." Since 1986 the rate of imprisonment for drug law violations has increased dramatically. By 1990 nearly one-third (32.1%) of all new imprisonments for both men and women were for drug offenses (Gilliard, 1993).

Possession of drugs and the probation and parole revocations for drug use inferred from positive urine analyses substantially increased the number of women arrested and rearrested. The number of women arrested for drug offenses, including possession, manufacturing, and sale of drugs increased over 300 percent between 1980 and 1989 (Bureau of Justice Statistics, 1991). Larceny/theft offenses very likely associated with drug use also increased during this time.

The Bureau of Justice Statistics (BJS) in 1992 estimated that 72 percent of women in state prisons had used drugs at some time in their lives prior to admission. Over half of the women reported using "major" drugs such as heroin, methadone, cocaine, PCP, or LSD. Nearly 25 percent of the incarcerated women used some of these drugs on a daily basis one month before they began serving time, and just under half of the women were using alcohol or drugs (or both) at the time of the offense for which they were arrested. Data from this national study indicate that women in prison are more likely than are men to have used heroin.

Substance abuse among women in prison is often tangled up with histories of mental illness (co-occurring disorders); sexual and physical abuse; poverty; and living as unemployed, single mothers with few coping skills and little social or family support. The BJS estimated that 41 percent of the women in prison had been either physically or sexually abused at some time in their lives. About half of these women had been abused as minors.

Half of the women prisoners in one state interviewed in a study conducted by Chandler and Kassebaum (1994) reported that they had been physically abused as children. About one third (36%) had seen a counselor about some type of abuse as an adult. Twenty-one percent said that at some time they had gone to court to get a temporary restraining order related to a domestic violence complaint. About 40 percent of the women reported sexual victimization as children, and 26 percent said that they had been sexually abused as adults.

Although the numbers of women in this study were small, there seemed to be a pattern in these data suggesting that the women who report using more of the most addicting drugs (heroin, crack, cocaine, and "ice") have higher-than-expected rates of physical abuse as adults. This pattern also holds for women who reported being sexually abused as adults. Of the women who report using at least three of the most addicting drugs, 70 percent also reported being physically abused as children; 55 percent reported a childhood sexual assault.

The association of adult problems with substance abuse and previous sexual abuse is now being documented in the research literature (Rohensow et al., 1988; Cohen & Densen-Gerber, 1982; Browne & Finkelhor, 1986). However, few substance abuse treatment programs are available to incarcerated women and even fewer are gender specific or focus on the dual issues of substance abuse and physical/sexual abuse.

The Newly Incarcerated

Historically, different concerns of the American people have influenced the codification of different laws. Today, newspapers are full of stories about violent crimes and murders. In fact, however, while the rates of violent crimes are dropping and the vast majority of crime consists of property offenses, it is the War on Drugs that has become the major referral source into prisons. Wellisch, Anglin, and Prendergast (1993) suggest that the accelerated rates of arrest and incarceration of women are probably due to changing attitudes about incarcerating women; the increased use of drugs and drug addiction among women; the increased number of serious crimes being committed by women; and mandatory sentencing for drug-related convictions. Kassebaum and Chandler (1994) contend that with new technology for measuring body chemistry, offenders on parole or probation who use drugs are much easier to detect. Consequently, parole or probation is easier to revoke. Routine screening now is a major source of parole and probation violations.

Bloom, Chesney-Lind, and Owen (1994) assert that the War on Drugs has become a "war on women." They say that the greatly increased use of mandatory prison sentences and higher sentence minimums are the major reasons for the explosion in the women's prison population. The percentage of women in prison for drug offenses rose from one in ten in 1979 to one in four in 1991. The drug crimes that women commit are most often "possession" and "possession for sale," which, for example, constitute over 65 percent of the drug offenses of the women in California prisons.

The special problems of incarcerated women have been slowly recognized. While the high rate of substance abuse has been well documented, only recently has the increase of injected drugs as a source of HIV transmission and the increasing number of drug-exposed infants become a corrections problem. Wellisch, Anglin, and Prendergast (1994) report that along with drug abuse problems, women in the U.S. correctional system come with physical and mental problems; poor educational/vocational backgrounds; and a variety of psychosocial problems (primarily low self esteem). Most of the single women with children also are reported to have little financial or emotional familial support.

Client Characteristics in the Criminal Justice System

Clients in the criminal justice system are extremely diverse, ranging from non-violent addicted men, rapists, and murderers to prostitutes and check-forging, single mothers. Age, ethnicity, previous criminal histories, and educational and skill levels vary widely among the population in America's correctional system but do not reflect the distribution of the general population. Racial and ethnic minorities and the poor are vastly over-represented. Greenfield and Minor-Harper (1991) reported that in 1986, 39.6 percent of women prisoners were Caucasian non-Hispanic; 46.1 African American; 11.7 percent Hispanic; and 2.5 percent of other ethnicities. Data show a wide age range, with 22 percent in their teens or early twenties; a similar fraction (19.6 percent) in their mid-thirties to mid-forties; and more than 7 percent forty-five or older. Most women in prison have been previously incarcerated or sentenced to probation, but female prison inmates are first timers more often than are male prisoners and are less likely than men to have a history of criminal violence.

The same survey showed that three-fourths (76 percent) of the women in prison had children, most under the age of eighteen, and an estimated 8 to 10 percent of them in foster care (Beckerman, 1994). The majority of incarcerated mothers (62 percent) were never married or were single parents, and 74 percent claim they wish to retain or regain custody of their children after release (ACA, 1990). Thus, on any given day, with over 75,000 women confined in the criminal justice system in the United States (Bloom, Chesney-Lind, & Owen, 1994), a large number of children are affected as well. Gaudin (1984) described the often sudden, traumatic, and extended separation that accompanies a mother's imprisonment. In most cases, the mother is quickly deprived of almost all contact with her children. Fewer than half of the incarcerated mothers see their children even once a month.

There are many obstacles to the maintenance of relationships between imprisoned mothers and their children. Prisons are often located in remote areas, making transportation difficult (Shover & Eisenstadter, 1988). Many correctional institutions severely restrict parental visits. Many foster care or child welfare workers are not cooperative in maintaining these relationships. Many incarcerated women are not aware of their parental rights or the legal ramifications of termination of parental rights proceedings (Beckerman, 1994).

Gender Differences

Early theories about the low rates of female offender incarceration hypothesized that most women were, by nature, "law abiding." Thus, those who got involved in crime must have been "led astray" by male perpetrators (Simpson, 1989, in Moyer, 1992). Other theories suggested that it was the "chivalry" of police departments and preferential treatment by judges that "shielded" women from criminal justice system involvement and incarceration (Pollock, 1978).

Baunach (1985) contends that this preferential treatment actually resulted in the further oppression of women. Since women were such a small percentage of the total in the criminal justice system, they were ignored and provided with few programs and services. Those that were available were often provided in isolated and substandard institutions. More and more research is now pointing out the special problems and needs of women in the correctional system (Wellisch, Anglish, & Prendergast (1993); Beckerman, 1994; Bloom,

Chesney-Lind, & Owen (1994), but the services being provided for women have clearly not kept pace nor are they yet focused on these newly identified needs.

Studies have consistently shown that women prisoners usually live in conditions that tend to be more limited than those in which men live. (This is not true everywhere, notably in the most recently constructed institutions for women, where some living accommodations are physically superior to good college dormitories.) Also, women tend to have "fewer educational and vocational programs; less opportunity for work release, recreation and visitation; fewer medical and legal resources" (Rafter, 1989, p. 89).

There has been and may still be an ideological tilt that results in female prisoners being dealt with in a paternalistic manner. (See *Cantering v. Wilson,* 1982, which found "restrictions are imposed solely because of gender with the objective of controlling the lives of women in a way deemed unnecessary for male prisoners.")

And there is the greater social and personal significance of the separation of mothers from dependent children and newborns. While parental contacts are important to male prisoners who are fathers, the need is considerably higher for female inmates. Legal challenges to traditional women's prison rules were mounted in 1979, resulting in greater equality of facilities and programs for men and women (Task Force on the Female Offender, 1990).

Probation and Intermediate Sanctions

With increasingly large case loads, probation perceived as providing relatively light supervision and imprisonment as being a major interruption of ordinary living (and each option being more and more overloaded with drug law offenders), interest rose in creating an action somewhere between punitive and controlling. These sentencing options came to be known as "intermediate sanctions." They were to be more punitive and more intrusive than regular probation, less costly than prison. Intermediate sanctions include Intensive Supervision (IS) on probation or parole, house arrest, electronic monitoring, residential programs, and several other variants. Although the name suggests the climate ("sanctions") that stimulated the creation of the new programs in many states, and even though deterrence and surveillance have priority, intermediate sanctions programs are not incompatible with correctional treatment. They have the potential to reduce prison commitments, improve the management of higher risk offenders, and better enforce court orders—all desirable outcomes.

Women offenders appear to be included in such programs in about the same proportion as they are in regular probation. Robinson (1992) details intensive probation, split sentence (brief incarceration, then probation), house arrest, and electronic monitoring tabulated participation in all fifty states on these programs and provides partial information on female offenders. (A number of states did not provide a breakdown of their data by gender.) The figures show that 15 percent of IS probationers are women (Robinson, 1992, p. 248).

Whether that is an advantage or a disadvantage for a women offender is hard to judge. Petersilia and Turner report a study of seven probation and parole IS programs. Each of the seven sites randomized the assignment of eligible cases to IS or regular controls. In comparisons, IS had lower new conviction rates in three comparisons, the control sample had lower new convictions in three other comparisons, and there was a tie in the seventh comparison. IS had lower technical violations in only two of the seven comparisons and logged fewer jail or prison days from arrests in four of the seven. Overall, the authors conclude, "it appears that IS did not reduce recidivism during the follow-up period as measured by official records" (Petersilia & Turner, 1993). Most of the IS units had some drug treatment enrollments. In each comparison there was more drug treatment in the IS sample than in the control, but the emphasis was on surveillance. These data are predominantly male; unfortunately, the report does not break out effects by gender. The report's general conclusions do not support the hope that watching probationers and parolees more cloesly or more often will reduce recidivism or commitments to confinement.

Social Work Practice in Corrections

The roles and tasks of social workers in meeting the needs of women offenders are changing as rapidly as are the issues in the corrections system (Severson, 1994). The profession of social work is dedicated to maximizing the dignity and worth of individuals; to fostering maximum self-determination on the part of clients; to advocating on behalf of clients; and to promoting equity and social justice (Johnson, 1990).

It is immediately apparent that these empowering and rehabilitative goals are not the goals of most correctional systems or penal institutions in which social workers are employed. Some have called this social work role an "uneasy partnership" (Handler, 1975), while others feel that "correctional social work" as a term might be an oxymoron. Many social workers are concerned about the coercive nature of correctional work and see their role in social control activities as contradictory to their helping role. DiNitto and McNeece (1990) see many of these activities as "not conducive to social work practice."

The professional training and affiliation of the social worker provides guidelines for working in various settings. Corrections is no different in many respects than are other practice settings, but it does have some characteristics that may be problems for social workers entering this field. Currently, and for the immediate future, there are several million adults on probation, parole, furlough, or serving suspended sentences. Because of more severe sentencing policies since the 1980s and subsequent prison crowding, more felons are now sentenced to probation than were before. In contemporary probation supervision there is greater emphasis on surveillance and enforcement of the orders of the court and more use of chemical testing for drug use. If liberty is conditional on clean urine and compliance with court orders such as child support, employment, and participation in training and abstinence programs, then social workers will de facto be a part of a wide social control network.

Social workers will have to be explicit about the implications of a relapse report for parole or probation revocation for their client. The National Association of Social Workers (NASW) will have to become familiar with the implications of these new issues, and the profession will have to take some position with regard to correctional and law enforcement responsibilities.

Work in secure institutions entails training, responsibilities, and risks that are different from those prevailing in open community settings. Structures of authority are more clearly drawn in correctional agencies, with a chain of command rising from the line staff and correctional counselor to the warden or superintendent via a custody staff (a captain or associate warden). Negotiating the social worker's employment details is different here than at a hospital or in a health department—the prison's organizational chart influences working styles. A drug treatment, therapeutic community in a prison, for example, is subject to the dual administration of a correctional agency and the attached therapeutic community. The relationship is not unlike landlord and tenant.

In general, along with an expanding professional employment market in institutional and community corrections, there is the need for a realistic assessment of different organizational practices and responsibilities. While these settings can be professionally challenging and intellectually stimulating, they can also be frustrating until or unless the social worker comes to terms with priorities such as security and risk management.

In today's legal climate, all professional personnel in human services agencies, including social workers, may be individually liable in lawsuits alleging violation of inmate or probationer rights under the Fourteenth Amendment, Chapter 1983 of the Civil Rights Act, and various other titles and entitlements. In addition, the newly emerging legal situation for persons who are HIV seropositive affects persons other than the patient, and this could include the social worker. Third-party lawsuits (involving employers, parents, co-workers) are not uncommon. Social workers in corrections should have adequate information about litigation and liability in their new work context.

Professional Issues for Social Workers

In no other social welfare field are the gender distinctions so apparent—over 88 percent of the correctional population is male, while the social work profession (even in corrections) is predominantly female. Social workers are involved in the treatment of clients in juvenile justice systems, courts, jails, prisons, and probation and parole offices. Netherland (1987) lists the following tasks of social workers in corrections: intake and screening, diagnosis and classification, supervision and treatment, and release planning. He suggests that the general case work and group-work skills taught in schools of social work are particularly appropriate for corrections work, as are the skills associated with interdisciplinary team work and the abilities for finding resources and referrals in the community.

Lister (1987) outlines a model of direct-practice social work that may be clustered into system development, system maintenance, system linkage, and direct client intervention. While his conceptualization focuses on direct practice roles, he includes some mezzo and macro roles such as planner, policy developer, researcher, administrator, consultant, team manager, and advocate. Direct client intervention with female offenders should not differ substantially from the traditional counseling of male clients or any clients not in the criminal justice system. However, social work's emphasis on self-determination is clearly limited when working with offenders. Moreover, as Johnson (1990) contends, involuntary clients exist in many social work fields and self-determination is not absolute. Child protective service workers, state hospital personnel, and social workers who counsel spouse abusers must wrestle with this philosophical dilemma each day.

The task of conducting comprehensive psychosocial assessments in multidisciplinary teams to design and implement treatment programs is certainly an essential social work function in the criminal justice system. However, it is clear that the female offender client profile is multifaceted and quite complex. After comprehensive assessments have been conducted, there are rarely empirically validated, effective interventions or programs that meet the specialized needs of female offenders. Previous assessments routinely documented that most female offenders had previous arrest records as juveniles and dropped out of school before graduation. Few worked in legitimate jobs or possessed the skills to do so. Chandler and Kassebaum (1994) found that most females incarcerated in a state prison reported serious drug addiction problems and admitted to long histories of substance abuse. Unexpectedly, many also reported they had previously enrolled in multiple alcohol and drug treatment programs, evidently with little success.

Empirical data indicate that most of the community-based treatment programs for women offenders are not designed for their special needs (Wellisch, Anglin, & Prendergast, 1993). Few residential programs permit children or have childcare facilities available. Fewer than half of the out-patient programs have obstetric/gynecological services available. Parenting training was available in 71 percent of the residential programs surveyed, and services related to economic survival (GED/vocational training) were found in 78 percent of the residential programs. But these crucial programs were found in only 56 percent of the out-patient programs, and the extent of the programming is not known. Legal advice, although clearly a need from the perspective of the women offenders, was available in fewer than half of the existing treatment programs.

Most of the jail and prison programs surveyed by Wellisch, Anglin, and Prendergast (1993) claimed to offer case management, relapse prevention, HIV/AIDS education, counseling, and twelve-step meetings. Many of these programs were offered through purchase-of-service arrangements, rather than through correctional staff. It is unclear if professionally trained persons are staffing these programs or if any effectiveness data have been gathered. The consistent empirical finding related to drug abuse treatment programs is that the efffects of treatment are positively related to the length of time in treatment (Hubbard et al., 1989; Simpson et al., 1986). Unfortunately, most of the programs available to women offenders are short-term, usually only a few hours a week. There are virtually no data on the efficacy of even highly intensive, well designed, short-term programs for women. Obviously, much correctional planning goes on with little data to guide it.

Social workers at the macro level (policy, planning, and administration) have not made a significant impact on the design or implementation of services in the corrections field. Social workers need to become more active in the examination of the effect of the laws and policies that influence the increasing rates of women in incarceration. And social workers need to become much more articulate in defining and delineating women offenders' special needs. Billions of dollars will be going into new prison construction and into new programs. Money must be directed towards programs designed for women as well as towards the development of appropriate, comprehensive, community-based programs. If social workers are to champion the cause of family preservation, then more voices must be heard advocating programs designed to prevent women's drift into crime and to assist their rehabilitation when they do offend.

Abandonment?

Williams and Hopps (1990) report data from a survey of the NASW membership that demonstrates a decline in the number of professional social workers practicing in the area of criminal justice. NASW membership data from 1993 also document extremely small numbers of professionally trained social workers practicing in corrections.

There are no data to explain why the area of corrections is a growth indus-try, yet the numbers of social workers in corrections is decreasing. One expla-nation may be that there has been a decrease in the numbers of "social work type" activities going on in correctional settings today. Another is that perhaps much traditional social work practice is now being conducted privately through purchase-of-service contracts. A third and most likely explanation is the increase of nonprofessional social workers doing the jobs trained social workers once did. In many states in which the M.S.W. degree is required for supervisory level correctional work, it is so difficult to recruit and retain M.S.W. workers that states have declassified social work positions or merely leave them vacant.

Ginsberg (1990) notes the small number of Master's degree students enrolled in corrections/criminal justice concentrations in schools of social work (1.6 percent) and that only 2.2 percent of the enrolled students were meeting practicum requirements in the corrections field. This suggests little interest among B.S.W./M.S.W. students in this field, making it unlikely that more professional social workers will enter the field in the near future. So while the job market in corrections is mushrooming, professional social work seems to be abandoning it (Specht & Courtney, 1994).

Clearly, professional social workers in corrections experience role con-flicts. Some contend that there is no place at all for social work in corrections. Others wonder if social work shuns these clients, who will provide counseling, family strengthening, and case work services to these multiproblem clients?

Social workers, like other professionals, are aware that the organizational work environment of the corrections system is bleak. Most state systems are understaffed and plagued with high turnover that results in poorly trained staff. Probation and parole officers and prison social workers all routinely work in understaffed environments, yet they are expected to conduct supervision over difficult, complex, multiproblem, and often violent offenders.

Social workers must deal almost daily with the frustration of having too heavy a case load, too few available program slots, and too few community-based treatment programs. Social workers are aware that most members of the offender population have substance abuse problems and need to be involved in structured drug rehabilitation programs for significant periods of time to stay clean and sober. Alcoholics Anonymous (AA), often the treatment of choice, is widely accessible, popular, and cheap but is rarely sufficient for addicted offenders. Several questions are now being raised about its appropri-ateness (or effectiveness) for women, yet it is often the only available program (Kasl, 1990).

Today, even more adults are under probation than are in the swollen U. S. prison system. Nearly one out of five probationers is a woman. Moreover, recent civil rights legislation has pushed open the doors to the employment of women as correctional, probation, and parole officers. But the occupational roles of women in probation and parole have changed. This is more apparent in probation. The earlier tradition of case work and advocacy in probation, as a kind of suspended sentence and leniency for offenders, gave way under pressure of greatly increased numbers of cases going to probation and the sentencing of more serious offenders to probation. A medical model, which considers criminal behavior in terms of illness or at least persistent personal problems, was incorporated in probation. Community supervision was conceptualized around classification (diagnosis), referral to appropriate treatment, and periodic reevaluation. A recent review of probation comments follows:

> The 1960s and 1970s have been regarded as the progressive era where rehabilitation was stressed by liberals for both incarcerated and nonincarcerated offenders. However, rising crime rates and the recidivism of probationers and parolees stimulated a public backlash against social reform programs. Studies conducted disclosed the apparent lack of success of rehabilitative programs including probation. . . . one result was the general condemnation of rehabilitation and specific probation alternatives. Despite these criticisms, rehabilitation continues to be a strong correctional goal. (Champion, 1990, pp. 18–19)

What succeeded the medical model has been variously called the justice model or the crime control model. Champion (1990) summarizes this view:

> Probation is a penal sanction whose [*sic*] main characteristic is punitive. Probation should be a part of a single graduated range of penal sanctions available at all levels of crime except for the most serious felonies. . . . Conditions should be justified in terms of seriousness of offense. Where conditions are violated, courts should assess additional penalties through "show cause" hearings. (Champion, 1990, p. 19)

Crime control itself has recently garnered more than its share of negative evaluations. The tension between a treatment model and probation's justice model appears to be resulting in a movement toward some kind of mix of both. Social workers entering probation as a career should expect to have a role in the enforcement of court orders and the assessment of risk as well as in meeting the needs of probationers.

Waning Support for Rehabilitation and Community-Based Alternatives

Correctional institutions today are synonymous with inadequate and insufficient educational, recreational, and treatment programs. Overcrowded prisons, whether long-standing or newly built, quickly become warehouses full of cells that merely contain people involuntarily for long periods of time under marginal conditions. The prisoners' rights movement and recent federal lawsuits have corrected some of the most deplorable institutional conditions. Nonetheless, public opinion favors building more prisons, giving longer sentences, and establishing life sentences without parole for persons convicted of three federal felonies (the "three strikes and you're out" rule). The new experimentation with tightly regimented boot camps for male first-time offenders, even without empirical evidence to support the effectiveness of such programs, is extremely popular in many states. There is very little public support (or money) for therapeutic communities or community-based rehabilitative and treatment programs. These were the types of programs that customarily hired social workers for counseling and case management tasks.

Studies have found a correlation between prison building and prison capacity—build them and they will be filled. Across the nation, legislatures are pouring money into expanding prison capacity, but little money has been provided for operational programs to meet either existing or newly emerging offender needs (Irwin & Austin, 1994). Since alternative programs and community facilities are not available, prisons become the "treatment" of choice and are likely to remain so in the near future. This is particularly troublesome for meeting the needs of women offenders.

Substantive and Practical Issues

The general issues for female offenders include those for male offenders, but special efforts must be made to ensure that women in confinement or on community supervision receive an equitable share of resources for all aspects of correctional life. Beyond that, the sentencing and supervision of female offenders is particularly important with respect to four problems: the offenses of prostitution; the relationship between a convicted mother and her young children; the necessity of adequate legitimate income and housing for a female offender who chooses to separate from a troubled or abusive marriage or cohabitation; and the special needs of women drug addicts.

The overwhelming majority of persons arrested for soliciting sex for money are females. Many states have enhanced penalties for prostitution or have mandated certain sentences. Where these enhancements use jail they constitute yet another contribution to institutional overload—albeit jail rather than prison. Where enhanced sanctions against prostitution include intermediate sentences such as house arrest and electronic monitoring, they raise the need for employment, housing, and child-care resources to qualify women for such sentences. Prostitution is often linked with drug addiction and greater risk of HIV infection and other health problems, making access to medical care important.

Most women offenders in prison have young children. Both their pre-prison parenting and the separation from children imposed by their sentences constitute potential problems for maintaining law-abiding lifestyles. In particular, transition housing and legitimate employment are important to help female offenders succeed once out of prison or while on probation.

Some parole divisions are trying special female units to better provide supervision. Research should be initiated on the possible differences and any advantages of female probation or parole officers supervising female offenders. The assessment and supervision of women in the community is likely to require special inputs. Professional social workers could be a factor in the development of such programs.

Remaining Issues

Five issues seem to us to have the highest priority. First, major problems of overcrowding and poor supervision continue to put many women at risk of abuse by more violent women and at risk for physical and sexual abuse from male correctional staff members.

Second, health problems have become an increasing concern since many incarcerated women receive little routine health care (such as gynecological exams or screenings) due to inadequate or unavailable medical care. That women are experiencing the highest rate of HIV infection of any population means prevention, screening, and treatment related to AIDS must become a paramount concern to the corrections system.

Third, the extreme shortage of effective substance-abuse treatment programs both for women confined to prison and after release is a tremendous factor in relapse and recidivism. There are currently too few substance-abuse programs designed for women only, as well as insufficient treatment slots available for pregnant women and women with babies and young children.

Fourth, preparing women for adequately paying legitimate jobs after release needs to be a high priority. This means not only more effective job training and assisted job entry but available day care for dependent children. (See Patterson and Starn [1993] for an exemplary program for chemically dependent mothers and newborns, although not one currently functioning in a correctional system.) Without legitimate employment and improved community empowerment, that is, the option of housing without the sponsorship of men whose association may have been detrimental in the past, continued recidivism and return to confinement are likely. Gender-specific programs for women need to address their lack of education and training skills for future employment as well as their low self-esteem and poor independent living skills.

Fifth, since perhaps over 80 percent of female inmates have dependent children, prison programs that do not address family issues such as parenting classes or family reunification issues are not meeting the needs of the female offender.

Data reported by Wellisch, Anglin, and Prendergast (1993) on the availability of treatment programs for women are quite disappointing. While there are more programs available for women offenders now than in the previous thirty years (Bureau of Justice Statistics, 1992), the increase has not been sufficient to reduce the discrepancy between those who need treatment and those who receive it. The percentage of those in need who are being served is no greater now than it was in the late 1970s (Wellisch, Anglin, & Prendergast, 1993).

Treatment effectiveness is also disappointing. Programs that enroll only women seem to orient their services more flexibly toward the special needs of women. While this may be a positive trend in the future, presently there are too few programs to evaluate. The dearth of programs that provide accommodations and activities for women and their children is also disappointing.

Likely Futures

What is the future for women in the criminal justice system? Is it likely that state governments will begin to re-orient and re-design their correctional programs toward the special needs of women? Will states begin to develop correctional programs, noting the huge numbers of minor children affected when a woman goes to prison? Will states increase their budget allocations toward the design and implementation of nontraditional training programs for women? Of parenting programs? Of substance abuse programs? Of literacy programs? Clearly the need is there, but public policy rarely is guided by need alone.

Dressel (1994) cogently argues that there is an intricately woven relationship between the more punitive regulations for means-tested social welfare benefits and the recent growth in the criminal justice system's population (particularly the prison population). She suggests that the evidence is clear if we examine the stagnant levels of welfare expenditures compared with the growing expenditures for prisons and police. What she sees is a growing commitment to social control (an expected budget increase of 21 percent in the next fiscal year) compared to a 2 percent increase for Aid to Families with Dependent Children (AFDC), which reflects our nation's loss of faith in its social welfare enterprise. Women cannot get out of poverty if dependent on AFDC. A woman with a child must earn over $8 an hour to earn as much as her welfare benefits—if she could find the appropriate job. But this is almost impossible for a person without a high school education, child care arrangements, or special training. Bane and Ellwood (1994) found that most poor women get out of poverty not through employment, but through marriage, which is a risky proposition for any woman. If women marry, they usually lose their benefits but may not learn to be economically self-sufficient.

When a society provides inadequate levels of social assistance and a sector of the population is structurally unable to enter the legitimate labor market, it becomes the target of social control measures. Dressel (1994) contends that due to racist and sexist policies, the primary targets of social control are African-American and Hispanic women. Laws also perpetuate this vast overrepresentation of ethnic minorities under correctional control, especially laws providing tougher penalties for the use of crack cocaine than for cocaine powder.

Policy Recommendations

Following are four recommendations for dealing with the needs of female offenders:

1. Women prisoners, in addition to their distinctive problems, share with male prisoners the current problems of overcrowded prisons. Racial conflict, organized predatory gangs, and idleness, as well as the vulnerability of some women for exploitation from violent women prisoners and male correctional staff, must be confronted. The old studies of incarcerated women do not provide an adequate guide to women's lives in the prisons of the 1990s. New ones must be conducted.
2. Schools of social work and the National Association of Social Workers should review available information on the employment of M.S.W.s in departments of probation, corrections, and parole. The interests of the profession are promoted by a greater understanding of the role demands and employment opportunities (and obstacles to them) in correctional work. Since most social workers are female, the probability is high that social workers in corrections and probation could influence intelligent supervision and assessment of women offenders.
3. Organizations supplying contracted substance abuse treatment services should be encouraged (or pressured) to design appropriate programs for chemically dependent mothers. Therapeutic attention to the likely problems of physical and sexual abuse need to be included in programming.
4. The development and expansion of postincarceration residential treatment support and assistance in housing and employment should be an important agenda item in local professional associations.

Conclusions

Clearly there is new information about women in today's correctional systems. This means there is a need for new knowledge and skills to be acquired from all of the people working with institutional or community-supervised women offenders. The huge numbers of women offenders using and abusing alcohol and other drugs suggest that staff must become familiar with the problems associated with polydrug abuse and become knowledgeable about effective treatment programs and regimens.

Furthermore, social workers need more information about preventing and counseling women with sexually transmitted diseases; this should become a routine part of social work practice. And since most women offenders are mothers, treatment and programs must be sensitive to these women's child care needs, parenting needs, and reentry problems. Women offenders without adequate job skills, education, and training cannot succeed in the community.

The odds are very high that social workers who work with women offenders will be working with women who have these problems. Clearly, the job of social workers in corrections is to be knowledgeable about their clients' problems and effective in providing services and designing programs to meet their special needs.

References

American Correctional Association. (1990). *The female offender: What does the future hold?* Washington, DC: St. Mary's Press.

Austin, J., Bloom, B., & Donahue, T. (1992). *Female offenders in the community: An analysis of innovative strategies and Programs.* San Francisco, CA: NCCD.

Bane, M. J., & Ellwood, D. T. (1994). *Welfare realities: From rhetoric to reform.* Cambridge, MA: Harvard University Press.

Baunach, P. J. (1985). *Mothers in prison.* New Brunswick, NJ: Transaction Books.

Beckerman, A. (1994). Mothers in prison: Meeting the prerequisite conditions for permanency planning. *Social Work, 39,* 9–14.

Bergman, C. (1987). Criminal justice reforms: The struggle continues, Jerico.

Bloom, B. (1994). Community based strategies and programs for women under correctional supervision in the United States. Paper presented at the John Howard Association of Hawaii Symposium, Honolulu.

Bloom, B., Chesney-Lind, M., & Owen, B. (1994). Women in California prisons: Hidden victims of the war on drugs. Unpublished manuscript.

Browne, A., & Finkelhor, D. (1986). Impact of child sexual abuse: A review of the research. *Psychological Bulletin, 99*(1), 66–77.

Bureau of Justice Statistics. (1991). *Drug and crime facts.* Rockville, MD: U.S. Dept. of Justice.

Bureau of Justice Statistics. (1992). *Women in prison* [Bulletin]. Rockville, MD: U.S. Dept. of Justice.

Bureau of Justice Statistics. (1993). *Capital punishment 1992.* Washington, DC: U.S. Dept. of Justice.

Champion, D. (1990). *Probation and parole in the United States.* New York: Macmillan.

Chandler, S. M., & Kassebaum, G. (1994). Drug-alcohol dependence of women prisoners in Hawaii. *Affilia: The Journal of Women and Social Work, 9,* 157–170.

Chesney-Lind, M., & Shelden, R. (1992). *Girls, delinquency and juvenile justice.*
Pacific Grove, CA: Brooks-Cole.

Cohen, F. J., & Caber, J. D. (1982). A study of the relationship between child abuse and
drug addiction in 178 patients. *Child Abuse and Neglect, 6,* 383–387.

DiIulio, J. (1987). *Governing prisons: A comparative study of correctional management.* Glencoe, IL: Free Press.

DiIulio, J. (Ed.). (1990). *Courts, corrections and the constitution: The impact of judicial intervention on prisons and jails.* Oxford: Oxford University Press.

DiNitto, D., & McNeece, C. A. (1990). *Social work: Issues and opportunities in a challenging profession.* Englewood Cliffs, NJ: Prentice-Hall.

Dressel, P. (1994). And we keep on building prisons: Poverty and the challenges to the
welfare state. *Journal of Sociology and Social Welfare, 21,* 7.

Fowler, L. T. (1993). What classification for women? In American Correctional
Association (Ed.), *A tool for managing today's offenders* (pp. 37–45). Laurel, MD:
ACA.

Gaudin, J. M. (1984). Social work roles and tasks with incarcerated mothers. *Social
Casework: The Journal of Contemporary Social Work, 65,* 279–286.

Giallombardo, R. (1966). *Society of women: A study of women's prison.* New York:
Wiley.

Gilliard, D. K. (1993). *Prisoners in 1992* [Bulletin]. Washington, DC: Bureau of Justice
Statistics.

Ginsberg, L. (1990). Selected Statistical Review. In *Encyclopedia of Social Work* (18th
Ed., 1990 Supplement, pp. 256–288). Silver Spring, MD: NASW Press.

Glaser, D. (1964). *The effectiveness of a prison and parole system.* Indianapolis, IN:
Bobbs-Merrill.

Goffman, I. (1961). On characteristics of total institutions. In *Asylums.* Garden City,
NY: Doubleday.

Greenfield, L. A., & Minor-Harper, S. (1991). *Women in prison* [Special Report].
Washington, DC: Bureau of Justice Statistics.

Handler, E. (1975). Social work and corrections: Comments on an uneasy partnership.
Criminology, 13, 240–254.

Hawkins, R., & Alpert, G. (1989). *American prison systems: Punishment and justice.*
Englewood Cliffs, NJ: Prentice Hall.

Heffernan, E. (1972). *Making it in prison: The square, the cool and the life.* New York:
Wiley.

Hubbard, R. L., Marsden, M. E., Rachel, J. V., Harwood, H. J., Cavanaugh, E. R., &
Ginzburg, H. M. (1989). *Drug abuse treatment: A national study of effectiveness.*
Chapel Hill: University of North Carolina Press.

Irwin, J. (1970). *The felon.* Englewood Cliffs, NJ: Prentice Hall.

Irwin, J. & Austin, J. (1994). *It's about time: America's imprisonment binge.* Belmont,
CA: Wadsworth.

Jacobs, J. B. (1977). *Statesville: The penitentiary in mass society.* Chicago: University
of Chicago Press.

Johnson, H. W. (1990). *The social services: An introduction.* Itasca, IL: Peacock.

Kasl, C. D. (1990). The Twelve Steps. *MS* Nov/Dec.

Kassebaum, G., & Chandler, S. M. (1994). Polydrug use and self-control among men and women in prison. *Journal of Drug Education, 24,* 333–350.

Kassebaum, G., Ward, D. A., & Wilner, D. M. (1971). *Prison treatment and parole outcome.* New York: Wiley.

Lister, L. (1987). Contemporary direct practice roles. *Social Work,* 384–391.

Maguire, K., Pastore, A., & Flanagan, T. (1993). *Sourcebook of criminal justice statistics (1992).* Washington, DC: Bureau of Justice Statistics.

Moyer, I. (1992). *The changing roles of women in the criminal justice system: Offenders, victims, and professionals* (2nd Ed.). Prospect Heights, IL: Waveland Press.

Netherland, W. (1987). Corrections system: Adult. In *The Encyclopedia of Social Work* (18th Ed., pp. 351–360). Silver Spring, MD: NASW.

Oregon Department of Corrections. (1991). *White paper: Oregon's women's offenders.* Salem, OR: Department of Corrections.

Patterson, K., & Starn, J. R. (1993). Program for women and infants exposed to drugs: A legal alternative. *Nurse Practitioner Forum, 4,* 224–230.

Petersilia, J., & Turner, S. (1993). Intensive probation and parole. In M. Tonry (Ed.), *Crime and justice: A review of research.* Chicago: University of Chicago Press.

Pollock, J. (1978). Early theories of female criminality. In L. M. Bowker (Ed.), *Women, crime, and the criminal justice system.* Lexington, MA: Lexington Books.

Rafter, N. H. (1985). *Partial justice.* Boston: Northeastern University Press.

Rafter, N. H. (1989). Gender and justice: The equal protection issue. In L. Goodstein & D. L. MacKenzie (Eds.), *The American prison: Issues in research and policy.* New York: Plenum Press.

Robinson, R. (1992). Intermediate sanctions and the female offender. In J. Byrne, A. Lurigio, & J. Petersilia (Eds.), *Smart sentencing* (pp. 245–260). Newbury Park, CA: Sage.

Rohensow, D., Corbett, R., & Levine, D. (1988). Molested as children: A hidden contribution to substance abuse. *Journal of Substance Abuse Treatment, 5,* 13–18.

Severson, M. (1994). Adapting social work values to the correctional environment. *Social Work, 39,* 451–456.

Shaw, M. (1994). Women in prison: A literature review. *Forum on Corrections Research, 6,* 13–18.

Shover, N., & Einstadter, W. (1988). *Analyzing American corrections.* Belmont, CA: Wadsworth.

Simpson, D. D., Joe, G. W., Lehman, W. E. K., & Sells, S. B. (1986). Addiction careers: Etiology, treatment and 12–year follow-up outcomes. *Journal of Drug Issues, 16(1),* 107–121.

Specht, H., & Courtney M. E. (1994). *Unfaithful angels: How social work has abandoned its mission.* New York: Free Press.

Sykes, G. (1958). *The society of captives.* Princeton, NJ: Princeton University Press.

Task Force on the Female Offender. (1990). *The female offender: What does the future hold?* Arlington, VA: American Correctional Association.

Ward, D., & Kassebaum, G. (1965). *Women's prison: Sex and social structure.* Chicago: Aldine.

Wellisch, J., Anglin, M. J., & Prendergast, M. (1993). Treatment strategies for drug-abusing women offenders. In J. Inciardi (Ed.), *Drug treatment and criminal justice*. Newbury Park, CA: Sage.

Williams, L. & Hopps, J. (1990). The social work labor force: Current perspectives and future trends. In *Encyclopedia of Social Work* (18th Ed., 1990 Supplement, pp. 289–306). Silver Spring, MD: NASW Press.

Chapter Eleven

▶ •••••••••••••••••••••• ◀

Juvenile Delinquency and Social Work Practice

Rudolph Alexander, Jr.

Some social workers have expressed several reasons for not working in corrections. They have stated that social work involves working with cases, not groups. They also have stated that because of prisoners' confinement, working with prisoners violates one of social work's cherished values—client self-determination. Finally, they have stated that because corrections work involves mostly social control (Never et al., 1990), social workers should not participate (Blagg & Smith, 1989; Handler, 1975). Included by social workers within the domain of corrections in the United States and England have been the juvenile justice system and juvenile delinquency (Blagg & Smith, 1989; Popple & Leighninger, 1993).

Despite these objections, a small but dedicated group of social workers have always worked directly or indirectly within corrections (Alexander, Butler, & Sias, 1993). Early social workers played very prominent roles in the creation of the first juvenile court in Chicago, Illinois, and have practiced within the juvenile justice system since then (Fox, 1983). The aim of this essay is to trace social work's involvement in creating the first juvenile court, to describe some of the early practices, to discuss the claimed conflicts between social work values and corrections (especially juvenile corrections), to depict contemporary roles that social workers play in the juvenile justice system, and to discuss challenges for the future.

Historical Discussions

Social Work's Involvement in Youth Issues and the Creation of the First Juvenile Court

One of the many byproducts of the industrial revolution was its negative effects upon children and youth (Trattner, 1970). In many cities, girls were drawn into prostitution, and boys were picking pockets, burglarizing homes, and engaging in such vices as drinking, smoking, and gambling (Klein & Kantor, 1976). Because of concern for misguided youth, Juvenile Protective Associations were started in many cities in the 1800s (Addams, 1930; Bloom, 1990; Roberts, 1983).

Additionally, settlement house workers became interested in youth problems. For example, when Hull House was opened in Chicago in 1889, the settlement house workers almost immediately began to intervene on behalf of boys who had been arrested and jailed. One of the Hull House workers, Ms. Stevens, held a semiofficial position at the nearby police station. The sergeant at the police station had agreed to give Ms. Stevens provisional responsibility for all boys and girls who had been arrested for trivial offenses (Addams, 1910).

Settlement house workers were also interested in youths who had been jailed for more serious offenses and provided services for them. As an example, in 1898, the Flanner House, a settlement house in Indianapolis, Indiana, developed programs to combat juvenile delinquency in the African American community (Crocker, 1992). As another example, Lucy L. Flower, Julia C. Lathrop, and Jane Addams, members of the Chicago Women's Club, persuaded the Chicago Board of Education to provide schooling for the more than five hundred boys housed in the Chicago House of Corrections. When their efforts failed to meet the boys' needs, they decided that these youths would be better served by another system, especially developed for them (Abbott, 1938; Needleman, 1983a). A committee was formed in 1898, consisting of the Illinois State Conferences of Charities, the Chicago Bar Association, and the women of Hull House, to seek fundamental changes in the criminal law with respect to juveniles. Their combined efforts influenced the Illinois legislature in 1899 to pass "An Act to Regulate the Treatment and Control of Dependent, Neglected, and Delinquent Children." This law created the first juvenile court in Chicago (Abbott, 1938). By 1917, forty-four states had established juvenile court systems (Schwartz, 1989).

Early Philosophies and Practices in the Fledgling Juvenile Justice System

The juvenile court established in Chicago was to encompass separate hearings, specialized judges, and probation (Richmond, 1917). Ms. Stevens, in her semiofficial position with the police, became the first and only juvenile probation officer during the early days. A year later, five other probation officers were added (Addams, 1910). The court itself was located across the street from Hull House, but after a few years it was moved to a new building and a detention home was added (Addams, 1910). In 1909, the Psychopathic Institute, headed by a psychologist named Healy, was added to the juvenile court in Chicago. Many social workers came there to be trained by Dr. Healy, who taught them that stealing was a symptom of a disease and that workers must understand the physical, mental, and social facts behind the symptoms before a cure could be achieved (Richmond, 1917). These views suggested that juvenile delinquency could be addressed at the micro level (Krisberg & Austin, 1993).

One of the states addressing youth problems at the microlevel was California. Social workers played prominent roles in the creation of the juvenile court in Los Angeles in 1903 and in its early practices and policies. Settlement workers, such as Evelyn Stoddard, Dr. Dorothea Moore, and Alice Stebbins Wells, convinced government officials to pay attention to female delinquents and to hire primarily professional women to deal with female delinquency. Toward that end, the Los Angeles Police created the Mother's Bureau within its department so that mothers who had problem daughters could refer them to a woman. The first female police officer was social worker Alice Stebbins Wells, whose job was to patrol the streets, dance halls, and amusement parks looking for girls in trouble. The referee and judge also were female. If a girl were committed to an institution, the institution itself was dominated primarily by female professionals—superintendent, physician, and psychologist (Odem & Schlossman, 1991).

Besides working directly with the juvenile court, social workers were also employed within juvenile correctional institutions in the 1920s. For example, the Whittier School in California, a home for delinquent boys, hired a psychiatric social worker to perform home rehabilitation. The social worker's job was to assess the family and educate parents about proper parenting skills so that when their delinquent sons returned home the parents could do a better job of supervising and correcting the delinquent behavior. The social worker was also expected to do preventive work by helping parents with younger children who were on the path to becoming delinquent (Schlossman & Pisciotta, 1986).

A similar rehabilitative program was initiated for the Pennsylvania State Industrial School for Boys. Earlier, the Family Society of Philadelphia had created a program to help federal adult offenders incarcerated by the Bureau of Prisons at the United States Northeastern Penitentiary at Lewis, Pennsylvania. According to historical accounts, the program created for the adult offenders was very similar to that developed later for the Pennsylvania State Industrial School for Boys (Middleton, 1939).

The Family Society of Philadelphia provided case work services for the family while it worked with the adult prisoners. Social workers assessed the home, family situation, economic status, the prisoner's childhood development, and the family's attitude toward the prisoner. When the study was completed, a report was prepared for prison administrators. The caseworker provided a full range of services to the family and to the prisoners after the prisoner was released. The caseworker helped the prisoners find jobs and engaged in crisis intervention. The program was considered a success and helped to explain why the Philadelphia juvenile justice system wanted something similar (Middleton, 1939).

Criticisms of the Fledgling Juvenile Justice System

Not everything was going well in the fledgling juvenile justice system, however. Discontent could be heard shortly after the courts were created. Some social workers stopped referring children to juvenile courts and because of dissatisfaction with how the courts were operating began referring them instead to child guidance clinics (Abbott, 1938). Other social workers used their Juvenile Protective Associations to reduce the number of children referred to juvenile courts (Addams, 1930).

Moran (1939) wrote that many juvenile courts were operating contrary to the principles upon which they were founded. Emphasis was placed on evidence and the facts of the crimes instead of on the offending child's needs and on helping him or her to become a productive member of society. Judges were part time and had little interest in this court system. Budgets were inadequate. If a child needed institutional care, the few institutions were severely overcrowded. Although the first probation officers in Chicago were children's advocates, many of the probation officers hired in other cities were undertakers, installment collectors, insurance agents, court attendants, and sign painters. These individuals simply did not understand what juvenile probation was about and that with the assistance of other social service agencies work needed to be done with the family (Moran, 1939).

The lack of trained professionals adversely affected juvenile courts. As Moran (1939) assessed the way the courts were functioning, he concluded that early juvenile courts were very limited in providing care to delinquents because of their hiring practices and lack of understanding of what good case work was. Quoting Joanna Colcord, Moran stated the view that "good probation work is simply good case work with the punch of the law behind it" (p. 534). But this has not been fully grasped by many persons working with juvenile offenders. Without a full understanding that good probation work must be performed by qualified men and women, juvenile courts, in his opinion, were sure to fail.

In addition to criticisms of the operation and personnel, other criticisms were being heard about recidivism. For instance, a study conducted in Boston, Massachusetts, found that 88 percent of 1,000 delinquents served by the juvenile court there after 1922 got into trouble again within five years (Abbott, 1938). Additionally, Harriet Vittum, head resident of the Northwestern

University Settlement, conducted a social investigation in Chicago and determined that recidivism was a problem, with most delinquents repeatedly coming from the worst part of the city (Addams, 1930). Perhaps because of criticisms directed at the operations of the courts and personnel, some social workers began to question their roles in corrections.

Conflicts with Social Work Values

The many social workers who have criticized social work's participation in corrections directed most of their criticism at adult corrections. They saw juvenile corrections somewhat differently because its goals were to treat children, whereas prisons were for punishment. Juvenile corrections was criticized because the treatment of juveniles strayed significantly from what advocates had intended. For instance, Clarke (1947) wrote that persons who operated juvenile correctional institutions ignored contemporary theories of adolescent behavior and continued to treat juveniles with contempt and scorn. Institutionalized juveniles were flogged, deprived of food, segregated, put in solitary confinement, given cold-water baths, and forced to take drugs that induced vomiting. Often, these practices were for done for trivial institutional violations, such as talking or insubordination (Clarke, 1947). So questions were raised about the participation of social workers in the state's control mechanisms. This question of corrections' social control functions has persisted.

When sociologists first began studying it, social control referred to cooperation and cohesion. George Herbert Mead defined social control as the degree to which persons in common endeavors are able to adopt the attitudes of each other. E. A. Ross defined social control as encompassing an understanding of how individuals live closely together in harmony. Both Mead and Ross suggested that social control involved an understanding of "the sources of empathy and harmony, how people associated together to perform common endeavors, [and] how voluntaristic cooperation marked social activity" (Rothman, 1983, p. 107).

Townsend, writing about social work and the family, discussed social control and conveyed an understanding similar to that of Mead and Ross. Social control was discussed in terms of the government maintaining the state and protecting citizens against health hazards such as communicable diseases, inadequate housing, contaminated food and water, and injurious working environments. Additionally, social control involving human welfare required the state to provide citizens with education, recreation, gainful employment, and freedom to practice their religion (Townsend, 1926).

Yet somehow, social control later assumed the negative connotation of iniquitously suppressing and controlling citizens of the state (Rothman, 1983). Some social work historians then began to reanalyze the motives of settlement house workers and supporters (Karger, 1987).

Besides criticizing corrections as social control, some social workers observed that prisoners lacked self-determination. They saw that working with prisoners in a coercive relationship violated one of social work's cherished values (Fox, 1983). However, these voices appeared to be in the minority because while discussing working in corrections many early social workers did not indicate any ethical conflicts. Biestek and Gehrig (1978) wrote that social workers in corrections faced two major tasks. The first was to ascertain the philosophy and orientation of the correctional institution. This was somewhat difficult because the institution tended to have a dual purpose—to punish offenders by holding them and to reform them if possible. If the institution's primary role was to punish, social workers must then interpret their authority to help the offender understand the societal right to punish through incarceration. Social workers must also decide whether they identify with the institution or the prisoners and what their roles are when the institution punishes, deprives, or disciplines prisoners. If the purpose of the institution is to rehabilitate, the authority of social workers is offset by their helping roles (Biestek & Gehrig, 1978). Biestek and Gehrig were writing historically, with their discussion meant to clarify self-determination in corrections during the 1920s and 1930s.

Subsequently, client self-determination has been discussed in a variety of contexts, and these discussions do not indicate that self-determination is incompatible with working in corrections. Most persons probably realize that self-determination, like liberty, is limited and that no one has an absolute right to do whatever he or she wants anytime he or she wants. Clarifying this view, Spicker (1990) argued that the original concept of client self-determination no longer was tenable and suggested that some clients lack decision-making powers. Spicker used examples involving social workers who were employed as probation officers in Britain. Other social workers have stated that whenever an individual has a limited role in his or her decision-making, the social worker may need to outline what needs to be done and help the individual carry out the needed tasks (Proctor, Morrow-Howell, & Lott, 1993).

Offenders have been put in the broader context of involuntary clients (Behroozi, 1992; Harris & Watkins, 1987; Ivanoff, Blythe, & Tripodi, 1994). Popple and Leighninger (1993) rightly pointed out that social workers intervene with a number of involuntary clients, such as persons with mental illness and children in the child welfare system. For them the question is not whether social workers should work with involuntary clients but how. Ivanoff, Blythe, and Tripodi (1994) described the critical aspects in working with all types of criminal offenders, including mentally ill criminal offenders.

Behroozi (1992) discussed these critical aspects and how social workers should practice with involuntary juvenile and adult correctional clients. Behroozi particularly espoused the following three practice aims with such clients: (1) transform correctional clients into clienthood by developing a service contract; (2) process clients' sources of resistance up front; and (3) after the sources have been identified, begin work with one of the three types of clients: (a) those who come into the group because of the coercion but who are aware of their problems, accept responsibility to change, and believe that they can indeed change; (b) those who come into the group because of the coercion, are aware of their problems and accept responsibility to change but do *not* believe that change is possible; and (c) those who come into the group in response to the coercion but deny both their problem and the need to change (Behroozi, 1992). Behroozi's practice aims were for correctional clients in group treatment, but other social workers rejected serving such groups and preferred other areas of intervention.

For example, Popple and Leighninger (1993) recommended against social workers' involvement in the traditional corrections roles—prison social worker, juvenile officer, probation officer, and parole officer—because social workers eventually are coopted to become punishing agents and lose sight of client treatment. Instead, they recommended that social workers assume roles outside the corrections role of the criminal justice system. They pointed to community mental health centers that accept referrals from the criminal justice system, schools involved in working with predelinquents, and community programs that provide treatment for victims or drug offenders. Popple and Leighninger (1993) also recommended that social workers become police officers because most of a police officer's duty is to help people.

While Popple and Leighninger made some very good points, many believe that social workers can also work in traditional criminal or juvenile justice positions, such as juvenile probation officers and correctional counselors. Although helping professionals can be coopted for punitive functions in programs that serve children, the elderly, and persons suffering from mental illness. For instance, social workers do not have to adopt the punitive measures that some colleagues may use in dealing with a verbally abusive adolescent. Similarly, they do not have to adopt punitive measures with an institutionalized delinquent. In fact, a strong social worker who is on record as shunning brutal treatment of juvenile offenders may, just by his or her presence, prevent some juveniles from being beaten and brutalized.

Current Roles of Social Workers in the Juvenile Justice System

Administrative Roles

The skills taught to social workers not only allow the social workers to practice with correctional clients but also to perform administrative tasks (Needleman, 1983b; Raymond, 1983). At the micro level, for instance, social workers advocate on behalf of correctional clients to help the clients negotiate various systems. At the macro level, social workers use advocacy skills in testifying before state legislative bodies for policies beneficial to juveniles involved in the juvenile justice system. For example, Terry Kennedy, formerly Assistant Deputy for Parole, Court, and Community Service in the Ohio Department of Youth Services, who holds an M.S.W. degree, has written proposed legislation for her department, and testified before the Ohio legislature. Additionally, her duties included the development of programs, supervision of staff, employee and public relations, budgeting, and grant writing. Kennedy subsequently became Assistant Deputy for Staff Training, with responsibility for all Youth Services training and some court employee training. The director of the Ohio Department of Youth Services, as well as several other administrators in the central office, also hold M.S.W. degrees (Ezell, 1994; see chapter 1 on administration of juvenile justice in this text by Ezell).

Direct Services Roles

As rehabilitation became important to corrections, social work also became more important. Both were viewed as being oriented to the positivistic school of criminology (Trojanowicz & Morash, 1987). Their training in writing case plans and their social case work concepts made social workers desirable and suitable for the authoritarian environment of prisons (Allen & Simonsen, 1989). Lundman (1993) stated that his book on juvenile delinquency was intended in part for social work programs that address juvenile delinquency through case work, group work, and community organizations. From such discussions, the roles of social workers in juvenile institutions, probation, and parole were clarified. In addition, social work roles exist in addressing pre-delinquent behaviors in the school system, in juvenile mediation and restitution programs, and in community counseling programs.

Social Workers in School Settings

Juvenile courts are not situated to address adolescents' inchoate delinquency, but an ideal institution to address it is the school. The school environment has been recognized as a key for intervention to prevent future delinquency. The school is a key because some adjudicated delinquents are not institutionalized and remain in the community for treatment. As these delinquents are served in the community instead of in an institution, they attend community schools designed to meet their educational needs. In the school, they receive counseling, school psychology, and social work services (Nelson & Rutherford, 1990). According to delinquency experts, "home-school counselors acting as liaisons between the family and the school might be effective in preventing delinquency. These counselors try to ensure cooperation between the parents and the school and to secure needed services—academic, social, and psychological—for troubled students before serious delinquency becomes a problem" (Siegel & Senna, 1994, p. 363).

Juvenile Mediation and Restitution

In the 1970s, mediation developed as an alternative to criminal prosecution for nonserious disputes involving neighbors, acquaintances, and co-workers. As mediation became accepted policy, it was expanded to cover conflicts involving juveniles, including intra-family conflicts, parent-child conflicts, students' conflicts, and "interpersonal conflicts leading to minor criminal complaints against juvenile offenders" (Bush, 1991, p. 4). Although some professionals were saying that mediation was appropriate only for minor juvenile offenses, Klein (1991) argued that restitution, which sometimes has a mediation aspect, is also appropriate for high-risk violent juveniles (Klein, 1991). Whether mediation or restitution is or is not appropriate for certain juveniles, social workers have embraced this approach and have articulated roles for practicing it.

The United Kingdom, for example, passed the Children and Young Persons Act in 1969. The Act created the Exeter Joint Services Youth Support Team and directed police officers, social workers, and probation officers to work together to divert some juveniles from the criminal justice system. Among the objectives of the youth support team, besides diversion, were developing policies to prevent delinquency in the county and to build community involvement. Reparation had been a part of the requirement for deciding some juvenile cases. The team decided to improve the reparation process by adding mediation (Harding, 1989; Veevers, 1989).

In the United States, Umbreit (1993) discussed social work mediation involving crime victims and offenders. Although Umbreit presented a case study involving a twenty-year-old offender, he made it clear that the practice model he described could apply to juvenile offenders as well. He wrote that the mediation process involved four phases—intake, preparation, mediation, and follow-up. The *intake phase* is initiated when a referral is made from an agent of the criminal justice system, such as the prosecutor or judge. During the *preparation phase,* the social worker meets with the offender and solicits his or her involvement. If the offender agrees, the social worker meets with the victim. No coercion is used to get either party into the mediation process. Instead, the social worker endeavors to empower both parties. During the *mediation phase,* both parties are brought together by the social worker. The social worker explains all parties' responsibilities and duties, including the social worker's. The victim is provided with an opportunity to ask questions, and the offender is allowed to personalize his or her behavior. They agree upon the losses and how restitution is to be made. The social worker is a passive participant at this stage and does not force an agreement on the parties. During the *follow-up phase,* the social worker presents the agreement to the referral person, monitors agreed-upon tasks, and solicits the assistance of a referral agent if the offender is not complying with his or her agreement. If another mediation is needed, the social worker must arrange it and then close the case when the issues have been resolved. A case may also be closed when the offender is removed from the mediation program for noncompliance and referred back to the judge for a typical criminal justice sanction.

Umbreit (1993) acknowledged that a significant limitation of mediation was that it may not be sufficient to meet the acute needs of some offenders and victims, but its major strength of empowering both offenders and victims makes it important for social work practitioners.

Community Halfway Houses

Palmer (1991) reviewed the intervention programs used with juvenile delinquents during the past thirty years. He predicted that in the 1990s emphasis would be on more community-based services because of institutional overcrowding and the high cost of building new institutions. He also predicted that considerable emphasis would be put on programs to achieve the rehabilitation of young offenders by helping them conquer their problems, conflicts, and deficits. The aim would be to help offenders grow and develop more positively through counseling and social skills development.

However, some professionals, while endorsing the overall aims of juvenile intervention, have stated that it is difficult to rehabilitate many juveniles because they have not been habilitated by their families, schools, and other socializing institutions (Mullen, Arbiter, & Glider, 1991). Thus, special programs must be developed for juveniles, such as the Amity program in Pima County, Arizona, which has served juveniles who are chronic abusers of mind-altering substances. Such programs are especially needed for girls, whose problems may be compounded by sexual abuse in childhood (Mullen, Arbiter, & Glider, 1991).

The fact that some youths have not been habilitated calls for the development of specialized programs of intervention with them. Greenwood (1986, p. 213) reviewed the theories concerning chronically serious juvenile offenders and concluded that an intervention program for them should do the following:

1. Provide opportunities for success and the development of a positive self-image.
2. Facilitate the development of bonds of affection and respect between juveniles and their guardians and involvement by them in conventional activities.
3. Provide frequent and accurate feedback for both positive and negative behavior.
4. Reduce or eliminate negative role models and peer support for negative attitudes or behaviors.

5. Require delinquents to recognize and reflect on inappropriate thought processes that led to negative behavior.
6. Create opportunities for juveniles to discuss early family experiences with appropriate staff.
7. Vary the sequence and exposure to various program components to adapt to the needs of each youth.

Leone, Walter, and Wolford (1990) also discussed new directions in services for youth and advocated a multidisciplinary, community-based program for seriously delinquent youth. They argued for an expansion of views from a problem-centered or person-centered focus to one that understands "that problems experienced by some youths suggest a poor fit between youths and their ecologies" (p. 297). Greenwood (1986) argued for alternative approaches to correctional institutions for juveniles such as wilderness camp programs. These calls by some juvenile advocates for multidisciplinary, comprehensive, and wilderness programs for juvenile offenders have all been tried.

One such specialized program is based on moral cognitive theory. Using Kolberg's stages of moral development, Gibbs (1993) wrote that because antisocial youths are at stage 2, treatment should be directed at remediation during this stage. According to Gibbs,

> moral judgment-delayed youths need an enriched concentrated dosage of social perspective-taking opportunity to stimulate them to catch up to an age-appropriate level of moral judgment. Subjects are given opportunities to consider the perspective of others vís-a-vís their own perspectives in the context of either a macrointervention or a microintervention strategy. In the macrointervention of "Just Community" strategy, attempts are made to restructure the institution (school or correctional facility) in accordance with principles of democracy and justice so that subjects (student or inmates) participate as much as is feasible in the rule-making and enforcement processes that affect institutional life. The narrower microintervention strategy focuses on group discussion of relevant sociomoral dilemmas or problem situations as a stimulus for perspective-taking experiences. Subjects must justify the reasons for their problem-solving decisions in the face of challenges from more developmentally advanced peers and from group leaders. (1993, pp. 169–70)

Gibbs's theory was tested in an experimental research design involving incarcerated juveniles in a midwestern state. Based on a modified version of Kolberg's theory of moral development, a program called Equipping Youth to Help One Another (EQUIP) was developed to help delinquent youth through stage 2. EQUIP was carried out by youth leaders, supervisors, teachers, and social workers employed in the institution. Several boys in the program were randomly assigned to an experimental group; two control groups consisted of a simple control group and a motivational control group. The researchers hypothesized that the boys receiving the EQUIP program would have increased degrees of mediating processes (i.e., moral judgment and social skills) and less dysfunctional behavior (i.e., institutional misconduct and postrelease recidivism) than did the two control groups. They found no significant difference in the amount of moral judgment exercised in the control group. But the boys in EQUIP did have significant favorable differences in the amount of social skills and the extent of institutional misconduct and post-recidivism (Leeman, Gibbs, & Fuller, 1993).

Although social workers played a role in the EQUIP program, and although Popple and Leighninger (1993) have recommended against social workers working in institutions, social workers still have another role to play in juvenile correctional institutions. (See chapter 2 in this text on juvenile corrections.) Like adults, juveniles undergo pains of imprisonment when they are incarcerated. They lose their freedom, which is a major loss. Institutional settings also involve a loss of autonomy. Additionally, confined juveniles must deal with possible victimization, such as robbery and physical and sexual assaults. Minority juveniles also may have to contend with discrimination within the institution. These pressures, either singularly or in combination, may produce serious mental health problems (Flowers, 1990). So even without a program such as EQUIP, ordinary mental health services may be needed. Social workers can provide these services.

Maryland has emphasized boot camps, group and foster homes, and other community-based programs. One new program is the Choice Program run by the University of Maryland. The Choice Program, recognizing that youth need attention and structure, provided a team of three case workers available to youths around-the-clock. A youth receives three to five face-to-face visits a day, seven days a week. The caseworker's job is to visit youths at home or school and to check on them in the evenings. Implemented in several states, the concepts operationalized by the Choice Program have been praised by the National Council on Crime and Delinquency (Maryland Uses New Tack, 1993).

Clagett (1992) described a wilderness camp for emotionally disturbed and delinquent boys in Apple Springs, Texas. Its program utilized reality therapy through group counseling. Caseworkers wrote a plan of service for each boy admitted to the program and conducted reviews with parents, the boy, and staff every ninety days. While the boy was in the program, caseworkers, many of whom hold Master's degrees in social work, kept in touch with his parents, meeting with them once a month. While the caseworkers worked with the parents, the live-in camp counselors worked with the boys. When a boy was ready to leave camp, aftercare services were provided to the boy and parents by the Hope Center for Youth (Clagett, 1992). Aftercare for juvenile offenders has been called a highly neglected area (Altschuler & Armstrong, 1991). (See chapter 3 in this text on aftercare.)

The Future of Social Work in the Juvenile Justice System

The juvenile justice system has come under recent criticisms. Some professionals have advocated its abolishment. Surprisingly held by many juvenile advocates considered liberal, the critics contend that serious offenders should be tried in the adult criminal justice system, where they would have more rights. They further suggest that juvenile offenders not be handled by the justice system at all. For the few juveniles who are convicted, professionally trained psychologists and social workers would have more time to work with them. Furthermore, juvenile prisoners would not be housed with adults (Bynum & Thompson, 1992). Despite the repeated calls for the abolishment of the juvenile justice system, it still exists and social workers must deal with it.

Conservative politicians and the media have been able to convince the public that because youthful offenders are not punished for their crimes the crime problem is getting worse. Thus, the movement to decriminalize juvenile offenders, deinstitutionalize some delinquents, and divert more juveniles from the criminal justice system has been halted. As a result, increasing numbers of juveniles are being institutionalized (Trojanowicz & Morash, 1992). Moreover, the increased incarceration of juveniles has racial implications. According to data compiled by McNeece and O'Quinn (1994), secure placement of white youth increased by only 1.9 percent from 1986 to 1990, but placement of African American youth increased by 34.5 percent during the same period. Additionally, the same data source showed that waivers to adult court increased for white youth by 22.5 percent but by 115.9 percent for minority youth.

In any event, social workers have a role to play in the treatment of juveniles. If the juvenile justice system is eventually abolished, youthful offenders still will need services. But the dominance of that system is increasing, and more juveniles are being institutionalized. Social workers can help in ameliorating and perhaps reversing the trend in the last few years of incarcerating more juveniles. Cox and Conrad (1987) wrote that improvement in the juvenile justice system really depends upon improving societal conditions, such as poverty, unemployment, and discrimination. Similarly, Bortner (1988) stated that professionals need to work more for social justice and help eliminate racism, sexism, poverty, and class discrimination.

Social workers can work for social justice so that the ecological fit between juveniles and their families is better, work to reverse the incarceration of some juveniles, and work with juveniles who have been diverted from the system. If the juvenile justice system is abolished, they can work directly with the more seriously disturbed delinquents.

References

Abbott, G. (1938). *The child and the state: The dependent and the delinquent child, the child of unmarried parents (Vol. 2)*. Chicago: University of Chicago Press.

Addams, J. (1910). *Twenty-years at Hull House.* New York: Macmillan.

Addams, J. (1930). *The second twenty years at Hull House.* New York: Macmillan.

Alexander, R., Jr., Butler, L., & Sias, P. (1993). Women offenders incarcerated at the Ohio penitentiary for men and the Ohio reformatory for women from 1913–1923. *Journal of Sociology & Social Welfare, 20,* 61–79.

Alexander, R., Jr., & Langford, L. (1992). Throwing down: A social learning test of student fighting. *Social Work in Education, 14,* 114–124.

Allen, H. E., & Simonsen, C. E. (1989). *Corrections in America: An introduction* (5th ed.). New York: Macmillan.

Altschuler, D. M., & Armstrong, T. L. (1991). Intensive aftercare for the high-risk juvenile parolee: Issues and approaches in reintegration and community. In T. L. Armstrong (Ed.), *Intensive interventions with high-risk youths: Promising approaches in juvenile probation and parole* (pp. 45–84). Monsey, NY: Criminal Justice Press.

Behroozi, C. S. (1992). A model for social work with involuntary applicants in groups. *Social Work With Groups, 15*(2/3), 223–238.

Biestek, F. P., & Gehrig, C. C. (1978). *Client self-determination in social work: A fifty-year history.* Chicago: Loyola University Press.

Blagg, H., & Smith, D. (1989). *Crime, penal policy and social work.* Harlow, UK: Longman.

Bloom, M. (1990). *Introduction to the drama of social work.* Itasca, IL: Peacock.

Bortner, M. A. (1988). *Delinquency and justice: An age of crisis.* New York: McGraw-Hill.

Bush, R. A. B. (1991). *Mediation involving juveniles: Ethical dilemmas and policy questions.* Ann Arbor, MI: Center For The Study of Youth Policy.

Bynum, J. E., & Thompson, W. E. (1992). *Juvenile delinquency: A sociological approach* (2nd ed.). Boston, MA: Allyn and Bacon.

Clagett, A. F. (1992). Group-integrated reality therapy in a wilderness camp. *Journal of Offender Rehabilitation, 17*(3/4), 1–18.

Clarke, H. I. (1947). *Principles and practice of social work.* New York: D. Appleton-Century.

Cox, S. M., & Conrad, J. J. (1987). *Juvenile justice: A guide to practice and theory* (2nd ed.). Dubuque, IA: W. C. Brown.

Crocker, R. H. (1992). *Social work and social order: The settlements movement in two industrial cities, 1889–1930.* Urbana: University of Illinois Press.

Ezell, M. (1994). The advocacy practice of social workers. *Families in Society, 1,* 36–46.

Flowers, R. B. (1990). *The adolescent criminal: An examination of today's juvenile offender.* Jefferson, NC: McFarland.

Fox, F. (1983). Foreword. In A. R. Roberts (Ed.), *Social work in juvenile and criminal justice settings* (pp. ix–xv). Springfield, IL: Charles C. Thomas.

Gibbs, J. C. (1993). Moral-cognitive interventions. In A. P. Goldstein & C. R. Huff (Eds.), *The gang intervention handbook* (pp. 159–185). Champaign, IL: Research Press.

Greenwood, P. W. (1986). Promising approaches for the rehabilitation or prevention of chronic juvenile offenders. In P. W. Greenwood (Ed.), *Intervention strategies for chronic juvenile offenders: Some new perspectives* (pp. 207–233). New York: Greenwood Press.

Handler, E. (1975). Social work and corrections: Comments on an uneasy partnership. *Criminology, 13,* 240–254.

Harding, J. (1989). Reconciling mediation with criminal justice. In M. Wright & B. Galaway (Eds.), *Mediation and criminal justice: victims, offenders and community* (pp. 27–43). London, UK: Sage.

Harris, G. A., & Watkins, D. (1987). *Counseling the involuntary and resistant client.* Washington, DC: American Correctional Association.

Ivanoff, A., Blythe, B. J., & Tripodi, T. (1994). *Involuntary clients in social work practice: A research-based approach.* New York: Aldine De Gruyter.

Karger, H. J. (1987). *The sentinels of order: A study of social control and the Minneapolis settlement house movement, 1915–1950.* Lanham, MD: University Press of America.

Klein, A. R. (1991). Restitution and community work service: Promising core ingredients for effective intensive supervision programming. In T. L. Armstrong (Ed.), *Intensive interventions with high-risk youths: Promising approaches in juvenile probation and parole* (pp. 245–268). Monsey, NY: Criminal Justice Press.

Klein, M., & Kantor, H. A. (1976). *Prisoners of progress: American industrial cities 1850–1920.* New York: Macmillan.

Krisberg, B., & Austin, J. F. (1993). *Reinventing juvenile justice.* Newbury Park, CA: Sage.

Leeman, L. W., Gibbs, J. C., & Fuller, D. (1993). Evaluation of a multi-component group treatment program for juvenile delinquents. *Aggressive Behavior, 19,* 281–292.

Leone, P. E., Walter, M. B., & Wolford, B. I. (1990). Toward integrated responses to troubling behavior. In P. E. Leone (Ed.), *Understanding troubled and troubling youth* (pp. 290–298). Newbury Park, CA: Sage.

Lundman, R. J. (1993). *Prevention and control of juvenile delinquency* (2nd ed.). New York: Oxford University Press.

Maryland uses new tack with young delinquents. (1993, June). *New York Times,* p. A8.

McNeece, C. A., & O'Quinn, N. K. (1994, March). Disturbing trends in juvenile offenses and case disposition. Paper presented at annual meeting of the Southwestern Social Science Association, San Antonio, TX.

Middleton, J. B. (1939). Parole and family agency. In F. Lowry (Ed.), *Readings in social case work* (pp. 626–634). New York: Columbia University Press.

Moran, F. A. (1939). New light on juvenile courts and probation. In F. Lowry (Ed.), *Readings in social case work* (pp. 527–536). New York: Columbia University Press.

Mullen, R., Arbiter, N., & Glider, P. (1991). A comprehensive therapeutic community approach for chronic substance-abusing juvenile offenders: The amity model. In T. L. Armstrong (Ed.), *Intensive interventions with high-risk youths: Promising approaches in juvenile probation and parole* (pp. 211–243). Monsey, NY: Criminal Justice Press.

Needleman, C. (1983a). Conflicting philosophies of juvenile justice. In A. R. Roberts (Ed.), *Social work in juvenile and criminal justice settings* (pp. 155–164). Springfield, IL: Charles C. Thomas.

Needleman, C. (1983b). Social work and probation in the juvenile court. In A. R. Roberts (Ed.), *Social work in juvenile and criminal justice settings* (pp. 165–179). Springfield, IL: Charles C. Thomas.

Nelson, C. M., & Rutherford, R. B., Jr. (1990). Troubled youth in the public schools: Emotionally disturbed or socially maladjusted? In P. E. Leone (Ed.), *Understanding troubled and troubling youth.* (pp. 38–60) Newbury, CA: Sage.

Never, D., Piliavin, I., Schneck, D., & Henderson, M. (1990, March). *Criminal justice and social work education: Lost opportunity for the profession and the client.* Paper presented at the National Field Work Symposium, 36th annual program meeting of the Council on Social Work Education, Reno, Nevada.

Odem, M. E., & Schlossman, S. (1991). Guardians of virtue: The juvenile court and female delinquency in early 20th-century Los Angeles. *Crime and Delinquency, 37,* 186–203.

Palmer, T. B. (1991). Intervention with juvenile offenders: Recent and long-term changes. In T. L. Armstrong (Ed.), *Intensive interventions with high-risk youths: Promising approaches in juvenile probation and parole* (pp. 85–120). Monsey, NY: Criminal Justice Press.

Popple, P. R., & Leighninger, L. (1993). *Social work, social welfare, and American society* (2nd ed.). Boston: Allyn and Bacon.

Proctor, E. K., Morrow-Howell, N., & Lott, C. L. (1993). Classification and correlates of ethical dilemma in hospital social work. *Social Work, 38,* 166–177.

Raymond, F. B., III (1983). Administration in probation and parole. In A. R. Roberts (Ed.), *Social work in juvenile and criminal justice settings* (pp. 203–229). Springfield, IL: Charles C. Thomas.

Richmond, M. E. (1917). *Social diagnosis.* New York: Russell Sage Foundation.

Roberts, A. R. (1983). The history and role of social work in law enforcement. In A. R. Roberts (Ed.), *Social work in juvenile and criminal justice settings* (pp. 91–103). Springfield, IL: Charles C. Thomas.

Rothman, D. (1983). Social control: The uses and abuses of the concept in the history of incarceration. In S. Cohen & A. Scull (Eds.), *Social control and the state: Historical and comparative essays* (pp. 106–117). Oxford, UK: Martin Robertson.

Schlossman, S., & Pisciotta, A. (1986). Identifying and treating serious juvenile offenders: The view from California and New York in the 1920s. In P. W. Greenwood (Ed.), *Intervention strategies for chronic juvenile offenders: Some new perspective* (pp. 7–38). New York: Greenwood.

Schwartz, I. M. (1989). *(In)justice for juveniles: Rethinking the best interests of the child.* Lexington, MA: Lexington Books.

Siegel, L. J., & Senna, J. J. (1994). *Juvenile delinquency: Theory, practice and law* (5th ed.). St. Paul, MN: West.

Spicker, P. (1990). Social work and self-determination. *British Journal of Social Work, 20,* 221–236.

Townsend, H. (1926). *Social work a family builder.* Philadelphia, PA: W. B. Saunders.

Trattner, W. I. (1970). *Crusade for the children: A history of the national labor committee and child labor reforms in America.* Chicago, IL: Quadrangle Books.

Trojanowicz, R. C., & Morash, M. (1987). *Juvenile delinquency: Concepts and control* (4th ed.). Englewood Cliffs, NJ: Prentice-Hall.

Trojanowicz, R. C., & Morash, M. (1992). *Juvenile delinquency: Concepts and control* (5th ed.). Englewood Cliffs, NJ: Prentice-Hall.

Umbreit, M. S. (1993). Crime victims and offenders in mediation: An emerging area of social work practice. *Social Work, 38,* 69–73.

Veevers, J. (1989). Pre-court diversion for juvenile offenders. In M. Wright & B. Galaway (Eds.), *Mediation and criminal justice: Victims, offenders and community* (pp. 69–81). London, UK: Sage.

Chapter Twelve

Intervention with Adolescent Sex Offenders

Karen S. Knox and Allen Rubin

The roles of social workers and other mental health professionals have been expanding in the criminal justice system. Opportunities for clinical work with juvenile offenders have increased in several areas, including gang prevention, chemical dependency, and sexual abuse. Common practice roles within the criminal justice system include crisis intervention and victim services workers, probation/parole officers, jail/prison counselors, mental health providers working with juvenile offenders and their families, and court advocates. Professionals in these roles must be knowledgeable about the specialized services and treatment modalities found in these practice fields, as well as the interdisciplinary nature of working within the complex setting of the criminal justice system.

The increase in direct practice with offenders and their families has been due to more emphasis on rehabilitation and counseling in the identified problem areas. Sexual abuse has been identified as high risk for recidivism and reoffending behaviors, and many communities now have mandatory counseling for both adult and juvenile sex offenders in corrections and probation/parole systems. Chemical dependency has also been associated with recidivism rates, and specialized programs have been implemented to address this problem as well. Prevention of chemical dependency and gang involvement has been targeted by educational programs that are coordinated efforts by law enforcement agencies, the school districts, and the communities.

The focus of this chapter is to discuss direct practice interventions and roles for working with adolescent sex offenders. An overview of the problem of juvenile sex offending and changes in the way juvenile justice and mental health professionals have dealt with this client population is presented. An example of a community-based program for adolescent sex offenders is discussed. Information on different treatment issues, modalities, interventions, and programs is provided, including a review of the literature and research studies on adolescent sex offenders. Direct practice and research roles for mental health professionals, as well as several issues associated with these roles, such as social control, cultural diversity, and effectiveness of services, is also discussed.

Overview of the Problem

During the past decade, recognition by both mental health professionals and the criminal justice system of the problem of sexual abuse by adolescents has increased. As a result, there have been changes in the way criminal justice and mental health professionals intervene with this client population. There is evidence of these changes in several areas.

First, there has been an increased awareness of the problem itself. While the exact incidence of adolescents being charged with a sexual offense is not known, some findings indicate that 20 to 30 percent of all rapes and 30 to 50 percent of all child molestations are committed by juveniles (Deisher et al., 1982; Abel et al., 1984). More recent data indicate that males under the age of nineteen accounted for 19 percent of forcible rapes and 18 percent of other sexual offenses (Borduin, Henggeler, & Mann, 1989).

The following example illustrates an increase in awareness and intervention at the community level. A study conducted in Austin, Texas, by Knox and Laredo (1991) from 1985 to 1991 tracked the sexual assault cases involving adolescent offenders to determine the numbers of referrals, the outcomes of the investigations, whether charges were filed, and adjudication outcomes. The findings of the study were reported to the Adolescent Perpetrator Sub-Committee of the Travis County Child Welfare Unit, a multidisciplinary team of professionals from law enforcement, child protective services, the criminal and juvenile court systems, and mental health professionals. The goals of this subcommittee were to identify the extent of the problem in the community, to monitor the cases through the criminal justice system, to make recommendations for improving and coordinating services, and to develop and implement a long-term treatment program for adolescent sex offenders through the Travis County Juvenile Court.

The report indicated that in 1986, twenty-two sexual offenses by adolescents were substantiated and charges filed; however, an equal number of investigations were closed without legal action. Of the twenty-two cases, only ten of the juveniles were adjudicated, placed on probation, and provided with counseling services. In contrast, the Austin police department filed charges on fifty-five juveniles in 1990 and there were fifty-nine arrests in 1991. The counseling services were serving a total of forty-four clients in 1990 and seventy-five in 1991. All of these clients had been referred through Travis County Juvenile Court and were on probation during the time of treatment.

These increases in the arrest, adjudication, and treatment rates for adolescent sex offenders in Travis County may have been the result of several policy changes implemented by law enforcement and the juvenile court system due to recommendations by the Adolescent Perpetrator Sub-Committee. One of these changes involved monthly staffings with all involved agencies to coordinate cases, provide continuum of care, and develop a long-term treatment program. Specialized case loads for juvenile probation officers, who received additional training and education about juvenile sex offenders, were also implemented in order to provide consistency in probation rules and referral for counseling, and to obtain a level of knowledge and expertise about sexual offenders for those working with this client population and their families. Another important policy change was to court-order both the adolescent perpetrator and the family into treatment, which was essential to ensure that they followed through with the counseling program.

A second area of change in the area of sexual abuse by adolescents was observed in the 1980s, when there was an increase in the numbers of researchers and clinicians who began developing treatment models and programs for working with this client population (Groth & Loredo, 1981; Groth et al., 1981; Knopp, 1982; Stickrod, Hamer, & Jones, 1984; Lane & Zamora, 1985; Smets & Cebula, 1987). A corresponding increase occurred in treatment programs, both residential and outpatient, with approximately twenty programs identified nationally in 1982 and over 520 specialized treatment programs serving juvenile sex offenders in 1988 (National Adolescent Perpetrator Task Force, 1988). However, it must be pointed out that until recently, few research studies had been conducted specifically on this client population, with treatment models and intervention strategies often based on literature and research about adult sex offenders.

As professionals have begun to coordinate and improve services for juvenile sex offenders, it has been necessary to establish consistent guidelines for legal definitions, diagnostic criteria, and treatment models. There has been much confusion and debate over what is "normal" adolescent sexual activity and how to define adolescent sexual offending behaviors. Several guidelines have been agreed upon by many clinicians in the field, but legal definitions are not always consistent with clinical priorities.

The issue of age is an example of this problem. The Texas Family Code (1988), the basis for juvenile court rules and procedures, defines a child as a person who is between ten and seventeen years of age, but the Texas Penal Code (1988) defines persons seventeen years of age as adults for criminal proceedings. However, there are certain criminal offenses, including sexual assault, for which juveniles as young as fourteen years of age can be certified as adults for criminal proceedings. Also, the legal system in Texas has no authority to file charges or to prosecute children under the age of ten, so prepubescent perpetrators are usually not identified through this system for intervention. In some cases, child perpetrators are targeted through Child Protective Services whenever the abuse occurs in the home, and treatment services may be implemented through the civil court system.

Both clinicians and the legal system agree that difference in age is another guideline in defining sexual offending. Generally, a two-year age difference between the offender and the victim is considered an appropriate time frame for this guideline, but other factors may need to be considered as well. Age differences also contain the elements of power if the perpetrator is physically bigger or has some perceived control over the victim. Developmental differences and the capability of giving consent vary with age, knowledge, and experience. In Texas, consensual sexual activity between youths who are at least fourteen years of age and who have less than a two-year age difference would not be considered a criminal offense, unless the victim is incapable of giving consent due to mental or physical impairment. Guidelines on age of consent differ across the states.

The use of force, regardless of age, constitutes a sexual offense. Force can involve a variety of behaviors, ranging from physical acts of aggression to the use of threats or weapons. The use of force in sexual offending needs to be taken very seriously. It indicates an underlying psychopathology that is more difficult to treat than for offenders who use other types of actions, such as bribery, manipulation, and seduction. Additionally, the elements of psychological harm and potential or actual physical injury to the victim are disregarded by the offenders, which may indicate sociopathic tendencies. The combination of sexuality and violence often results in the development of more deviant sexual patterns, where the victim's pain or injury stimulates the offender. This pattern is associated with serial killers and rapists and undifferentiated pedophiles whose violence escalates, resulting in injury or death for the victim (Hazelwood & Warren, 1989).

These two factors—difference in ages and the use of force—are considered by both the criminal justice system and clinicians as essential to a working definition of adolescent sexual offending. The legal system is more specific in defining certain actions as criminally enforceable, with hands-off offenses such as exhibitionism, voyeurism, and obscene phone calls typically being misdemeanor charges of less seriousness, and hands-on offenses such as fondling, fellatio, and intercourse generally being felonies. Most clinicians would argue that hands-off offenses should be considered as serious components of a continuum of sexual-offending behaviors that may precede or co-exist with hands-on acts. Additionally, while the juvenile offender is generally charged with the most recent incident, offending behaviors may in reality have been documented as long-term problems, involving a variety of sexual contacts over a number of years, often with more than one victim. Therefore, the client's continuum of sexually offending behaviors is the focus of clinical intervention, while the focus of law enforcement and the courts is to file charges on the most prosecutable incident.

One of the reasons that the problem of adolescent sexual offending has been overlooked by both the legal and mental health systems in the past is the issue of underreporting. It is common for both the offender's family and the victim's family to minimize the seriousness of the sexually offending behaviors, especially when the young offender is a relative or friend of the victim. Families also try to handle the problem among themselves and are reluctant to report the adolescent to law enforcement or child protective services. Additionally, human service providers may not have been trained to identify and intervene with juvenile sex offenders, and most offenders do not disclose any behaviors that could result in negative legal or social consequences.

These factors associated with underreporting also reflect several issues that need to be dealt with by both clinicians and the legal system. The dynamics of denial and minimization by those involved, including the offender and his or her family, the victim and his or her family, and even the mental health and juvenile justice professionals are critical issues to be addressed in the initial intervention strategies. This dilemma in reporting sexually offending behaviors reinforces denial and minimization through fears of legal consequences and stigmatization by others.

A second issue is involvement by the legal system and coordination and cooperation between treatment providers and juvenile justice professionals. The legal authority to court-order counseling and supervision services for the offender and the family members helps to ensure follow-through with the treatment program. Lack of participation by the offender's parents had been an on-going problem in the counseling program in Travis County, until the judge implemented a fine for nonattendance at the monthly parents group meeting. Prior to that change, fewer than one-fourth of the parents would attend the mandatory meeting.

Distrust is a third issue. Since these clients are involuntary, and often defensive and resistant to treatment, issues of power and authority by mental health and juvenile justice professionals are also important dynamics to be addressed in treatment. Distrust of those professionals may lead to power struggles and an adversarial relationship. Lack of education and training about this client population can contribute to these problems. Additionally, cultural and class differences must be considered in relation to power issues. For example, adolescents, who already are struggling with the developmental task of autonomy, often view being uncooperative and resisting the system as a way of asserting control and power. This positive value of not being coopted into the system is also shared by many ethnic minorities, due to their group history of institutional oppression and discrimination. Approximately two-thirds of the clients in the sex offender program in Austin are from ethnic minorities and low-income families, which underscores the importance of training and education on multicultural and class issues for both mental health and juvenile justice professionals.

Review of the Literature

A review of the available literature concerning the problem of adolescent sexual offending indicates a focus on two major areas: (1) characteristics and profiles of adolescent sex offenders and (2) treatment issues and programs. Most of the literature consists of descriptive studies, rather than empirical research evaluating theoretical approaches or treatment interventions. However, most of the authors cite the need for more empirical research, and recent studies reflect a move in this direction (Becker, Kaplan, & Kavoussi, 1986; Guthmann, 1986; Blaske & Borduin, 1988).

Even though studies prior to the 1960s tend to be moralistic and define sexual offenses according to societal mores, their findings are consistent with those cited in more recent literature. Several early studies cite the positive nature of early intervention by the courts and clinicians, and the need for professionals to understand sexually offending behaviors as important issues in working with this client population (Doshay, 1969; Markley, 1950). Other studies note the need for family intervention, finding that emotionally non-supportive families are characteristic of the population and the most likely source of sexual maladjustment (Markley, 1950; Maclay, 1960). More recently, Kaplan, Becker, and Cunningham-Rather (1986) concluded that treatment factors associated with parents of juvenile sex offenders include lack of appropriate sex education, parental denial or cover-up, and a cycle of abuse (modeling).

Studies profile the adolescent sex offender as a socially and sexually immature loner who has minimal social skills and a lack of peer interaction, preferring the company of younger children or adults. (Shoor, Speed, & Bertelt, 1962; Groth & Loredo, 1981; Fehrenbach et al., 1986). An emphasis on diagnostic criteria continued through the 1970s with profiles of types of adolescent sex offenders, development of measurement and testing instruments, and research on family dynamics being the focus of many studies (Lewis, 1976; Groth, 1977; Whalley & McGuire, 1978; Anderson & Kunce, 1979).

A shift in focus occurred in the 1980s, with more research specifically on treatment issues, interventions, and program models. Several issues that studies have identified as critical to the treatment process were the offender's need for power and control, cognitive distortions contributing to denial and minimization, and acceptance of responsibility for the sexually offending behaviors (Breer, 1987; Ryan, et al., 1987; Gil, 1987). Dynamics such as poor self-esteem, sexual victimization in the offender's history, and depression were cited as characteristic of juvenile sex offenders (Fehrenbach et al., 1986; Ryan et al., 1987; Gil, 1987). Other treatment issues for adolescent sex offenders include poor impulse control, problems with anger management and aggressive behaviors, learning and developmental disabilities, chemical dependency, and other delinquent behaviors.

Interventions targeting deficits in social skills, empathy, and sex education were emphasized by these same studies, and many clinicians began to develop programs and models for working with juvenile sex offenders during this time. An analysis by Knopp (1982) of nine treatment programs, which included both outpatient and residential facilities, reflected agreement among clinicians on the importance of addressing the following treatment issues: (1) acknowledgement of sex offending behaviors, (2) addressing the offender's own victimization, (3) sex education and values clarification, (4) assertiveness and social skills training, (5) development of victim empathy, (6) cognitive restructuring, and (7) disruption of the deviant sexual assault cycle.

These same issues were included in Ryan's (1986) criteria as typical of most programs working with adolescent sex offenders: (1) acknowledgment of accountability for the sexual abuse, (2) emphasis on sex offense specific treatment, (3) peer group treatment, with individual and family therapy as adjunct, (4) risk assessment criteria regarding safety issues, and (5) court involvement with probation to ensure follow-up services. Ryan also noted that "a multidisciplinary team approach wherein law enforcement, the courts, clinicians, and communities work together promises to have a significant impact on stemming the development of a new generation of sex offenders" (Ryan, 1986, p. 126).

The preference for group treatment as the modality of choice for most clinicians working with juvenile sex offenders is based on several reasons, including the elements of peer pressure and interaction, which are important in confronting denial and minimization. The group setting also provides an atmosphere that reduces isolation and anxiety, and many adolescents find it easier to disclose and take responsibility when communicating with peers who share similar histories and experiences. Additionally, the group allows for a social-learning setting where skills can be developed and practiced through interaction with others.

The use of a male and female therapy team has been cited as crucial to the quality of the group (Smets & Cebula, 1987; NAPTF, 1988). Contact with appropriate male and female role models provides the opportunity to improve social skills and interaction, which can then be used in age-appropriate relationships with both genders.

The length of treatment can vary across cases; however, most programs require a minimum of twelve months of clinical intervention, with some clients needing more extensive services depending on the individual circumstances and needs. Factors such as a high level of family dysfunction, a lack of motivation or capacity of the client, the presence of other antisocial and delinquent behaviors, and the severity of the sexual abuse history can contribute to the need for an increased time frame for intervention. This necessitates long-term treatment plans, including follow-up services and legal mandates, to ensure cooperation and participation in the treatment process.

The relationship between treatment interventions, theoretical approaches, and research has not been clearly defined in this area. While many programs espouse a cognitive-behavioral theoretical approach, few have attempted to evaluate its effectiveness with this client population (Breer, 1987; Becker & Kaplan, 1988). O'Brien (1985) acknowledged that clinicians working with adolescent sex offenders "have been playing it by ear for the most part, and we must begin to validate our hunches, hypotheses, and models by undertaking sound and comprehensive research" (p. 163). One recent study conducted with the sex offender program in Travis County evaluated the effectiveness of cognitive-behavioral, self-instructional training with adolescent sex offenders (Knox, 1994), and other researchers have been researching and developing theory-based models (Becker, Kaplan, & Kavoussi, 1986; Lane & Zamora, 1985; Monasterski & Smith, 1985; Smets & Cebula, 1987).

Cognitive-Behavioral Therapy with Adolescent Sex Offenders

The cognitive-behavioral approach has been documented as an effective treatment modality when working with children and adolescents, especially in a group setting (Kendal & Braswell, 1985; Santostefano, 1985). Feindler's (1987) work with adolescent anger control training is based on the premise that clients with anger control problems have behavioral and cognitive deficits. Her self-management program, designed to modify emotional arousal and aggressive responses, has been found to be effective in both outpatient and residential settings (Feindler, Marriott, & Iwata, 1984; Feindler et al., 1986). Cognitive-behavioral self-instructional programs have also been used with children and teens who have problems with impulse control, poor social skills, and empathy training (Meichenbaum, 1977; DeLange, Barton, & Lanham, 1981; Copeland, 1981; Corcoran, 1982; Jackson, 1987; Lochman, White, & Wayland, 1990).

Cognitive deficiencies and distortions have been identified by clinicians as targets for intervention with adolescent sex offenders. Their numerous thinking errors, or cognitive distortions, help to support and justify their deviant behaviors. These thinking errors include misperceptions, such as making excuses for the sexually offending behaviors, misinterpreting affectional cues as sexual in nature, blaming the victim, minimizing the impact of the offense, and denial of sexually offending problems.

Cognitive deficits, which involve insufficient or limited cognitive activity, are associated with this client population by a lack of problem-solving and coping strategies, poor social skills, a lack of empathy, and learning and developmental disabilities. These deficits usually have been due to a lack of appropriate socialization and learning experiences and impairment in cognitive processing capabilities. Social-skills training and developing an increased repertoire of problem-solving and coping skills are as essential to the treatment process as the cognitive restructuring techniques that address thinking errors and cognitive distortions.

Cognitive restructuring begins in the first phase of treatment with acknowledgment of responsibility for the sexually offending behaviors and overcoming denial and minimization. To facilitate this process, self-monitoring is implemented in this phase to target both prosocial and antisocial behaviors to be worked on in therapy. This process also identifies the specific types and frequency of target behaviors for intervention.

Cognitive restructuring continues with process recording in a daily journal about the experiences, feelings, and thoughts of the client. The purpose of this procedure is to facilitate awareness of the interrelatedness of these processes and to assist the client in identifying patterns. Specific techniques are also implemented to increase self-awareness and to develop problem-solving and coping skills. Modeling and role play are methods that engage clients in experiential learning exercises with other group members and the therapists. They enable clients to process alternative interpretations and solutions, and provide an opportunity to practice new skills. Positive reinforcement and response-cost methods involve rewarding desired behaviors and punishing negative or inappropriate actions. These methods can be supplemented by parents to support treatment goals and ensure consistency in therapy. Homework assignments provide the client with actual experience in trying out the alternative skills.

The process of cognitive restructuring also involves identifying cues or triggers to high-risk situations and dysfunctional behaviors. The client's understanding of the relationships between feelings, physiological reactions, and behaviors is integral to this component of therapy. The client is helped to identify the faulty information-processing errors that maintain or support continuation of inappropriate thoughts, emotions, and actions. Figure 12.1 presents a

Figure 12.1:   Cognitive-Behavioral Framework for Adolescent Sex Offenders

	I. Cognitive Level	II. Affective Level	III. Behavioral Level
A	Distortions Thinking errors Blaming others Minimizing Miscues Misinterpretation Denial	Anger Depression Frustration Displeasure Hurt Offended Threatened	Aggression Offending Violence Delinquency Threatening Fighting Antisocial
B	Coping self-statements Problem-solving Cognitive processing	Empathy Range of Feelings Expression of Feelings	Social skills Assertiveness Communication
C	Id cues and triggers Id problem Generate solutions Evaluate consequences Select solution Reinforce self	Id feelings Id autonomic reaction Deep breathing Relaxation methods Emotional release	Self-monitor Self-reinforce Self-control Role play Homework Response cost
D	Decrease/eliminate cognitive distortions and develop coping and problem-solving skills.	Increase awareness, range, and expression of feelings. Develop empathy.	Improve social skills and communication and decrease aggression.

framework that conceptualizes how this approach is used in clinical work with adolescent sex offenders.

Section *A* of this framework identifies specific *treatment issues* for juvenile sex offenders at the *cognitive, affective,* and *behavioral* levels. Section *B* presents the various *deficit areas* at each level that require intervention in order to impact on the identified treatment issues. It should be noted that clients vary developmentally in skills levels and deficits, with some of them having more problems than others. An advantage to working in the group setting is that clients who have more appropriate, prosocial skills can model them for other group members. Interaction between peers facilitates the social learning process, and it provides an environment in which the client can practice new skills.

Section *C* includes the specific *intervention techniques* used to effect change in the client. It is important to remember the interactive nature at each of the three levels, which means that change at one level will impact on the other levels as well. This also means that in order for the client to reach the goals of treatment, interventions should target all the levels, since the client must learn and develop more appropriate coping and problem-solving skills that involve making changes in cognitions, feelings, and behaviors.

Section *D* contains the treatment goals for each of the three levels. To meet these goals, the client has to learn and develop new skills as well as eliminate or reduce other behavior problems and cognitive distortions. Clients often show change at the behavioral level immediately, with the cognitive and affective levels requiring more time and work in treatment. Unless change is made at those levels as well, most clinicians would consider the client still at high risk for reoffending, since it is more difficult to control or change behaviors unless one has also worked on the cognitive distortions and emotional issues that have helped maintain those behaviors in the past.

This framework does not include all the areas targeted for treatment with adolescent sex offenders; however, it does provide a format for understanding the relationships between the cognitive, affective, and behavioral levels, as well as the interrelatedness between the issues/deficits, interventions, and goals of treatment. While the effectiveness of cognitive-behavioral techniques has been documented in other problem areas with children and adolescents, there has been little research into the effectiveness of this approach with juvenile sex offenders. Areas of treatment that may benefit from using this model include social and communication skills, impulse control, anger management, self-esteem, empathy building, and the sexual offending cycle and behaviors. Although many clinicians working with this client population espouse a cognitive-behavioral approach, empirical study is needed to develop a systematic theoretical model for working with adolescent sex offenders.

Direct Practice Roles and Ethical Issues

Direct practice roles with adolescent sex offenders can be found in several settings within the overall juvenile justice setting. The traditional role has been that of probation/parole officer, which includes many responsibilities such as case management, supervision, brokering and referral, crisis intervention, counseling, advocacy, and education. Specialized case loads for adolescent sex offenders have been implemented in many communities, so that training and education about this client population can be ensured for those professionals working with them. In the Travis County program, specialized case loads and training have been critical to providing consistency and coordination of services between probation and treatment providers. One problem experienced in this program prior to the implementation of specialized case loads was that treatment providers had to contact numerous probation officers. This required more time and paperwork than in the current situation, where only three probation officers are working with the juvenile sex offenders. It has also been helpful in scheduling meetings and staffings for clients and their families, and when providing training workshops for other involved professionals.

These clients and their families are difficult to work with, having multiple problems and requiring more supervision and case management than other types of offenders. This results in burnout and high turnover rates for probation officers, whose case loads are specialized with this client population. Also, personal issues may be triggered for some professionals, who themselves may have experienced sexual abuse or know someone who has. Support and case supervision services for probation/parole officers working with adolescent sex offenders, such as peer supervision and support groups, team-building experiences and workshops, staff retreats, and referral for counseling can be helpful in addressing these issues.

Working with juvenile sex offenders requires a multidisciplinary approach, as it is common to have contacts with law enforcement, attorneys, court judges and personnel, mental health providers, and school teachers and administrators. The team approach reflects the need for consistency and coordination of services and treatment goals, which can be difficult when those involved have different perspectives and priorities. It is important that the professionals involved in this setting be knowledgeable about all of these systems, so that potential problems can be minimized. Dilemmas associated with confidentiality, social control, and power/authority can become problems when working within these complex systems, and being familiar with the different legal and ethical issues is vital.

Problems with confidentiality, for example, led to policy changes in providing counseling services for juvenile sex offenders in Travis County. Initially, clients would be accepted into the treatment program prior to adjudication, if the juvenile and his or her family admitted responsibility and cooperated voluntarily. However, confidential information from the counseling sessions was then used by the prosecutors. This often resulted in juveniles receiving sentences of incarceration, instead of probation, which had been recommended by both the probation officer and the counselors.

Confidentiality issues also arise after adjudication, when information revealed by clients in counseling sessions should be reported to the probation officers. Therapists have to ensure that their clients understand which information will be shared with others, including parents or other involved professionals, and which will remain confidential. When probation rules or supervision guidelines have been violated, the clients should be encouraged to take responsibility and report them directly to their probation officers; the therapists should offer to help with that process—if the client wants the assistance. Of course, mandatory child-abuse reporting laws should be explained to the clients and their families before entering treatment, since any reoffending behaviors or disclosures of other child sexual abuse have to be immediately reported.

One of the most difficult roles for probation officers is that of social control agent. Responsibilities of the probation officer include monitoring and supervising the probation rules and guidelines for each client. (Sex offenders generally have very strict curfew and supervision guidelines.) It is common for sex offenders not to be allowed any unsupervised contact with children two or more years younger than themselves, and to have no contact with their victims unless approved by the therapists and probation officer. Some may be required to wear electronic monitors, which can be an effective tool for dealing with infractions of these rules.

Other issues of social control and power/authority are apparent when working with an involuntary client population, particularly those with high levels of denial and minimization. For those clients who maintain their innocence, even after being adjudicated and placed on probation, a period of time is needed for participation in treatment to help the client to admit to the sexually offending behaviors. If after a reasonable length of time (perhaps six to eight weeks), the client is still denying the offense, a polygraph examination may be required. Should the client pass the polygraph test, a review hearing can be scheduled to revise the case treatment plan; however, there has never yet been any one who has passed a polygraph. Those who fail typically come back to the group ready to talk about the sexual abuse.

Another issue with power/authority is trust in the client/therapist relationship. Treatment providers are often associated with the juvenile justice system, and prior contacts with law enforcement, the courts, and the juvenile justice system tend to arouse suspicions and distrust among clients referred for mandatory counseling. A written treatment contract that clients and their families must sign might enhance client trust. Issues of confidentiality and reporting can be addressed in the contract, as well as other information about the treatment program, such as group and supervision rules and treatment issues and goals.

This issue of authority is very different for the therapist than for the probation officer, who is the one expected to have such power. Since there are more opportunities for mental health professionals to practice directly with juvenile offenders, ethical dilemmas experienced in these areas of confidentiality and power require careful deliberation. A common problem is that of disclosure of other offending behaviors. Clients are expected to be honest about their offending behaviors and past histories, but to do so may jeopardize them. For example, a client who had been making good progress in treatment disclosed on probation that he had also sexually abused another relative several years ago, an incident that had never been reported. From the therapist's perspective, this disclosure is positive indication of the client's progress in treatment, but from the legal perspective, the disclosure must be reported to authorities. This could result in other penalties or incarceration for the client. When faced with this type of situation, therapists may feel torn between the therapeutic issues and the legal mandates.

Direct-practice opportunities with adolescent offenders have increased in the past decades. For counselors working with adolescent sex offenders, opportunities can be found in the juvenile justice system itself, with specialized programs and services provided through criminal justice funding and other child abuse grants available through local, state, and federal programs. The Austin Police Department Victim Services Program received a five-year grant that funded three counselor positions to work directly with child abuse investigators—jobs that eventually were funded through the City of Austin after the grant period ended.

The Travis County Juvenile Court budget has funded its sex offender program for the past eight years, providing outpatient counseling services and residential placement. The probation department also utilizes student interns and volunteers to work directly with youth through a variety of programs. The University of Texas School of Social Work has a field intern unit at the court, where opportunities for counseling, tutoring, role modeling, recreational activities, and group work are available. Other local universities also have opportunities for their students to work with juvenile offenders in gang prevention and drug abuse counseling and prevention programs and in programs aimed at keeping at-risk youth out of the criminal justice system.

Another direct-practice role involves working with the families and victims of the juvenile offenders. A collateral support service used in Travis County has been the Family Preservation Program, administered through the Austin-Travis County Mental Health and Retardation Department (ATCMHMR). Counselors there have small, specialized case loads, providing family therapy in a home setting. This type of service is essential for adolescent sex offenders who have molested a relative or person in the home. Many juvenile offenders are separated from their families and placed with relatives, in shelters, or in residential treatment facilities. For reunification to occur, the offenders, the family, and the victim(s) must all participate successfully in individual, group, and family therapy. For therapists working with the offenders, collateral services must be implemented with the families, but community resources or financial problems sometimes create barriers to this goal. Contracts with other treatment providers may be needed to provide such services for low income families or those without insurance and funds to obtain other counseling.

Other clinical settings are available for direct practitioners working with adolescent sex offenders. Many residential treatment programs offer specialized services and counseling for adolescent sex offenders, but even now it is difficult to place this client population for lack of bed space and financial funding. It is also understandable that many residential treatment facilities are reluctant to accept juvenile sex offenders into their programs without access to specialized services and personnel, due to safety and supervision concerns for their other clients. Several of the clients in Travis County are placed in residential programs, where they are transported to the offense-specific group treatment program sponsored by Travis County Juvenile Probation. Coordination and collateral contacts between mental health providers is critical in these settings to ensure consistency in treatment goals.

Incarcerated juvenile sex offenders can receive counseling services through inpatient programs. In some programs, intensive group and individual therapy is available on a daily basis. Clients may be required to participate and graduate successfully from the program before release or parole. Even after release, juvenile sex offenders are often referred for follow-up outpatient counseling services as a condition of parole, to ensure maintenance of behaviors and provide support for the transition back into the community.

Other roles encountered in the juvenile justice system include that of researcher and educator. Opportunities to conduct research through the sponsorship of juvenile courts are increasing for several reasons. There is an increased demand and interest in evaluating the effectiveness of treatment services, both for validation of client improvement and for substantiating funding requests. Research studies focusing on juvenile offenders are being conducted through joint efforts by the juvenile justice system and higher education institutions. The emphasis on conducting research to evaluate direct practice with clients has also increased at the academic level.

The opportunities for leadership roles by juvenile justice professionals and educators in the areas of research and direct practice are challenging for the future. With the increase of juvenile crime being reported nationwide and the resulting reactionary fears of the public and the press, empirical research and theory-based treatment models will be more important than ever. There is great concern and debate on how to deal with juvenile offenders, and there are many different opinions on how to best serve this client population as well as to ensure the public's safety. Sound empirical research and documentation and validation of services will be essential to recommendations for rehabilitation programs for juvenile offenders.

Direct Practice Issues with Adolescent Sex Offenders

One of the most difficult issues in direct practice with juvenile sex offenders is that of social control. The legal sanctions concerning client confidentiality have already been introduced in this chapter, but other problems associated with social control include reporting other criminal or delinquent behaviors, testifying at revocation or review hearings, and sharing information with other collateral contacts, including parents, teachers, or other professionals.

Since mental health professionals may be seen as part of the juvenile justice system, many young offenders try to give the socially desirable response or withhold information that may have negative legal or social ramifications. So reliance on self-reports for evaluation, assessment, or research can result in biased data. Counselors may be perceived as having both direct and indirect control over their clients; indirectly, through the therapeutic relationship with the client, and directly, through the authority invested by the court or probation system.

These social-control issues address community and victim safety concerns. For example, juveniles on probation for a sexual offense may not be permitted to go to the public parks, recreation centers, or swimming pools where younger children are, unless accompanied by a responsible supervising adult—one who knows why the youth needs strict supervision. Such supervision may extend to friends' homes and schools, which creates dilemmas for these teenagers, who may not want their friends, teachers, or neighbors to know about their sexual offending or probation status.

Certain clinical interventions also incorporate elements of power and control, such as administering polygraphs or plethysmographs, covert sensitization techniques involving masturbation satiation and disruption of the deviant sexual cycle, aversive conditioning with electric shock or olfactory aversion to reduce deviant fantasies, and chemical castration with Depo-Provera. Plethysmographs measure penile erection rates, while the client views sexually explicit material, to evaluate inappropriate arousal patterns. Masturbation satiation requires that the client masturbate for a long period of time to an inappropriate fantasy, until the exercise becomes painful or the client has negative responses, which is supposed to deter future similar fantasies. Aversive conditioning techniques also intend to produce negative conditions when the client is presented with inappropriate sexual material. There are ethical concerns about the use of these methods with adolescent sex offenders, especially considering the lack of empirical research on the effectiveness and consequences of such techniques with this client population.

Cultural diversity is another issue for direct practitioners in many communities. For instance, bilingual services may be needed for parents who do not speak English. Cultural and class differences can be issues in groups as well, with adolescents gaining knowledge about other cultural traditions and experience in relating to individuals of different races or ethnicities. Respect for others' beliefs and values is stressed, and racist or sexist comments should not be allowed in group sessions. Of course, issues of gender and homosexuality are two other areas for discussion and exploration in group sessions, particularly when the clients are trying to develop healthy, appropriate attitudes and values about sexuality.

Most adolescent sex offenders in treatment programs are males, but sometimes female perpetrators are referred as well. Underreporting and bias in sexual standards for adolescent boys and girls contribute to the low rates of female sex offenders involved in the legal system. Many still believe the old adage that a young male is "lucky" to be initiated into sexual activity by an older woman, whereas similar contact between a young female and an older man would be clearly viewed as child abuse. Female sex offenders are generally treated in separate groups or in individual therapy; however, coed groups have been successfully tried with adult sex offenders and could be an option for some programs.

With the trend toward more diversity in our communities, the increased need for education and emphasis on ethnic- and gender-sensitive practice is apparent. A multicultural perspective should be espoused by both mental health professionals and the juvenile justice system. Research instruments and treatment interventions need to be evaluated in relation to cultural and language differences for client populations. And, of course, the problem of institutional discrimination in the criminal justice system looms over the debate about juvenile crime and what to do with adolescent offenders.

This debate rages between those who maintain that the hard-line approach is needed versus those who believe in rehabilitation and treatment. A few programs try to combine these approaches. The controversy over boot camps and work details for certain juvenile offenders is fueled by suspicions that probation and counseling services are not punitive enough or effective in reducing recidivism. Research into the effectiveness of these different programs and services is needed to validate what works and what doesn't. In these days of shrinking budgets, it is imperative that in addressing both funding priorities and client problems, the need for services and the outcomes of the programs are documented.

Research to build upon the knowledge and theoretical base for working with juvenile offenders is also important. Empirical validation of a theory-based model has been emphasized by educators, researchers, and professionals working with adolescent sex offenders. Long-range studies have been difficult to conduct due to problems with tracking clients, confidentiality of juvenile records, and lack of coordination between adult and juvenile justice records. Hopefully, the increase in juvenile crime will be accompanied by a corresponding increase in funding and research to address this problem.

Evaluating Self-Instructional Training
with Adolescent Sex Offenders

A review of a study conducted with adolescent sex offenders in Travis County, Texas, is presented as an example of the type of research that can be useful to clinicians and juvenile justice professionals. The primary purpose of this study was to evaluate the effectiveness of cognitive-behavioral, self-instructional training in reducing the incidence of problems with "aggressive" and anti-social behaviors. A necessary assumption associated with this purpose is that adolescent sex offenders give evidence of problems with these behaviors in the clinical range. However, there is little documentation of the extent of these problem behaviors with this client population, so the study also empirically tested this assumption.

The second purpose of this study was to determine if cognitive-behavioral intervention techniques are effective in developing and increasing prosocial behaviors and problem-solving skills in the client population. The assumption that this client population has the capacities and capabilities to achieve these goals must take into account the age and developmental level of the juveniles. The age range can be a factor in that the developmental capacity for cognitive restructuring and problem-solving varies, depending on the level of maturity of the client, and many of the adolescents have learning disabilities and attention deficit disorders that can also impact on their capabilities.

The sample for this research study consisted of twenty-five subjects who were on probation for sexual offenses through Travis County Juvenile Court during the time frame of this study. These subjects were already participating in the juvenile sex offender program group therapy sessions that had been court ordered as a condition of probation. There were forty clients in the program when the study was implemented, but because client participation was voluntary, data on only 63 percent of the clients in the treatment program were collected.

All of the subjects were male adolescents, ranging in age from thirteen to eighteen, with a mean age of fifteen. Hispanics comprised 56 percent, African Americans 24 percent, and Caucasians 20 percent. Twenty-three of the subjects were attending school, with the majority being in the eighth or ninth grade (64 percent). Eight (32%) of the subjects were attending special education classes, and 60 percent had a history of academic or behavioral problems at school.

Only 56 percent of the subjects lived at home or with relatives, while the others were in institutional treatment. Seventeen (68%) of the subjects had been or were receiving other types of mental health treatment, including in-home services, individual and family therapy, residential or in-patient services, and medication. Three of the subjects were on medication for Attention Deficit Hyperactivity Disorder, and one was on an antidepressant.

Fifteen (60%) of the parents or primary caregivers of the subjects participated in the research study. They completed daily monitoring forms and other standardized testing instruments used in the study. The adolescents also completed the daily self-monitoring forms and standardized measures, and participated in the weekly group therapy sessions (three groups) during the four-month period of this study.

The research design consisted of two components. The first component involved standardized tests, used to measure the extent of the problems shown by the subjects in the areas of antisocial and prosocial behaviors and as pre-post test measures to evaluate the effectiveness of the self-instructional training. Both the parents and the adolescents completed these tests, which included the Child Behavior Checklist (CBCL) and Youth Self-Report (YSR) (Achenbach & Edelbrock, 1983a), Matson's Evaluation of Social Skills with Youngsters (MESSY) (Matson, 1990), the Revised Behavior Problem Checklist (RBPC) (Quay & Peterson, 1987), and the Social Problem-Solving Index (SPSI) (D'Zurilla & Nezu, 1990).

The second component of the research design was the multiple baseline, single-case design that used the daily self-monitoring forms to evaluate treatment effectiveness. Only twenty-three of the subjects participated in this component, with the adolescents being distributed among the three therapy groups in the treatment program. The baseline phase for the groups consisted of fourteen days, twenty-one days, and twenty-eight days, respectively, with an intervention phase of eight weeks for each group.

Follow-up phases for the groups were conducted for a two-week period one month after the intervention phase had been completed.

Each subject completed a daily self-monitoring form that measured both antisocial and prosocial behaviors (See Appendix 1, Behavior Checklist). The data were then charted on graphs for visual analysis and to determine any statistical significance. The parents also completed the daily monitoring form, and their data also were graphed to evaluate significance and for triangulation with the adolescent self-reports.

During the baseline phase, the adolescents completed the self-monitoring Behavior Checklist every day and attended the regular group sessions, which did not include cognitive-behavioral self-instructional interventions. At the start of the intervention phase, the adolescents began completing Daily Thought Record I (Stark, 1990), which is the first step in the process of cognitive restructuring (see Appendix 2). By identifying their feelings and accompanying thoughts and behaviors, this thought record helped the client identify environmental cues or triggers that elicit certain emotions. It also emphasized the interactive nature of emotions, thoughts, and behaviors, so that clients would begin to understand the patterns and dynamics of this interaction in their own life situations.

During the first group session, the purposes of the thought record were explained and examples were discussed to provide information about completion of the forms. The adolescents were asked to think about the last time each had experienced either happiness, sadness, or anger. They then completed the sample thought records by writing what was happening, what he or she was doing, and what he or she was thinking at the time of that feeling. The group then discussed the completed forms to identify any particular patterns or interactions between the feelings, behaviors, and thoughts. After the discussion, the group leaders distributed a binder with seven behavior checklists and thought records to each of the group members, with instructions to complete and return the forms at the next group session.

At the second group session, the completed behavior checklists and thought records were turned into the group leaders, and the adolescents each received seven more of both forms for the next week. The self-instructional training continued with discussion of the types of feelings the clients had experienced and monitored the previous week. After identifying the specific emotions, the group members discussed their autonomic reactions accompanying the feelings. As most of the adolescents did not understand the term "autonomic reactions," the therapists asked them instead to identify their body or physical reactions when experiencing the emotions. For example, one of the adolescents related that whenever he started to get angry, he would get flushed in the face, start breathing rapidly, and clench his fists. The importance of identifying such autonomic reactions was so the client could begin to cue into the triggers and use self-control and coping statements to minimize the emotional reactions.

The use of coping self-statements to minimize or control autonomic reactions is a critical step in self-instructional training, since externalizing behaviors and impulse-control problems are generally reactive in nature. By enabling the client to identify and process feelings and physiological reactions and begin self-control methods, the client can then begin coping and problem-solving. Coping self-statements are devised to calm down or focus the client to a level where emotional reactions are not interfering with problem-solving.

Each adolescent was asked by the therapists to think of at least one coping self-statement, something they usually said to themselves to calm down or relax when upset or emotional. The clients then wrote these statements on index cards, which they were to keep handy for easy reference during the week. Examples of some of the coping self-statements are "blow it off," "chill out," "it's not worth it," and "be cool."

The homework assignment for that week was to continue identifying the physical reactions and environmental cues for certain emotions or situations, and to also use their coping cards whenever they got angry, upset, sad, frustrated, or out of control. The goal of this assignment was to provide practice in developing these skills in real-life situations.

At the third week of the intervention phase, the subjects again turned in their behavior checklists and thought records and received another week's supply. The group now focused on learning deep breathing and relaxation methods. The therapists had the adolescents learn and practice deep-breathing exercises and also identify any physiological changes or reactions from the exercises. The group members also participated in a relaxation exercise, where the therapists instructed them on muscular tension building and release techniques. This technique enabled the client to physically experience muscle stress and tension and compare those physiological reactions to more relaxed states. The relaxation exercise was one that the adolescents could easily use on their own, and the homework assignment for the week was, if possible, to practice the deep breathing and relaxation exercises whenever they got upset, stressed out, or angry, or at night before going to bed. The goal of the assignment was for the subjects to become more familiar with ways to self-control autonomic reactions, and to begin incorporating the relaxation techniques every day.

Week four of the intervention phase introduced Daily Thought Record II (Stark, 1990) (see Appendix 3), to replace the Thought Record 1. This thought record continued the self-instructional training by adding the problem-solving process to the form. The client was to identify his or her feelings, thoughts, and behaviors as on the first thought record, but then to identify the evidence that supports the validity of those feelings, thoughts, and behaviors. This step was critical in identifying cognitive distortions or miscues from the social environment, by asking clients to identify specific evidence or information to validate their beliefs.

The next step was to identify and generate alternative ways of thinking or other possible solutions to the situation. The purpose of this step was to provide clients with the experience of trying to figure out other available options, instead of reacting in the same identified pattern of behaviors and thoughts. This was aimed at increasing their ability to solve problems more appropriately.

The last step in this process was to identify the possible consequences of the alternative thoughts or behaviors in order to analyze them and choose the best available option. The homework assignment for the week was to complete the second thought record every time they felt sad or angry, and to continue the coping self-statements and relaxation techniques as needed.

The second thought record was completed, along with the daily behavior checklist, throughout the rest of the intervention phase. Week five focused on discussion of the completed thought records to identify specific situations or problems the clients were experiencing, and then to collaborate with other group members on possible alternatives or solutions. The group members were then asked to role-play the specific situations to gain experience and practice in developing appropriate prosocial skills when dealing with the problems. When adolescents were successful in the role plays, positive reinforcement was given by both the therapists and the group members to encourage using these new skills. When the clients were unsuccessful in the role plays, the group members and therapists tried to point out positives but also discussed ways to improve the process or their social skills.

Homework assignments at this point began to be more individualized to the subject's specific situation or problem area. For example, if the adolescent was shy and introverted, the homework assignment would be to talk to at least three people each day or to try to make a new friend at school. If the subject was having behavior problems, such as getting into fights, then the assignment would be to use the new social and problem-solving skills learned in therapy whenever the problem arose. The goals of the homework assignments were to have the subjects practice and use their problem-solving and coping skills in social situations, and to reinforce the self-instructional training by applying it every day.

Week six built upon the initial emotional work done with the deep breathing and relaxation exercises by exploring other appropriate methods of emotional release. The subjects' repertoire of emotional release methods was limited, and typically included such tactics as listening to music or going for a walk. Other possible methods were identified by the therapists and the group members, and the subjects selected several that fit their specific situations or problem behaviors.

For example, if getting mad or angry was a problem, then more appropriate ways of releasing those feelings were identified as possible alternatives to the established pattern. One adolescent would hit his bedroom walls or door whenever he got mad—which damaged both the property and his hands. Several alternatives suggested were to hit a pillow or stuffed animal, to get a punching bag, to tear up old phone books or newspapers, or to pound clay. The homework assignments for week six were also individualized to the specific emotional release work needed by the subjects. This encouraged them to use and practice the new methods identified and explored in the group session.

Weeks seven and eight of the intervention phase continued with more social skills and assertiveness training. The group discussion for week seven focused on the differences between aggression and assertiveness, with the goal of providing the adolescents with more appropriate ways to interact and communicate with others. Learning how to make "I" statements and other appropriate ways of communicating their thoughts or needs to others was important, since many antisocial behaviors and problems stem from the inability to be assertive with others and reliance on aggressive tactics as a defense mechanism.

The subjects and the therapists participated in role plays and used modeling techniques to learn and practice the new social and communication skills. One of the benefits of the group setting was that those members who were higher functioning and had more appropriate social skills were able to be role models for the others. Homework assignments continued to be individualized to each subject's specific needs or problem areas.

Self-reinforcement and response-cost consequences were also implemented at this time. If the subject was successful in applying the problem-solving and coping skills learned in the group to life situations, then some reward system was negotiated with the parents to reinforce the use of these new skills. Reward systems included earning points toward material items, social activities, or extra privileges. The parents were also encouraged to provide other forms of positive reinforcement, such as praise or reminders of their child's success in reaching the treatment goals.

Response-cost systems were also negotiated to provide some form of consequence for continued antisocial behaviors and failure to use the new skills. Examples of response cost would include losing points earned, assignment of extra chores or homework, and restriction of privileges. Shaming or negative feedback from the parents was discouraged, with the focus of the response cost on behaviors and skills, not personal attributes.

Week eight was the final week of the intervention phase, and group discussion focused on reviewing the new skills that had been learned. Feedback from the group members and therapists included observations on change and improvements achieved by the subjects, as well as reflecting on behaviors or problems still needing work. It must be noted that the subjects expressed great relief at no longer having to complete the behavior checklists and thought records. Questions regarding the use of the data were answered by the therapists, and expressions of gratitude and positive feedback about the subjects' participation in the research projects were given to the adolescents.

One month after the intervention phase, the two week follow-up phase was implemented to evaluate the maintenance of change in the target behaviors. Only seven of the adolescents and two parents participated in this phase, reflecting the problems of monitoring burn-out and retention in the program for this sample. The behavior checklists were completed on a daily basis for the two-week period by the adolescents and the parents. Group treatment at that time was not cognitive-behaviorally oriented, with the subjects receiving education on birth control methods and sexually transmitted disease.

This description of the components and techniques used in self-instructional training has provided specific information to elaborate on the cognitive-behavioral framework for working with adolescent sex offenders. These components and techniques targeted all three intervention levels—cognitive, affective, and behavioral. The effectiveness of self-instructional training was measured on the cognitive and behavioral levels only, since the primary purpose of this study was to examine the levels of antisocial and prosocial behaviors and social problem-solving skills.

While affect is an integral part of the change process, the focus for this project was on behaviors and skills, which are more easily monitored than emotions. While empathy training using cognitive-behavioral interventions has been found to be effective with other adolescent populations, this variable was not included for evaluation in this study. Further research in this area would be beneficial, since empathy building is one of the most difficult components of sex offender treatment to address.

Research Findings and Implications

The findings of the research project in Travis County indicated that this client population does evidence problems in the clinical range for antisocial behaviors and deficits in prosocial skills. Results from the Child Behavior Checklist (CBCL) and Youth Self-Report (YSR) (Achenbach & Edelbrock, 1983b) show that these subjects had high T-scores for both internalizing and externalizing behavior problems, with 73 percent scoring within the clinical range on the CBCL and 71 percent scoring within the clinical range on the YSR. Social competence T-scores within the clinical range showed that 73 percent had social deficits, 55 percent had school problems, and 55 percent scored in the clinical range for total social competence problems.

The parental ratings on the Revised Behavior Problem Checklist (RBPC) (Quay & Peterson, 1987) support these findings with the percentage of T-scores within the clinical range as follows: conduct disorder (54%), socialized aggression (23%), attention problems/immaturity (62%), anxiety/withdrawal (77%), psychotic behavior (54%), and motor excess (38%). For scores in the Matson's Evaluation of Social Skills with Youngsters (MESSY), 44 percent scored within the clinical range for having deficits in appropriate behaviors, and 20 percent scored within the clinical range for having inappropriate behaviors. For the parents' MESSY scores, 25 percent indicated deficits in appropriate behaviors, 42 percent showed problems with inappropriate behaviors, and 33 percent fell in the clinical range for the total scores.

The findings from the standardized measures validated the assumptions that this sample shows evidence of problems in the clinical range for externalizing and internalizing behaviors, thought disorders, and social competence. In particular, the high T-scores for depression, anxiety/withdrawal, and attention problems/immaturity reflect significant problems with internalizing behaviors that are not generally a focus of treatment with this client population.

Pre- to post-intervention change was measured via T-tests on the pre-post test scores on the Matson Evaluation of Social Skills with Youngsters (MESSY) (Matson, 1990) and the Social Problem-Solving Index (SPSI) (D'Zurilla & Nezu, 1990). The adolescents completed both measures while the parents completed only the MESSY. Only eight of the adolescents completed both the pre- and post-tests for statistical analysis, and only two of the parents completed the MESSY pre- and post-tests, so statistical tests were not run on the parents scores.

No statistical significance was found with the SPSI; however, on the adolescents' MESSY, significance ($p<0.05$) was found in the social skills scores. The change in the pre- to post-test means was nine points, from 71.1 (pre) to 80.4 (post). The effect size was 0.64, in the average range for clinical studies, according to Rubin & Babbie (1993). Of course, issues of low statistical power (0.11) and the high probability of the risk of a Type II error (0.89) are clearly apparent (assuming on an a priori basis a moderate effect size), due to the low N of the sample size (N=8).

Visual analysis of the single-case, graphed data was done by four independent raters. All of the raters were clinicians who have been in private practice or direct practice settings and had received graduate-level education on single-case research. Interrater agreement was found for only 63 percent of the graphs, and they expressed difficulty in interpreting visual significance, due to ambiguous outcomes on the majority of them. By and large, the findings were therefore inconclusive.

Even though there were several issues and problems associated with this research study, there were benefits as well. The demographic information obtained on the subjects and their parents were the first such data gathered on this client population in the history of the study. This provided valuable information for the clinicians and juvenile court staff that will be used as a data base for further research. The data gathered from the standardized measures brought insight into the different problem areas evidenced by this client population, and were helpful in identifying specific behaviors and patterns to be worked on in counseling. The self-monitoring forms were also beneficial in identifying the frequency and specific types of antisocial and prosocial skills to target for treatment for each client.

Although clear-cut results were not obtained on the majority of the graphs, it remains conceivable that cognitive-behavioral, self-instructional training can be effective with this type of client population. Both the single-case and standardized measures indicated that approximately one-third of the subjects already had acceptable levels for both prosocial and antisocial behaviors, and were not evidencing current problems in these areas. Another third of the subjects indicated improvement in the right direction, which may mean that the intervention was beneficial despite the problems with ambiguity in interpreting the graph data. And, the statistical significance on the pre-post tests for appropriate social skills on the adolescent MESSY supported treatment effectiveness, even considering the low N of eight subjects (one-third of the sample).

The length of treatment and the issues of denial and minimization also need to be considered when analyzing the study's results. Although this project had an eight-week intervention phase, sufficient to gather enough data points recommended by single-case design text, it was probably not enough time to reflect significant behavior changes in this client population. In other words, the reason that most of the graphs were found to be ambiguous but improving may have been that cognitive restructuring is generally considered to be longer-term treatment of one or more years. This time frame for at least one year of therapy is also typical for most programs and clinicians working with juvenile sex offenders.

From the clinical perspective, this research experience brought about additional benefits. The learning process of being able to design, implement, and conduct a project such as this was professionally rewarding. With the current emphasis in mental health professions on evaluating clinical practice and treatment programs, the actual hands-on education was exciting and fulfilling, regardless of the results obtained. Also from the clinical perspective, it is often difficult to evaluate a client's progress in treatment, and the data were particularly helpful in showing the client and his or her parents the specific types and patterns of behavior problems that still needed to be worked on or addressed.

It was also remarkable that this client population cooperated and participated in the study to the extent they did. Considering that this was a voluntary study that required a lot of time and effort by the clients to complete the monitoring forms, it was very surprising that most of the adolescents were motivated enough to follow through. Since denial and minimization are so prevalent with this client population, the clinicians had some doubts that the subjects would report negative, antisocial behaviors. However, the self-monitoring forms reflected reliable data that were triangulated with other sources, such as parental reports and feedback from teachers and probation officers. The honesty of the subjects in identifying and recording these types of problem behaviors was appreciated and speaks to the trust that these clients had in the treatment providers.

An overlooked clinical issue that became apparent from this testing were the extensive problems with internalizing behaviors, such as depression, anxiety, and immaturity. The relationship of these factors to sexually offending behaviors is not clear from current literature on this client population. Future research into these dynamics is needed to evaluate their importance and inclusion in sex offender treatment.

It seems clear that more emphasis in education and specialized curriculum on criminal justice systems and working with juvenile offenders will be needed by higher education in the future. Considering the current situation with violent young offenders in our country, the need for more research and study into the most effective ways of working with this client population is required to try to have a successful impact.

With the opportunities for more direct practice experiences with juvenile offenders by mental health professionals, the knowledge base on which this work is based must be strengthened with empirical research, as well as practice wisdom. Clinicians must also face the challenges of working within a multidisciplinary field in a team approach, which requires knowledge of those other systems and professionals involved with the clients. Many communities are implementing specialized services and programs for adolescent sex offenders, and it is hoped that the examples from the sex offender program through Travis County Juvenile Court have been helpful in giving ideas on how to set up such programs and to access other available community services for this client population.

Appendix 1: Behavior Checklist

Date:_____   Name:_____

Verbal Behaviors
___ Argue/threaten/yell/scream
___ Yell/scream
___ Swear/cuss
___ Talk with adult
___ Make racist/sexist remark
___ Talk back/disrespectful
___ Lie
___ Make assertive statement
___ Make polite remark
___ Compliment another

Task Behaviors
___ Obey rules
___ Disobey rules
___ Do homework
___ Have good grades/job
___ Have poor grades/job
___ Be truant/tardy
___ Be suspended
___ Do chores
___ Be on time
___ Participate

Physical Behaviors
___ Fight/hit
___ Push/shove
___ Pinch/scratch
___ Destroy property
___ Avoid trouble
___ Steal
___ Be sexually inappropriate
___ Show appropriate affection
___ Help another
___ Use coping skills

Personal Behaviors
___ Show positive attitude
___ Show negative attitude
___ Cheat
___ Cooperate
___ Lose temper
___ Use drugs/alcohol
___ Have bad friends/gangs
___ Solve problems
___ Make new friend
___ Control temper

Appendix 2: Daily Thought Record I

Remember to complete this form whenever you have these feelings. Bring your booklet to the group meeting.

Happiness

What was happening:

What I was doing:

What I was thinking:

Sadness

What was happening:

What I was doing:

What I was thinking:

Anger

What was happening:

What I was doing:

What I was thinking:

Appendix 3: Daily Thought Record II

Remember to complete this form whenever you feel sad or angry. Bring your booklet to the group meeting.

What was happening:

What I was doing:

What I was thinking:

The evidence:

Alternative ways of thinking

1.
2.
3.
4.
5.

What might happen:

The thought that I choose to believe:

References

Abel, G., Becker, J., Cunningham-Rather, J., Rouleau, R., Kaplan, M., & Reich, J. (1984). The treatment of child molesters: A manual. Unpublished manuscript. New York State Psychiatric Institute.

Achenbach, T., & Edelbrock, C. (1983a). *Manual for the child behavior checklist and revised child behavior profile.* Burlington: University of Vermont.

Achenbach, T., & Edelbrock, C. (1983b). *Manual for the youth self-report and profile.* Burlington: University of Vermont.

Anderson, W., & Kunce, J. (1979). Sex offenders: Three personality types. *Journal of Clinical Psychology, 35,* 671–676.

Becker, J., & Kaplan, M. (1988). The assessment of adolescent sexual offenders. *Advances in Behavioral Assessment of Children and Families, 4,* 97–118.

Becker, J., Kaplan, M., & Kavoussi, R. (1986). *Measuring the effectiveness of treatment for the aggressive adolescent sexual offender.* Unpublished manuscript. Columbia University College of Physicians and Surgeons, New York.

Blaske, D., & Borduin, C. (1988). *Individual, family, and peer characteristics of adolescent violent offenders and sexual offenders.* Unpublished manuscript.

Borduin, C., Henggeler, S., & Mann, B. (1989). Individual, family, and peer characteristics of adolescent sexual offenders and assaultive offenders. *Developmental Psychology, 25,* 846–855.

Breer, W. (1987). *The adolescent monster.* Springfield, IL: Charles C. Thomas.

Copeland, A. (1981). The relevance of subject variables in cognitive self-instructional programs for impulsive children. *Behavior Therapy, 12,* 520–529.

Corcoran, K. (1982). Behavioral and non-behavioral methods of developing two types of empathy: A comparative study. *Journal of Adolescent Health Care, 2,* 279–286.

D'Zurilla, T., & Nezu, A. (1990). Development and preliminary evaluation of the social problem-solving inventory. *Psychological Assessment: A Journal of Consulting and Clinical Psychology, 2*(2), 156–163.

Deisher, R., Wenet, G., Paperney, D., Clark, T., & Fehrenbach, P. (1982). Adolescent sexual offense behavior: The role of the physician. *Journal of Adolescent Health Care, 2,* 279–286.

DeLange, J., Barton, J., & Lanham, S. (1981). The wiser way: A cognitive-behavioral model for group social skills training with juvenile delinquents. *Social Work with Groups, 4,* 37–48.

Doshay, L. (1969). *The boy sex offender and his later career.* Montclair, NJ: Patterson Smith.

Fehrenbach, P., Smith, W., Monastersky, C., & Deisher, R. (1986). Adolescent sexual offenders: Offender and offense characteristics. *American Journal of Orthopsychiatry, 56*(2) 225–233.

Feindler, E. (1987). Clinical issues and recommendations in adolescent anger control training. *Journal of Child and Adolescent Psychotherapy, 4,* 267–274.

Feindler, E., Eaton, R., Kingsley, D., & Dubey, D. (1986). Group anger-control training for institutionalized psychiatric male adolescents. *Behavior Therapy, 17,* 109–123.

Feindler, E., Marriott, S., & Iwata, M. (1984). Group anger control training for junior high school delinquents. *Cognitive Therapy and Research, 8*(3), 299–311.

Gil, E. (1987). *Children who molest: A guide for parents of young sex offenders.*
    Walnut Creek, CA: Launch Press.
Groth, A. (1977). The adolescent sex offender and his prey. *International Journal of
    Offenders Therapy and Comparative Criminology, 21,* 249–254.
Groth, A., Hobson, W., Lucey, K., & St. Pierre, J. (1981). Juvenile sex offenders:
    Guidelines for treatment. *International Journal of Offender Therapy and
    Comparative Criminology, 25*(3), 265–272.
Groth, A., & Loredo, C. (1981). Juvenile sex offenders: Guidelines for assessment.
    International Journal of Offender Therapy and Comparative Criminology, 25(1),
    31–39.
Guthmann, D. (1986). Snohomish County sex offender project: An assessment of the
    project's impact on client behavior. Unpublished manuscript.
Hazelwood, R., & Warren, J. (1989). The serial rapist: His characteristics and victims.
    FBI Law Enforcement Bulletin, 11–25.
Jackson, E. (1987). Behavior in groups as a predictor of internal empathy and commu-
    nicated empathy. *Social Work with Groups, 10*(1), 3–15.
Kaplan, M., Becker, J., & Cunningham-Rather, J. (1986). Characteristics of parents of
    adolescent incest perpetrators: Preliminary findings. Manuscript submitted for
    publication.
Kendall, P., & Braswell, L. (1985). *Cognitive-behavioral therapy for impuslive chil-
    dren.* New York: Guilford Press.
Knopp, F. (1982). *Remedial intervention in adolescent sex offenders: Nine program
    descriptions.* Syracuse, NY: Safer Society Press.
Knox, K. (1994). Effectiveness of cognitive-behavioral therapy: Evaluating self-
    instructional training with adolescent sex offenders. Ph.D. diss., University of
    Texas, Austin.
Knox, K., & Laredo, C. (1991). Adolescent sexual assault referrals and investigation
    outcomes in Travis County, Texas, 1985–1991. Unpublished manuscript.
Lane, S., & Zamora, P. (1985). A method for treating the adolescent sex offender. In R.
    Mathias (Ed.), *Sourcebook for treatment of the violent juvenile offender* (pp.
    347–354). San Francisco, CA: National Council on Crime.
Lewis, D. (1976). Diagnostic evaluation of the juvenile offender: Toward classification
    of often overlooked psychopathology. *Child Psychiatry and Human Development,
    6,* 198–213.
Lewis, D. O. (1976). Diagnostic evaluation of the juvenile offender toward the clarifi-
    cation of often overlooked psycho-pathology. *Child Psychiatry and Human
    Development 6(4),* 198–213.
Lochman, J., White, K., & Wayland, K. (1990). Cognitive-behavioral assessment and
    treatment with aggressive children. In P. Kendall (Ed.), *Cognitive behavioral ther-
    apy with children and adolescents* (pp. 23–65). New York: Guilford Press.
Maclay, D. (1960). Boys who commit sexual misdemeanors. *British Medical Journal,
    11,* 186–190.
Markley, O. (1950). A study of aggressive sex behavior in adolescents brought to juve-
    nile court. *American Journal of Orthopsychiatry, 20,* 719–731.
Matson, J. (1990). *Matson evaluation of social skills with Youngsters: Manual.* Baton
    Rouge: Louisiana State University Press.

Meichenbaum, D. (1977). *Cognitive-behavior modification: An integrative approach.* New York: Plenum Press.

Monastersky, C., & Smith, W. (1985). Juvenile sexual offenders: A family systems paradigm. In E. Otey & G. Ryan (Eds.), *Adolescent sex offenders: Issues in research and treatment* (pp. 164–175). (DHHS Publication No. ADM 85-1396). Rockville, MD: U.S. Dept. of Health and Human Services.

National Adolescent Perpetrator Task Force. (1988). Preliminary report from the national task force on juvenile sexual offending. *Juvenile & Family Court Journal, 39*(2), 5–67.

O'Brien, M. (1985). Adolescent sexual offenders: An outpatient program's perspective on research. In E. Otey & G. Ryan (Eds.), *Adolescent sex offenders: Issues in research and treatment* (pp. 147–163). (DHHS Publication No. ADM 85-1397). Rockville, MD: U.S. Dept. of Health and Human Services.

Quay, H., & Peterson, D. (1987). *Manual for the revised behavior problem checklist.* Coral Gables, FL: University of Miami, Department of Psychology; New Brunswick, NJ: Rutgers State University, Graduate School of Applied and Professional Psychology.

Rubin, A., & Babbie, E. (1993). *Research methods for social work.* Belmont, CA: Wadsworth.

Ryan, G. (1986). Annotated bibliography: Adolescent perpetrators of sexual molestation of children. *Child Abuse and Neglect, 10,* 125–131.

Ryan, G., Lane, S., Davis, J., & Isaac, C. (1987). Juvenile sex offenders: Development and correction. *Child Abuse and Neglect, 11,* 385–395.

Santostefano, S. (1985). *Cognitive control therapy with adolescents.* New York: Pergamon Press.

Shoor, M., Speed, M., & Bertelt, C. (1962). Syndrome of the adolescent child molester. *American Journal of Psychiatry, 122,* 783–789.

Smets, A., & Cebula, C. (1987). A group treatment program for adolescent sex offenders: Five steps toward resolution. *Child Abuse and Neglect, 11,* 247–254.

Stark, K. (1990). *Childhood depression: School-based intervention.* New York: Guilford Press.

Stickrod, A., Hamer, J., & Jones, B. (Eds.). (1984). *Informational guide on the juvenile sex offender: Three Oregon programs.* Hillsboro, OR: Jim Hamer.

Texas family code. (1988). St. Paul, MN: West.

Texas penal code. (1988). St. Paul, MN: West.

Whalley, L., & McGuire, R. (1978). Measuring sexual attitudes. *Acta Psychiatrica Scandinavia, 58,* 299–314.

Chapter Thirteen

▶ •••••••••••••••••••••• ◀

Social Work Practice with African-American Juvenile Gangs: Professional Challenge

Mary S. Jackson and David W. Springer

The discussion of gangs in this chapter is designed to provide the social worker with an alternative to the common negative perception of African-American gangs/gang members, and to encourage the formation of therapeutic gangs within juvenile correctional facilities. If social workers are not able to alter their negative perceptions about gangs/gang members, effective intervention strategies may not be feasible. A major gap in social work practice would then continue.

There are three images sure to evoke fear in the American public: drugs, gangs, and African American males. All three have generated a great deal of research among criminologists and social workers, yet services provided to gangs/gang members as a result of this extensive research are limited. There is a fear, or reluctance, by social workers to utilize nonquantitative research (Fox, 1985). This feeling among social workers, together with a common fear of working with gangs has severely hampered social work practice with gangs/gang members.

Writings on gangs have generally been negative and thus have fostered negative practice implications. For example, many social workers do not want to work with gangs/gang members because they are perceived as too violent and too resistant to change. However, similar statements could be made about drug-using clients, child molesters, spousal batterers, rapists, and homicide offenders. Yet, social workers do continue to work with these populations.

Why are African-American gangs/gang members viewed differently in social work practice? One speculation is because of an increasing fear permeating both the media and research interpretations. We are bombarded every day with news media stories about young children shooting other youths in rival gang activity. We are constantly reading research about tough, impenetrable, gang members in which most of the results imply the need for social control efforts when working with gangs.

It has also been speculated that African-American gangs are viewed differently because social work practice is changing. Cloward and Epstein (1965) identified this trend three decades ago when they stated that social workers are "upgrading" their clients and leaving the poor behind. With the enactment of licensure laws, a new wave has emerged of social workers who seem to feel quite comfortable with private practice and more uncomfortable in public agencies. The primary objectives of this chapter are to (1) dispel some of the myths and stereotypes surrounding gangs; (2) provide a theoretical framework to guide social work practice with gangs; and (3) illustrate intervention strategies that can be utilized in social work practice with gangs, specifically with therapeutic gangs in the juvenile justice setting. A historical context will first be provided.

History of Social Work Practice with Gangs

Based on documented trends in social work practice with gangs, it appears that historically there have been major gaps in the delivery of services to this population. Spergel (1992) notes: "Professional social workers' interest in gangs has never been strong, even during the heyday of youth outreach or street work programs in the 1950s and 60s" (p. 21).

Though social work practice with African American gangs officially began in the 1880s with the settlement house movement, it actually started long before then. Social workers had been working with gangs before social work was even officially acknowledged as a discipline and before Thrasher (1927) formally acknowledged gangs as a population in need of services. In social work's infancy as a discipline, many social work clients were not specifically identified in workers' notes as gang members, although they themselves may have been very well aware of their status within gangs.

From the time that African Americans were brought to America, gangs have been an integral part of their culture. These gangs originated as a positive force in Africa, where groups of young men would together experience the rites of passage to adulthood. They would continue associating with this same group of individuals, engaging in positive activities and overcoming numerous developmental and societal obstacles. Parents and other village members taught the youngsters to become effective gang members by enhancing their social skills (e.g., hunting) so that they could contribute to the village. As slavery was introduced in America and the African heritage was stripped away (Wiltse, 1965), gangs took on a negative connotation among the African slaves. Just as gangs are known to do today, they met in secret places. They planned escapes, communicated by hand signals understandable only to the gang members, identified each other by distinct clothing, and sent messages through songs. These gangs of slaves often fought violently to claim their turf. Children and women were admitted to gang membership for the same reasons as today—they were less suspicious, and laws regarding children and women were more lenient.

It can be argued that no documentation exists on the presence of African-American gangs during slavery, perhaps because African Americans were allowed almost no formal education until the late nineteenth century, after emancipation. Even abolitionists wrote nothing about African-American gangs, indicating either that they were not aware of gangs within the African-American subculture, or knew it would have been unwise to write about African-American gangs at that time because it would have placed them and their families in danger. Any gang activity then documented in the literature was termed "revolutionary" and not considered to be "gang" activity. Thus, historical documentation of African American gangs during times of slavery is nonexistent. This, in turn, helps to explain the absence of a necessary cognitive framework for researchers and practitioners to follow when attempting to define these gangs from a historical perspective. Furthermore, if we simply rely on current literature to guide our thoughts in deciding what or who constituted such gangs, it becomes apparent that there is no agreement among scholars today (Spergel, 1992).

Our definition of gang is derived from the old African-American notion that "when one of us stands on the corner it is an individual, when there are two of us, it is a gang," as well as from Thrasher's (1927) concept, which defines gang membership both in terms of the interstitial group and by the esprit de corps criteria. Thus, the definition of gang proposed here is similar to that provided by Short (1990): "a group whose members meet together with some regularity, over time, on the basis of group-defined criteria of membership and group-determined organizational structure" (p. 239). Our specific definition of a gang is two or more individuals who have formed bonds for the purpose of meeting basic human needs such as safety and love, who meet regularly, and who have a social system specific to the group.

Social work among gangs evolved from the adverse conditions surrounding slavery, in coordination with the emergence of slave gang activities. People who performed what today is termed social work were in some instances called abolitionists, since they provided services to those slave gang members who were considered by the larger society to be violent packs of ignorant animals who could be easily eradicated (Wiltse, 1965).

Documented work with gangs is sparse, even during the settlement house movement when the primary focus of social workers was the elimination of poverty (Fox, 1985). During the 1950s and 1960s there emerged a renewed interest in social work with gangs, as evidenced by the classic work by Cohen (1955), *Delinquent Boys: The Culture of the Gang,* as well as Liebow's (1967) classic sociological ethnographic work, *Tally's Corner: A Study of Negro Streetcorner Men.* These works, along with the political climate in the United States at the time, provided social workers with a positive base from which to consider practice with African-American gangs. The political climate was instrumental in enabling practitioners to focus their human rights concerns on human dignity within gang populations.

The social and political climate changed during the 1970s and 1980s. Americans developed a heightened outrage toward the violent nature of our society. Thus, there began a movement to target those components of society considered to be the root of the problem: drugs, gangs, and African-American males. Some would argue that there has always been an unofficial war on African-American males (Wiltse, 1965). Gangs were often the recipients of much attention, due to the movement to curb violence. Furthermore, there was an official proclamation from the White House declaring "a war on drugs." Social work practitioners became very active in this war on drugs and have not only provided relevant research in the field (McNeece & Dinitto, 1994), but have also continued to delineate intervention strategies specific to chemical-using populations (Delgado, 1990; Jackson, in press).

During the 1990s, the government has been concerned with implementing social control efforts. However, there continues to be fear in the hearts of the American people both for violent domestic incidents (e.g., the bombing of the Alfred P. Murrah Federal Building in Oklahoma City in April 1995) and for violent incidents abroad (e.g., the Gulf war). The current climate of social work practice is indicative of a fearful societal climate. Additionally, there is a need to identify and suppress all acts that may be considered violent. African-American gangs/gang members have been classified as violent in nature and thus are placed in a position of lesser importance in social work practice and of greater importance in the research about gangs by sociologists and criminologists. Numerous conceptualizations are presented in the literature on gangs.

Literature Review

Current literature on gangs has focused primarily on violence, drugs, and gang migration (Howell, 1994). The literature on African-American male gangs provides varying perspectives on how to view this population. Thrasher's (1927) conceptualization demonstrated an important perspective on how to look at African-American male gangs. He suggested that they evolved as a result of limited opportunities for success within American society. Cloward and Ohlin (1960) later termed this occurrence as "blocked" opportunity. Klein (1971) viewed gangs as being a natural phenomenon in which adolescents caught up in identity crises (Erikson, 1955) could find some means of satisfaction. Yablonsky (1966) promulgated a notion of a personality deficit in African-American gang members. He considered them to be extremely violent sociopathic youths who lived primarily in ghettos.

As the current emphasis in the social and political arena has been to control gangs, the literature has likewise moved in this direction. With few exceptions, contemporary literature on African-American gangs focuses on the need to provide youth service programs and gang units (Siegel & Senna, 1994). Spergel (1992) has noted a major gap in the research, as there is very little focus on gangs in juvenile correctional facilities. Realization of the need for such services has been intensified by the personal autobiographies of former African-American gang members (Scott, 1994), as well as by a new challenge to social work professionals to become more involved in practice with gangs (Spergel, 1992). An integral aspect of this challenge is that social workers should be aware of the prevalence of illicit drug use among delinquent juveniles.

The literature addressing delinquent juveniles' behavior as it relates to drug use is widespread. This issue is mentioned in an attempt to demonstrate a positive correlation between gang members engaging in drug use and delinquent behavior, not to imply that all gang members are engaging in delinquent behavior or in using drugs. Kingery, Pruitt, and Hurley (1992) cited that adolescents who were using drugs, as compared with those who were not, engaged in violence more often, took risks that predisposed them to assault, and were assaulted more both at school and outside of school. Kang, Magura, and Shapiro (1994) found that of 427 inner-city male adolescents in a New York City jail, 23 percent had used cocaine or crack in the month prior to being arrested and 32 percent had reported chronic use. According to Irvin and Maag (1993), factors that contribute to the onset of substance abuse in adolescents include the adolescent's peer relations, sociocultural conditions, self-concept, familial matters, and social competence. Greenwood (1992) reported that adolescents raised in impoverished urban communities are at high risk for engaging in drug use and drug dealing, and that such juveniles often demonstrate behavioral problems and associate with delinquent peers. Furthermore, annual rates of delinquent activity among fourteen to twenty year old subjects increased directly with more serious drug activity (Johnson et al., 1991).

Debate on community involvement and implementation of community projects has been widespread in contemporary gang literature (Jackson, 1989; Miller, 1990; Spergel, 1986). However, there is limited information on these community intervention strategies. Goldstein and Huff (1993) and Fox (1985) are among the few who provide some actual practical intervention strategies for social workers.

There is a great deal of literature about African-American male gangs; however there is limited insight into how practitioners can effectively work with this population. As Davis and Proctor (1989) have stated, "There is no evidence which suggests that group treatment is more or less suitable for any particular ethnic group" (p. 116). Within the empirical literature found on gangs, there has been no discussion of the need to work with gangs from an African-American perspective. The closest we come to finding this perspective has been in considering implications of culturally sensitive models within the context of practice.

Services to African Americans are considered suspect because of the theoretical models utilized (Green, 1982). Many of these theoretical conceptualizations view the client as the problem and focus on the limitations of the client. Hill's (1972) classic work, *The Strengths of Black Families,* identified strengths of African Americans within the family context. Karenga (1994) and Asante (1988) utilized a systematic approach to formulate a theoretical conceptualization to guide social work practice with African-American male gangs. Asante has termed his theory *Afrocentricism.* This theoretical approach is beginning to appear more frequently in literature focusing on African-American drug users (Jackson, in press). Through reflecting on the notion held by Miller (1982) that gangs have become more violent, and by considering the view held by Goldstein (1991), which questions why some African-American youth become gang members and others do not, we discover that a significant component of gang membership is contingent on an individual identity. Fewer adolescents join gangs if they are clear about their history, understand their heritage, and feel good about who they are. Many gang members, prior to initial recruitment, feel helpless, hopeless, isolated, unsuccessful, and unworthy as human beings.

A method of social work that contains an Afrocentric perspective for working with gangs is therefore proposed. Afrocentricism is a cognitive framework that is an ongoing process (Asante, 1988; Karenga, 1994; Meyers, 1988). This theoretical approach should not be confused with culturally sensitive writings or training that is discussed extensively in social work literature. The Afrocentric framework incorporates the key elements of spirituality, respect for tradition, life as a series of passages, importance of community ("we"), and importance of elders. The Afrocentric world view is based on a holistic belief system (Brookins, 1994) that is immutable and operative (Asante, 1988). Through this world view a gang member is encouraged to consider every aspect of his life, and to transpose the strengths of his historical roots into his present situation. He is first taught to reach a better understanding and awareness of self, and also to consider his strengths and how these strengths can best be utilized. Initially, a gang member verbalizes what is considered to be negative. For example, a gang member may boast of his adventures in terms of a macho image. The role of the social worker is not to judge, display signs of shock, or lecture the adolescent, but to suggest alternative methods of channeling these attributes into avenues that would assist the adolescent with his self-assessment.

One means of rechanneling gang members' energies that has been proven effective by one of the authors, Mary Jackson, is to have the gang members express their feelings on paper. In some instances, if they are unable to write, they can be asked to tape record their feelings. Not only is this process therapeutic for the gang member, but it also provides him with a sense of pride because he has accomplished something that is valued by greater society (e.g., a poem, a painting). For example, the following poem was written by a gang member who had been deemed stupid, unteachable, uneducable, and a "loud mouth" without a serious thought in his mind:

Locked-Down, But Not Out

My little red brother did some dirt,
Tryin' too hard to survive,
Doin' whatever he knew, just to stay alive.

When one-time showed up, to barry him away,
This Piru Love heart said "hell-naw, no-way, not today!"
Since I knew what went down, I said "I did it."
God, how my little brother frowned,
One-time got glad, and threw me to the ground.
My set and my brother is all the real family I got,
Whatever I need, they're here on-the-spot.

U gotta understand,
I will never B alone,
As long as I got my G's,
I know I got a home.
(Anonymous)

Gang members seek a number of values shared by the larger society: security, a sense of identity, love, respect, and a sense of success. An Afrocentric approach to working with gangs/gang members can offer them all of these attributes. This approach can last a lifetime and can hopefully provide a break in the cycle of intergenerational gang families. Any trained social worker can utilize an Afrocentric approach. In order to convince social work practitioners to utilize this approach, however, it is necessary to change current conceptualizations of African-American male gangs/gang members.

Contemporary Social Work Practice with Gangs

The first step social workers must take in order to work effectively with gang populations is to begin with a different opinion of African-American male gangs than is portrayed by the media. Gangs/gang members have been stereotyped as hostile, dangerous, difficult to reach, and a lost cause. Often, the media intermingles the images of drugs, gangs, and African-American males, evoking fear within general American society. This fear can limit social work when the social worker is faced with the possibility of working with clients who represent a combination of all three images. This is not to imply that common sense should be given up in the process, but gang members are no different than many other societal groups. In order to illustrate how other groups in society are similar to gangs, a comparison will be made between fraternities/fraternity members and gangs/gang members. In fact, gangs/gang members are very similar to fraternities/fraternity members (Jackson, 1989).

It is important for the social worker to consider the major similarities and differences between gangs and fraternities in American society. Members of both groups engage in violence (e.g., hazing in fraternities), use drugs, wear distinguishing colors, travel in groups as a show of identity, specify initiation procedures, use secret body language, are secretive about group business, and allow females to wear their colors or pins. This comparison can enable the social worker to view gangs in a different light. This correlation demonstrates how gangs/gang members, like fraternities/fraternity members, use group membership to find a place in the world and as an outlet to express themselves.

When similarities between gang members and members of other groups in society are recognized by social workers, it is more likely that gang members can be influenced by the social workers' efforts. For example, social workers can approach work with gangs/gang members as if the gang members were college students. It is then likely that the social worker can pull from gang members some of the same strengths—such as being creative, analytical, and thoughtful—that professors are able to pull from college students. Consider for a moment the ease with which a gang member memorizes rap songs and the gang alphabet. These same talents could be used to learn English literature. The energy a gang member uses to memorize gang history can be used to learn world history. The skills used to manufacture drugs can be applied to learning chemistry. These attributes can be rechanneled through the efforts of social workers who are willing and patient enough to work with this population. Thus, the social worker's role becomes didactic and empowering.

Special Issues in Contemporary Social Practice with Gangs

Beliefs, attitudes, and values of gangs do not differ greatly from those of other groups within society, as they too seek the same American dream. Because of blocked opportunities, gang members' methods of fulfilling that dream may differ, but their actions can still be rechanneled into acceptable societal behaviors.

Contemporary social work has evolved from a middle-class-value perspective. Consequently, social workers may struggle with ethical issues and conflicts when working with gangs. The workers must be careful not to impose their own personal value system on the clients. For example, a ten-year-old runner explaining how to make crack should not be scolded or made to feel guilty for having this knowledge. Instead, he should be asked to explain why there is a need to use baking soda as opposed to some other substance, or how he determines the correct amounts of cocaine, soda, and water when making crack. The social worker can inquire into how the runner knows that crack should not be placed near acidic substances. All of this information can be related to other subject areas by the social worker, who either individually or in a group can facilitate the client's learning by using the client's experiences, thus "beginning where the client is." For example, the social worker can demonstrate that the client can learn things that may not be drug related by transposing drug-related experiences to socially accepted experiences. From the gang member's perspective this may be all that he knows how to do well, but he will be delighted to discover that he is capable of expanding his knowledge base.

The social worker should not exhibit surprise or shock at information expressed by a gang member. Within the Afrocentric perspective, every occurrence should be treated as part of the developmental cycle and therefore should be expected. All matters should be considered of equal importance in the gang member's life. Further, the mystique, shock value, and degradation of some events should be minimized, diminishing the need for the gang member to exaggerate and to maintain secrets.

Within the Afrocentric perspective, the notion of social support can be incorporated into a treatment philosophy that holds the community responsible for its individuals. The old African proverb "It takes a village to raise a child" illustrates this notion. Some projects funded by the government have been developed by using components of this community approach. However, the difference between a naturally occurring Afrocentric community approach and a planned community project lies in the fact that many of these community projects (1) are not a naturally occurring order because they are rooted in conflicting belief systems and agendas; (2) are superficially imposed onto the community while funding is available and plentiful; (3) solicit and select gang members to meet the needs of project directors or principal investigators; and (4) have the primary purpose of collecting data, or studying a particular gang or community, with little effort invested in the long-range welfare of the community.

Social workers should be encouraged to return to the practice approaches utilized when group work was emerging in the settlement houses in the late

1800s and early 1900s. Group work in the settlement houses provided citizens with opportunities for education, recreation, social action, and the arts. People such as Jane Addams, founder of Hull House in Chicago, used group work to prevent delinquency and to rehabilitate those who were not well adjusted to the demands of society (Addams, 1909). As Toseland and Rivas (1995) write, "settlement houses offered groups as an opportunity for citizens to gather to share their views, gain mutual support, and exercise the power derived from their association for social change" (p. 48). Therefore, contemporary social workers are encouraged to actually go into communities with the primary goal of assisting gangs and communities to better understand their historical strengths. This conceptualization is not limited to working with individuals in the community, however group work as an intervention within juvenile correctional facilities has also proven beneficial both to staff and gang members.

Social Work Practice with Gangs in the Juvenile Justice Setting

In juvenile correctional facilities, administrators have typically expressed concern over the number of gang members incarcerated in their facilities. They claim that the gang members create more problems for staff by increasing the number of altercations and pointless disputes, thus purposely upsetting the unit. The administrators have consistently made attempts to isolate gang members from the larger population only to discover that this is not feasible.

One method of working with incarcerated gang members is for the social worker to form *therapeutic gangs* within the facility, thus providing (1) a sense of security and control conducive to working together, and (2) therapeutic interventions for helping members to address and to explore methods of resolving some of their problems. One reason for forming a therapeutic gang may be to improve security and control within the facility. However, the major purpose is to assist the young men in finding positive alternatives to the negative attitudes, behaviors, and values used in the past.

In the therapeutic gang, members soon discover they have basically experienced many of the same problems. Yalom (1985) refers to this concept as "universality," noting that as members realize that others in the group have similar concerns they will often report "feeling more in touch with the world and describe the process as a 'welcome to the human race' experience" (p. 8). In order to effectively carry out the tasks of forming and maintaining therapeutic gangs, the social worker should have some knowledge of both group and gang dynamics.

Group dynamics is defined by Toseland and Rivas (1995) as the "forces that result from the interactions of group members" (p. 69). Thelen (1954), in his classic group work research *Dynamics of Groups at Work,* explicitly delineated for social workers the properties of group dynamics that should be considered when working with groups: membership, shared purpose, expectations or guidelines, leadership policies/roles, and status system. These group properties should be considered and utilized by the worker who is facilitating the therapeutic gang.

One way the social worker can utilize both group and gang dynamics when working with therapeutic gangs is by implementing the same mechanisms gang members use to begin and maintain gangs. In the same way that gang members *recruit*, social workers should consider each individual's strengths that can be utilized within the group. Gang leadership attempts to *retain* members within the gang. The worker should consider group projects that will not only build the self-esteem of individual group members but will also foster the concept of cohesion within the group. *Cohesiveness* has been defined by Festinger (1950) as "the resultant of all the forces acting on all the members to remain in the group" (p. 274). Cohesiveness is significant to therapeutic gangs, because in order for the therapeutic gang to exist, the members must be motivated to attend, interact within the group, and carry out tasks. Furthermore, as gang members strive to *establish a long lasting bond*, the social worker should also provide an atmosphere that allows members to establish relationships with one another that foster not only working together in the institution but also maintaining ties when they are released into the community.

Working with gangs/gang members in the juvenile justice system takes on a different connotation than when working with them in the community. For example, in the juvenile justice system the social worker is bound by structural constraints, policies, and laws. However, these factors do not negate the potential for positive outcomes. The primary objective remains the same: focus on the strengths of the individual and demonstrate how these strengths can become a positive force for the adolescent when he is released into the community. To ensure that members benefit from the group experience, the worker must recognize some of the constraints and obstacles encountered within the juvenile justice setting.

One such obstacle is that delinquents in the juvenile justice setting will likely be affected by what Garvin (1987) calls the *inmate code*. This norm demands that inmates maintain their respective status with other inmates by maintaining secrecy within their natural circle and aligning with one another against staff. This norm often arises within the context of the therapeutic gang and must be dealt with by helping members comply with it. It is through the group that members are best able to challenge and reevalute their norms.

Garvin (1987) stresses that the social worker must also recognize that the behavior of the member is socially deviant. There are conditions, both within and outside of the juvenile justice setting, that are oppressive in nature. The therapeutic gang needs to adress these social forces in an attempt to increase the possibility of members shedding their deviant roles and taking on more positive alternative ones.

Therefore, it is imperative that the social worker act as a mediator between the agency and the group to ensure that the group's needs are being met. To an extent, in other words, the worker is protecting the group from the agency's social control functions. Agency conditions that could have an impact upon the group are the types of resources the agency makes available to the members, agency policies for disciplining group members, and oppressive attitudes among staff. The worker must be active in helping group members establish goals that complement those of both the group and the agency. The social worker serves as a mediator between agency policy and group objectives, thus making the group a therapeutic experience for the group. Group members can not be expected to challenge their own value and belief systems if the worker and agency are not supportive of their cause.

According to Empey and Erickson (1972), there are various techniques that can be utilized by the social worker throughout the development of a guided group interaction approach. This approach has substantial empirical support and can be applied effectively when working with therapeutic gangs in the juvenile setting. We will provide an overview of guide group interaction, along with specific techniques for working with therapeutic gangs, so that a conceptual framework is established. It is through using this framework and such techniques that the worker will hopefully be able to address various issues within the group such as chemical dependency, behavioral problems, and socialization skills.

Prior to meeting in a group, the social worker's role is to interview each prospective group member individually, informing the member of the group's purpose and goals. Individual contracts should be used to state specific rules and guidelines, such as allowing no communication via hand signals, no physical confrontation and, as a way of ensuring members' confidentiality, no discussion outside of the group about personal information shared by group members.

Garvin (1987) raises an important ethical issue that needs to be addressed in this type of setting. The members of juvenile gangs are not legal adults, and some may have severe mental or emotional problems. When group members are thus incapable of establishing goals for themselves, the social worker is obligated to communicate with their families or legal guardians. Informed consent for such communication should be obtained from the juveniles if at all possible.

When the group is beginning, there will be a considerable amount of conflict and a lack of trust directed at the social worker and the institution by the members. Therefore, "the concern of a group leader should be with fostering interaction among group members and instilling some confidence that it might eventually be effective and rewarding" (Empey & Erickson, 1972). In other words, the social worker needs to be concerned with involving members in the group process, and also with placing a certain amount of responsibility on the members for the success of the group. This involves directing questions asked by members back to the group, for them to struggle with themselves, and hopefully share ideas. It is also appropriate to explore members' feelings about being in the therapeutic gang. Additionally, each member should be invited to tell his story, thus providing history for the rest of the group and necessary information for the social worker to assess the members. The worker will, of course, continuously assess the functioning of both individual members and the group as a whole throughout the life of the group.

It is important to determine, preferably at the first meeting, how new therapeutic gang members will be selected to replace those who may drop out. Because membership selection should be a group decision, the social worker should ensure an equal distribution of individuals from different gangs. Criteria to be considered in the membership selection process are length of commitment to both the juvenile justice setting and the group, as well as prior or present gang affiliation. Having too many members from the same gang, or having members who have absolutely nothing in common, may stifle group processes in this therapeutic gang. The worker should be concerned primarily with cohesiveness when composing the gang.

We realize that achievement of this ideal in the juvenile justice setting may not always be possible; it is meant as a guideline when composing the therapeutic gang. It is likely that members will encourage deviant behavior from each other. Once the group is established and a sense of trust has emerged, the social worker can address deviancy by constructively confronting members on various values and belief systems that lead to such behavior. It is important to mention that the use of strong confrontation in groups has led to much controversy and debate among group workers. Utilizing members who have been in the group for a while as role models is often effective. They can provide encouragement and guidance to those members who are new to the group experience and thus more vulnerable to the social conditions that foster deviance.

After members agree to the guidelines outlined in individual contracts—during the first meeting—the rules and sanctions for the entire group should be established through the use of a group contract. These rules and sanctions should be written and posted at each subsequent group meeting. They should include meeting time, meeting place, the need for confidentiality, and a list of infractions. The treatment team, if there is one at the facility, should agree to rules and sanctions before the group adopts them, because gang norms dictate consistency and the ability to "follow through." This therapeutic gang should function no differently.

Though the group will have input on decisions regarding tasks, projects, and topics for discussion, it is important for the social worker not to allow the first project to be too large, so as to court failure. It should be designed instead to enhance success. The members might first discuss how they can work together as a group and identify some projects that they want to work on. The worker can also have them each identify their own individual strengths as they perceive them; at later meetings group members can identify each other's strengths. Additional projects will emerge as members become more comfortable with each other and develop group trust, thus evolving into a cohesive entity.

As with most involuntary clients in groups, the members will not form a cohesive bond until the later stages of development. It is important that the social worker serve as a model for the group members on how to provide feedback on any confrontation within the group, so that members learn to act constructively in a safe environment. This atmosphere can help members overcome their resistance to the group, although it is likely they will continue to encounter obstacles as the group develops. The group should address obstacles as problems to be solved, while encouraging interaction among members. If these obstacles are not dealt with, there is as greater likelihood that members' motivation will decrease.

Eventually, group members will become bored and impatient with merely sharing their histories and exploring feelings, and they will begin to view the group as a forum for problem solving. Thus, the "planning and orientation" stage of group development will be coming to an end (Northen, 1969), while the stage of "stereotyped problem solving" begins (Empey & Erickson , 1972). During the stereotyped problem-solving stage, members ask the types of questions and give the types of answers they think the leader expects. The social worker must be patient during this period, careful not to confront members too early on their responses. The worker can facilitate this process by helping members realize the here-and-now of what has been occurring in the group up to now, by discussing why the group is ready to move forward and by mediating any conflicts between members. One possible reason for the group to be entering this stage of development is that members may begin to realize they need to do more in the group if this experience is to lead to discharge from the agency.

The next stage is termed "awareness of individual differences and alternatives" (Empey & Erickson, 1972). Members begin to challenge one another, moving away from the somewhat predictable responses found in the previous stage. Thus, there is an atmosphere of openness and honesty about oneself and toward others. The social worker can expect the members to engage in this process gradually, while he or she occasionally reintroduces the notion of deviance. As this period progresses, members will more frequently tend to view each other as unique individuals.

Empey and Erickson (1972) refer to the next stage of development as "group awareness." The social worker's objective in this period is to educate members about group structure and group process, while promoting problem solving within the therapeutic gang. As members learn about norms, types of leadership power, and group dynamics, they will naturally increase their investment in the group as a whole. The assumption that deviance is a result of social forces underlies this educational component of group leadership. The intent is that as members learn more about group processes, they will in turn better understand the social processes that contribute to their deviant behavior.

Finally, Empey and Erickson (1972) call the termination stage "integration of group and program structure." If this stage is reached successfully, members can effectively share what they gained from the therapeutic gang with others throughout the agency and with others in the community after discharge.

Forming therapeutic gangs can be successful within juvenile correctional facilities, although only limited follow-up research has been done to determine the extent of members' involvement with each other after they are released into the community. More research is needed in this area to help guide the effective use of therapeutic gangs in the future.

The Future of Social Work Practice with Gangs

Just as social workers feel the need to become involved in issues of health-care reform, they also have a professional responsibility to develop a greater awareness of factual information about gangs. This greater awareness will allow social workers to dispel some of the myths that may be attributed to limited practice with this population.

There is an immense need for social workers to consider devising and implementing intervention strategies that will aid gangs/gang members. Recently social workers have become alarmed at the number of prisons planned for construction as a result of passage of the crime bill with its specific gang provisions. However, the combined efforts of criminologists, sociologists, psychologists, and social workers could provide a national strategy that may have more positive effects on the "gang problem" than will the construction of more prisons.

As the field of social work becomes more privatized, less attention will be focused on this high-risk group, even though undergraduate programs in social work officially adhere to a generalist model. Social work students are prepared to intervene on micro, mezzo, and macro levels of practice. They are taught social work values and the social work code of ethics, which emphasize the need to respect the human dignity of each client. All accredited social work programs are mandated by the Council on Social Work Education (CSWE) to ensure inclusion of minority/special populations content in their curriculums. Yet even though gangs are considered to be a national problem, most of the programs never mention gangs in the curriculum. But when the students are assigned to their practicum, it is highly likely they will encounter gang members at some point.

CSWE, as the governing educational body, should take greater responsibility in implementing training that allows social workers to become more involved in practice with gangs. If it is in fact true that the social and political climate influences social work practice (Fox, 1985), then we need to consider and assess why gang intervention strategies have not been a major concern in social work practice. Criminologists and sociologists have been continuously involved in researching and devising strategies to work with gangs. However, their strategies have a macro level focus, generally leaving gaps at the micro and mezzo levels. If social work is truly a helping profession, social workers must meet the future challenges of working with gangs.

Conclusion

This chapter provided a discussion of African-American male gangs/gang members, along with a history of social work with gangs and the relevant literature. Contemporary social work with this population was then explored, including special issues to be considered. Additionally, working with gangs in the juvenile justice setting through the use of therapeutic gangs was addressed. Finally, the future of social work with gangs was discussed.

References

Addams, J. (1909). *The spirit of youth and the city streets.* New York: Macmillan.

Asante, M. K. (1988). *Afrocentricity.* Trenton, NJ: Africa World Press.

Brookins, C. C. (1994). The influence of Afrocentric values and racial identity attitudes: Validation of the belief systems analysis scale of African-American college students. *Journal of Black Psychology, 20*(2), 143–156.

Cloward, R., & Epstein, I. (1965). Private and social welfare's disengagement from the poor: The case of family adjustment agencies. In M. N. Zald (Ed.), *Social welfare institutions: A sociological reader.* New York: Wiley.

Cloward, R., & Ohlin, L. (1960). *Delinquency and opportunity: A theory of delinquent gangs.* Glencoe, IL: Free Press.

Cohen, A. (1955). *Delinquent boys: The culture of the gang.* Glencoe, IL: Free Press.

Davis, L., & Proctor, E. (1989). *Race, gender & class: Guidelines for practice with individuals, families, and groups.* Englewood Cliffs, NJ: Prentice Hall.

Delgado, M. (1990). Hispanic adolescents and substance abuse: Implications, research, treatment and prevention. In Larry Davis & Arlene Stiffman (Eds.), *Ethnic issues in adolescent mental health.* Newbury Park, CA: Sage.

Empey, L., & Erickson, M. L. (1972). *The Provo experiment: Evaluating community control of delinquency.* Lexington, MA: Heath.

Erikson, E. (1955). *New perspective for research on juvenile delinquency.* Helen Witmer & Ruth Kotinsky (Eds.), U.S. Department of Health, Education, and

Welfare; Social Security Administration (pp. 9–10). Washington, DC: U.S. Government Printing Office.

Festinger, L. (1950). Informal social communication. *Psychological Review, 57*, 271–282.

Fox, J. R. (1985). Mission impossible: Social work practice with black urban youth gangs. *Social Work, 30*(1), 25–31.

Garvin, C. (1987). *Contemporary group work* (2nd ed.). Englewood Cliffs, NJ: Prentice Hall.

Goldstein, A. (1991). *Delinquent gangs: A psychological perspective.* Champaign, IL: Research Press.

Goldstein, A., & Huff, C. R. (1993). *The gang intervention handbook.* Champaign, IL: Research Press.

Green, J. W. (1982). *Cultural awareness in the human services.* Englewood Cliffs, NJ: Prentice-Hall.

Greenwood, Peter W. (1992). Substance abuse problems among high-risk youth and potential interventions. Special issue: Drugs and crime. *Crime & Delinquency, 38*(4), 444–458.

Hill, R. (1972). *The strengths of black families.* New York: Emerson-Hall.

Howell, J. (1994). Recent gang research: Program and policy implications. *Crime and Delinquency, 40*(4), 495–515.

Irvin, D. M., & Maag, J. W. (1993). Substance abuse among adolescents: Implications for at-risk youth. *Special Services in the Schools, 7*(1), 39–64.

Jackson, M. S. (1989). Juvenile gangs: An analysis. In Willa Hemmons (Ed.), *The state of black Cleveland.* Cleveland, OH: Urban League Publishers.

Jackson, M. S. (in press). Afrocentric treatment of African-American women and their children in a residential chemical dependency program. *Journal of Black Studies.*

Johnson, B. D., Wish, E. D., Schmeidler, J., & Huizinga, D. (1991). Concentration of delinquent offending: Serious drug involvement and high delinquency rates. *Journal of Drug Issues, 21*(2), 205–229.

Kang, S. Y., Magura, S., & Shapiro, J. L. (1994). Correlates of cocaine/crack use among inner-city incarcerated adolescents. *American Journal of Drug and Alcohol Abuse, 20*(4), 413–429.

Karenga, M. (1994). *Afrocentricity and multicultural education: Concept, challenge and contribution.* Department of Black Studies. Long Beach: California State University.

Kingery, P. M., Pruitt, B. E., & Hurley, R. S. (1992). Violence and illegal drug use among adolescents: Evidence from the U.S. National Adolescent Student Health Survey. *The International Journal of the Addictions, 27*(12), 1445–1664.

Klein, M. (1971). *Street gangs and street workers.* Englewood Cliffs, NJ: Prentice Hall.

Liebow, E. (1967). *Tally's corner. A study of Negro streetcorner men.* Boston, MA: Little, Brown.

McNeece, C. A., & DiNitto, D. (1994). *Chemical dependency: A systems approach.* Englewood Cliffs, NJ: Prentice Hall.

Meyers, L. (1988). *Understanding an Afrocentric world view: Introduction to an optimal psychology.* Dubuque, IA: Kendall/Hunt.

Miller, W. (1982). *Crime by youth gangs and groups in the United States.* Washington, DC: U.S. Dept. of Justice, Office of Juvenile Justice and Delinquency Prevention.

Miller, W. (1990). Why the United States has failed to solve its gang problem. In C. R. Huff (Ed.), *Gangs in America* (pp. 263–287). Newbury Park, CA: Sage.

Northen, H. (1969). *Social work with groups.* New York: Columbia University Press.

Scott, C. (1994). *The autobiography of an L.A. gang member.* New York: Penguin Books.

Short, J. F. (1990). New wine in old bottles? Change and continuity in American gangs. In C. R. Huff (Ed.), *Gangs in America.* Newbury Park, CA: Sage.

Siegel, L., & Senna, J. (1994). *Juvenile delinquency: Theory, practice, and law.* New York: West.

Spergel, I. (1986). The violent gang problem in Chicago: A local community approach. *Social Service Review, 60*(1), 94–131.

Spergel, I. (1992). Youth gangs: An essay review. *Social Service Review, 66*(1), 121–140.

Thelen, H. (1954). *Dynamics of groups at work.* Chicago: University of Chicago Press.

Thrasher, F. (1927). *The Gang: A study of 1,313 gangs in Chicago.* Chicago: University of Chicago Press.

Toseland, R. W., & Rivas, R. F. (1995). *An introduction to group work practice* (2nd ed.). Boston: Allyn and Bacon.

Wiltse, C. (1965). *David Walker's appeal.* New York: Hill & Wang.

Yablonsky, L. (1966). *The violent gang.* Baltimore: Penguin Books.

Yalom, I. D. (1985). *The theory and practice of group psychotherapy* (3rd ed.). New York: Basic Books.

PART IV

Educating/Preparing
for the Future

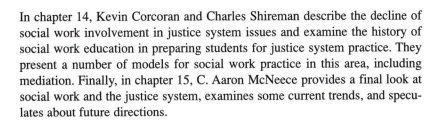

In chapter 14, Kevin Corcoran and Charles Shireman describe the decline of social work involvement in justice system issues and examine the history of social work education in preparing students for justice system practice. They present a number of models for social work practice in this area, including mediation. Finally, in chapter 15, C. Aaron McNeece provides a final look at social work and the justice system, examines some current trends, and speculates about future directions.

Chapter Fourteen

M.S.W. Education for the Justice System: From the Rehabilitative Ideal to Generalist Practice

Kevin Corcoran and Charles Shireman

Social work education for the justice system has changed dramatically since its beginnings at the turn of the century. From the philosophical and ideological optimism of the Progressive Era through the high-water mark of the 1960s, master's-level social work education provided a meaningful influence in juvenile justice and corrections. Today, however, social work education has little influence. This decline would appear to result from a variety of factors. First, a sort of "de-professionalization" has taken place in many public services. Further, criminal justice philosophies and practices tended in recent years to shift away from problem-solving, helping roles toward greater emphasis upon repression and retribution. At the same time, social work education's attention has been drawn more toward other areas of opportunities and need, including work with youth in settings ancillary to official justice agencies, occupational social work, private practice, and others. However, social work's contemporary emphasis on the generalist perspective does increasingly contribute to enabling M.S.W. graduates to practice in a wide variety of settings. This may well contribute to an early repenetration of the traditional correctional agencies, as well as to theory-building and work in other settings related to the justice system.

This chapter reviews the history of M.S.W. education related to the justice setting from its origins to current practice. It traces professional development to the current state of generalist and advanced generalist practice, and considers models of education for social work practice in the justice system.

History of Social Work Education in the Justice System

Social work and social work education's commitment to the justice system has had a long history, dating back to the turn of the century. In 1899 there came the statutorily created juvenile court in Cook County, Illinois—the first such court in the United States and probably in the world. Among the court's founders were some of those who founded the first graduate school of social work housed in a major university—namely, the School of Social Service Administration at the University of Chicago. From that and similar schools came a history of early scholarship on crime and juvenile delinquency.

Social work and social work education's commitment to crime and delinquency grew out of relationships with psychiatry, criminology, charity, and corrections. Work in the juvenile courts, along with medical social work and charity organizations, were the foundations of Mary Richmond's theory of social diagnosis (Richmond, 1917). An early organization of social workers was the National Conference of Charities and Correction, a one-time highly influential organization dating back to 1893. Recognized areas of practice included psychiatric social work in clinics closely aligned with local criminal and juvenile courts. Chief among these were the Juvenile Psychopathic Institute, which began in Chicago in 1909, and the Judge Baker Foundation, founded in Boston in 1916. By 1920 the National Committee on Mental Hygiene included a Division of Delinquency.

One of the intellectual leaders of that early development of social work was William Healy, who Lubove (1971) credits as the person most responsible for introducing social/community psychiatry to the mainstream of social work thought. Healy's views found early enthusiasm at a conference of Chicago's Juvenile Protection Association, held at Hull House in 1908. Healy examined a wide variety of theories of delinquency, including those on hereditary and on biological and social predictors (e.g., cigarette smoking). His major conclusion was that delinquency was not as simple as thought at the time, but that it had numerous causes and required interventions based on social assessment and differential diagnosis (all in the tradition of Mary Richmond's scientific casework).

Programs similar to Healy's developed in other areas of the juvenile justice system. Most noted was Boston's Juvenile Court and the Judge Baker Foundation, founded in 1916. This program used trained social workers as probation officers and offered field placements for social work students. The Judge Baker Clinic functioned in cooperation with the National Committee for Mental Hygiene and its Division of Delinquency. Members of the division, which included Healy, made recommendations for expanded study and treatment of delinquent youth and for training of personnel—including social workers.

For much of their history, social work and social work education have been primarily concerned with juvenile justice and adult corrections. Culminating some three years of study, in 1958 the Council on Social Work Education (CSWE) published its thirteen-volume report on the desirable educational objectives and content of social work education. Included in that formidable report was volume 5, *Education for Social Work in the Correctional Field* (Studt, 1959). Although this volume was markedly the slimmest of the set, it made clear that corrections had a broader scope than simply postadjudication. It included then, as now, the functions of arrest and detention, judicial disposition, probation, incarceration, and parole, as well as wider concerns for juvenile delinquency and its prevention. The inclusion of Volume 5 was an affirmation of social work education's commitment to the total criminal justice system.

During this same period there was a very active CSWE committee, the Committee on Correction, which had published *Perspectives and Guides in the Expansion of Social Work Education for the Correctional Field* (1958) and *A Casebook in Correctional Casework* (1958). Funding also was secured for a project to foster and improve social work training of correctional personnel, and Eileen Younghusband, an internationally known social work educator and juvenile court magistrate, was brought from London, England, to help launch the project. Younghusband's (1960) report was widely recognized in social work education circles.

Additionally, with federal financial support CSWE organized a regional institute on personnel standards for corrections. Both the National Council on Crime and Delinquency and the American Correctional Association were involved in that effort to promote high standards for the education and staffing of correctional personnel. This institute was followed in 1964 by a White House Conference on Corrections, out of which grew a Joint Commission on Correctional Manpower and Training charged with forging a national plan for action.

These efforts were abetted by CSWE's employment for some five years of a staff person charged with promoting social work education's dedication to training for employment in the justice system. The final report illustrated a substantial increase in the number of students, field placements, and faculty numbers identified with corrections (Prigmore, 1964).

Social work education's role in and contribution to juvenile and criminal justice may have reached its high-water mark in 1966, when the United States Children's Bureau, the National Council on Crime and Delinquency, and the National Council of Juvenile Court Judges published *Standards and Guides for Juvenile and Family Courts* (HEW, 1966). This document stated that "since 1923 professional organizations have held graduation from an accredited school of social work as the most appropriate standard for training in correctional work." Similar endorsements of social work education came from the National Council on Crime and Delinquency, which included in its recommended personnel standards "a master's degree from a recognized school of social work" (1962, p. 19) for probation officers.

From the Rehabilitative Ideal to Crime and Punishment

So what happened as a result of all this enormous effort and early success? Today's picture of the relationship of social work, social work education, and the justice system appears quite different than might have been anticipated. The CSWE has not employed a corrections specialist since 1965. The earlier and quite active NASW Council on Corrections no longer exists. Only a handful of social work schools emphasize criminal justice or corrections, and this emphasis is often not profound. Few students express interest in careers in juvenile or criminal justice, and those who do often have difficulty in finding rewarding positions.

Underlying these changes was a shifting philosophy in the justice system. The tide of thinking about the relationship between society and offender has largely been shaped by the tensions stemming from two conflicting philosophies. The social services and their allied social sciences rest their theoretical framework largely upon a deterministic conceptualization of human behavior. From this perspective, behavior is seen as being in large part determined by a complex totality of familial, cultural, socio-economic, and other environmental forces impinging upon the individual. This philosophy led to a helping, problem-solving approach to criminal justice. By contrast, the philosophy of ordered liberty (i.e., law, law enforcement, and the criminal justice system) is based on a "free will" perception of human behavior. Under this framework, citizens are necessarily held responsible for their actions and are either rewarded or punished. It is, thus, the state's obligation to administer legally defined punishment to societal wrongdoers.

Social work education's investment in the justice system was in large part an aspect of the deterministic perspective during a period cogently termed by Frances Allen (1974) "the era of the rehabilitative ideal." (Ironically, Allen coined this term in writings that predicted the early demise of that ideal!) The period of the rehabilitative ideal was a significant aspect of the proud heritage of the Progressive Era and the leadership of such pioneers as Healy and Judge Harvey Humphrey Baker. The ideal rested, as Allen noted, on the conviction that human behavior is the natural result of antecedent causes, and that the behavior of wrongdoers could be altered if these antecedents were identified and understood. The challenge to society was, thus, to eliminate the antecedent causes of antisocial behavior and provide opportunities for productive social living.

The deterministic view of human nature, societal goals of ordered liberty, and social responsibility provided the basis for social work's entry into the criminal justice system. It led to the development of probation and parole as means of intervention beyond mere surveillance. It led as well to development of the juvenile court, separation of juvenile from adult corrections, prison clinics and educational programs, the characterization of the prison as a "correctional" facility, and a myriad of other "progressive" services.

The rehabilitative ideal was quite different from the earlier "classical criminology," which dominated the field in the Western world since the early eighteenth century. Classical criminology had previously determined thought about the origins of crime as well as the belief that the essential pathway toward societal protection was through punishing wrongdoers. Punishment was to result from the application of law and to be commensurate with the seriousness of the offense. Awareness by citizens of which actions were defined by the law as crimes and of the resultant penalties would provide a deterrent to transgressions. The societal challenge was one of efficient detection, arrest, fair adjudication, and even-handed administration of penalties.

The gap between the perceptions of the nature of humankind on the part of law and law enforcement, on the one hand, and that of the social service professions on the other underlies the debate about the conflicting values of social work and criminal justice. In essence, this debate pits social work values and an emphasis on promoting an individual's well-being against the criminal justice system's reliance upon protecting society through punitive sanctions for wrongdoers.

Social work found refuge in the framework of the rehabilitative ideal, which was compatible with the value base of the profession. However, the justice system recently has emphasized a law-and-order, crime-and-punishment approach in the tradition of classical criminology. Some, such as Senator Carol Moseley-Braun (1994), for example, argue that society should try juveniles in adult courts for offenses that include the use of firearms. The danger is that this could undo many of the earlier accomplishments in both juvenile and criminal justice. As Nygaard (1994)—a judge with the Third U.S. Circuit Court of Appeals—recently summarized, "our answer to the question of crime has become singular: To correct we punish. To deter we punish. To rehabilitate we punish" (p. A17). The extreme law-and-order approach ignores ultimate sources of crime, those same sources that were recognized by Healy and were ultimately the focus of social work's early commitment to the justice system. Harsh poverty, increasing growth of an underclass, bias and prejudice, and the need for good education and job opportunities are all excluded from consideration by the punishment mentality.

Social Work Education in the Era of Crime and Punishment

During the same period of the rise of a crime-and-punishment mentality, social work education was redirecting curriculum from one based on a field-of-practice approach to one of generalist practice. The demise of the rehabilitative ideal and the move to generalist practice education has left social work education with considerably less coordinated focus on the needs of the justice system, in particular juvenile delinquency and corrections.

Social workers and social work education did not wholly stand aside during the wane of the rehabilitative ideal and the advent of the crime-and-punishment mentality. In many respects, social work education has addressed justice issues that are at least different from, and perhaps broader than, narrowly defined services for delinquents and criminal offenders. For example, throughout the 1980s numerous B.S.W. and M.S.W. programs offered courses on social policy and practice in the justice system. Moreover, course content has been available through introductory courses on social welfare policy and services. Thus, the advent of generalist practice allows social work education to embrace a broader role in both the criminal and civil justice system. Those systems currently include a wide array of areas for social work practice, including social justice, criminal and civil justice, and services to victims and families (including families of those incarcerated), as well as the traditional areas of juvenile delinquency and corrections.

Social work education for generalist practice is particularly suited for the development of the professional interested in employment in the emerging broader views of the justice system. A range of professional social work skills are necessary and common to a variety of developing settings. Generalist education emphasizes common methods, sanctions, purposes, and values, as well as a problem-solving perspective of the person in the environmental context (McMahon, 1994). While the field-of-practice approach does offer a specialist curriculum around one's potential employment setting, the generalist curriculum offers skills that are common to good social work practice with an emphasis on interventions useful for varying client needs and strengths. By design, generalist principle is intended to advance the notion that social work education's principal goal should be to teach knowledge, skills, and values that are applicable to a variety of practice settings (CSWE, 1992). The generalist practitioner, for example, would be as professionally prepared to be a court administrator as is a probation officer or a clinician in a prison or half-away house setting. Clearly, various professional activities may call for differing theories and skills. However, from the generalist perspective these specialized needs are more appropriately obtained pursuant to professional performance and not necessarily as part of one's graduate education.

Educational Models of Social Work Practice in Justice

While social work education in the present era focuses on generic preparation, in a further very important way it provides a theory and practice framework particularly appropriate for work with persons in conflict with the society in which they live. Social work's primary concern is with the transactional field, where the individual personality meets the opportunities and demands of the social environment. It provides a resource not offered by other more personality-oriented social sciences such as psychology or psychiatry. Nor is that resource available from the more theoretically oriented sociological disciplines, with their focus upon the responses of large groups and cultures to the social environment. The question becomes how this distinct role of social work can best be made available to practice in or related to the justice system. Education for generalist practice may provide one important step toward that goal.

Probably the most formalized examples are those few schools that offer a dual course of study leading to both the M.S.W. and a law degree (J.D.). There are two types of programs—those offering a joint degree that combines the social work and the law curriculum, and dual degree programs where the student completes the courses work for the two separate degrees with certain courses applicable to both. Similar programs are available with other disciplines, such as administration of justice.

The more typical model of education is a year of foundation course work in generalist practice followed by courses in a variety of topics and interventions, such as theories of violence, crisis intervention, victim services, program evaluation, and mediation. For example, the student interested in work with victims of domestic violence would find generalist skills necessary for a variety of activities, from coordinating a community or statewide coalition to managing a family crisis when a mother of three appears at a women's shelter. Such professional interest may best be met with a generalist education enriched by training in specific topics and interventions. Examples of relevant course work include crisis information, violence and oppression, women's issues, family social work, and a relevant field placement. Such a course of study would be furthered in the second year when a student's studies could emphasize relevant interventions, such as working with clients who are sexually abused or abusive, substance abuse treatment, program development, and another relevant field placement. All would contribute to a well-educated professional who is grounded in a generalist understanding and approach.

Another example is a program that offers advanced generalist practice with course work in crisis intervention, community-based mediation, family mediation, social work and the law, and interdisciplinary courses from the law school, including mental health and the law, juvenile law, and law and disabilities. Students selecting this rigorous course of study would find themselves not only prepared for practice in various settings (e.g., hospitals and psychiatric clinics), but with beginning skills useful in the justice system.

Two further examples of expanded social work roles are provided by what was once called "police social work" and mediation. The former reflects a traditional role of social work in the justice system; the latter illustrates the new practice area that is integral to numerous aspects of the justice system, criminal and civil.

Police Social Work

The waning of the rehabilitative ideal and the decrease in direct social worker involvement with police departments is in marked contrast to earlier times when such partnerships were promoted nationwide (Treger, 1981). However, the change may also be considered a redeployment from the role of specialist in a field of practice (e.g., criminal justice) to social work interventions regardless of the practice setting. While this area of practice has had a long and rich history (e.g., see Roberts, 1976), more recently it includes social work involvement in domestic violence, women and children emergency shelters, and child abuse investigation (Conte, Berliner, & Nolan, 1980). The social work interventions emphasized from generalist practice include crisis intervention, victim services, and an array of interpersonal and interviewing skills. The general outcome of the relationship between police and social workers often seems to be the provision of better services to individuals and community (Treger, 1981). Because of the variety of services needed and available in such police-related social work, the need for generic skills coupled with understanding of the person-situation configuration seems particularly important.

Mediation

A further example of new employment opportunities that cut across a broad range of justice settings is mediation (Nugent, 1992). While earlier relatively undiscovered as an area of professional practice outside of the legal profession, conflict resolution services are growing on many levels. Because of its apparent success, mediation has found welcoming consumers in a variety of settings, from the corporate board room and the ever present threat of litigation to the street corner where a conflict might escalate to a physical altercation, a police call for service, possible arrest, and involvement in the criminal justice system.

While mediation may not often be considered part of the field of practice of delinquency and corrections, the circumstances where it is used are those that most likely could result in work related to the formal criminal and civil justice system. Examples include services to victims of crimes, such as victim-offender reconciliation programs, school-based programs, community mediation, family mediation, and public policy mediation.

The example of victim-offender mediation is closely aligned with the traditional field of practice in juvenile and criminal justice. It has proven to be a valuable and effective service (Nugent, 1992). While relatively unheard of in the 1970s, such services have grown from just a few to numerous programs in over one hundred jurisdictions (Umbreit, 1990).

Mediation in school settings may well deflect and prevent violence. In addition, it may well relieve the current crisis of a crowded juvenile and criminal justice system. Among social work's greatest opportunities to actually prevent delinquency may well be the advent of conflict resolution skills that could become as integral to education as reading, writing, and arithmetic. School social workers should be poised to meet this unique challenge.

Similarly, community mediation has afforded social workers employment opportunities addressing a variety of interpersonal conflicts. Currently, there are nearly five hundred programs nationwide, having grown from just a few in the early 1980s. Participation in the civil justice system then was fairly limited, with a social work curriculum based on a field-of-practice approach. Generalist education, however, prepares professionals for such endeavors. Community mediation also intervenes in disputes that are civil was well as criminal. Examples include landlord-tenant disputes, merchant-consumer disputes, and contract disputes. Many times these disputes involve little or no financial value, even compared with the cost and time of a *pro se* appearance in a small claims court; moreover, small claims courts are increasingly using mediation in advance of adjudication.

Social work participation in the civil justice system is also seen in family mediation. Social workers, in fact, were among the founders of mediation in family settings and divorces, in particular (Haynes, 1978; Lemmon, 1985). Mediation not only helps a couple seeking a divorce to obtain a meaningful and less hostile dissolution of the marriage, but includes such critical judicial issues as child custody and support, visitation, and property (including equity in one's home and the ever-growing pension plan). Family mediation includes not only divorce cases but everyday family conflicts, which once may have resulted in some form of family therapy. Such personal decisions were once determined by a judge with the expensive assistance of "adversaries in blue suits" (i.e., his lawyer and her lawyer). Mediation, in contrast, has afforded family members an opportunity to determine for themselves what is a "just and right" division of property or what is in "the best interest" of one's children.

Finally, mediation interfaces with the justice system in the area of public policy mediation. Mediation of policy disputes includes those between the builders of a group home and a neighborhood association with a "not in my backyard" response and disputes between state agencies with overlapping jurisdictions or conflicting policies.

Social work may until recently have been slow to be vigorous in such endeavors as police social work, mediation in a wide variety of settings, and other functions related to the justice system. But the coming of the generalist perspective may well lead to many such activities, including those in family systems, school settings, administration, and other areas of professional social work. Conflict resolution affords an opportunity for the professionally trained social worker to truly help people resolve conflicts between family members, the community, businesses, and society.

Conclusion

Among the harsh aspects of current social reality is that at any one time more than three million persons live under some form of supervision by criminal justice agencies. This includes roughly one out of every thirty-five adult males, one of every nine African-American males, and one of every four African American males between the ages of eighteen and thirty. About 975,000 of those under criminal justice supervision are in prisons or jails. The prospect is that by the year 2000 the total number of citizens under supervision will reach four million (Dilulio, 1991). In light of the punishment mentality of current policy formulation, the number under supervision will probably continue to increase well into the twenty-first century.

It is our opinion that all social work students should be exposed to practice in the criminal and civil justice system. This should include critical examination of such accepted concepts as deviance and disorders, the volume, distribution, and consequences of delinquencies and crime, and the cultural, subcultural, and personality correlates of criminal behaviors. There should also be at least a beginning awareness of the social structures that give rise to criminality and society's past and present endeavors to control and react to unlawful acts.

In today's world, social work education's abdication of responsibility for sharing in the struggle to cope meaningfully with crime and delinquency should be unthinkable. During a period that has witnessed an unprecedented construction of new prisons, overcrowding of existing facilities, and heightened public awareness of crime, social work's role must increase, not decrease, as seems to be the circumstance. It seems imperative that the profession engage itself in two broad fronts. First, it should help prepare some social work graduates for practice with juvenile and adult wrong-doers, their families, and victims. Secondly, it should vigorously participate in public policy formulation, contributing rational emphasis upon the profession's value system, its professional knowledge of the social antecedents of human behavior, and the various approaches to shaping and rehabilitating behavior.

It seems essential to acknowledge that a narrow focus upon the current roles of generalist practice in the justice system has left delinquency, corrections, and the whole area of social conflict without the benefit of the value-based voice of social work. Consequently, the increasing mythology to the effect that the sole solution to crime and delinquency is more vigorous sanctioning of the offender is not countered with an argument emphasizing knowledge of societal and environmental factors, social work values, and an ecological approach to interventions. True, "three strikes and you're out" remains a politically almost irresistible rallying call. But also emerging is a degree of thoughtful awareness that limiting our focus to the crime that has already taken place is self-defeating. A window of opportunity may be almost at hand—an opportunity for social work and social work education to assert through a variety of channels the profession's historic concern for the offender, for the socioeconomic factors that contribute so powerfully to bringing about the offense, and for the most disadvantaged, alienated, and despairing members of society.

References

Allen, F. A. (1974). *The borderline of criminal justice.* Chicago: University of Chicago Press.

CSWE. (1958). *A casebook in correctional casework.* New York: Council on Social Work Education.

CSWE (1958). *Perspectives and guides in the expansion of social work education for the correctional field.* New York: Council on Social Work Education.

CSWE. (1992). *Curriculum policy statement for master's degree programs in social work education.* Washington, DC: Council on Social Work Education.

Conte, J. R., Berliner, L., & Nolan, D. (1980). Police and social worker cooperation: A key to child sexual assault cases. *FBI Law Enforcement Bulletin, 49,* 7–10.

Dilulio, J. J. (1991). *No escape: The future of American corrections.* New York: Basic Books.

Haynes, J. (1978). Divorce mediation: A new role. *Social Work, 23,* 5–9.

HEW. (1966). *Standards for juvenile and family courts.* Children's Bureau Publication Number 437–1966.

Lemmon, J. A. (1985). *Family mediation practice.* New York: Free Press.

Lubove, R. (1971). *The professional altruist.* New York: Atheneum.

McMahon, M. O. (1994). *Advanced generalist practice with an international perspective.* Englewood Cliffs, NJ: Prentice Hall.

Moseley-Braun, C. (1994). Should 13-year-olds who commit crimes with firearms be tried as adults? Yes: Send a message to young criminals. *ABA Journal, 40,* 46.

National Council on Crime and Delinquency. (1962). *Standards and Guides for Adult Probation.* New York: NCCD.

Nygaard, R. L. (1994). Punishing: Dead-end approach to crime. *The National Law Journal,* March 14, A17–A18.

Nugent, W. R. (1992). Mediation techniques for persons involved in disputes. In K. Corcoran (Ed.), *Structuring change* (pp. 272–291). Chicago: Lyceum.

Prigmore, C. (1964). *Manpower and training for corrections.* New York: CSWE.

Richmond, M. E. (1917). *Social diagnosis.* New York: Russell Sage Foundation.

Roberts, A. R. (1976). Police and social workers: A history. *Social Work, 21,* 294–299.

Studt, E. (1959). *Education for social work in the correctional field.* New York: CSWE.

Treger, H. (1981). Police-social work cooperation: Problems and Issues. *Social Casework, 62,* 426–433.

Umbreit, M. S. (1990). Mediating criminal conflict. In A. L. Greenspan (Ed.), *Handbook of alternative dispute resolution.* Austin: State Bar of Texas.

Younghusband, E. L. (1960). Report on a survey of social work in the field of corrections. *Social Work Education: Supplement, 8,* 1–24.

Chapter Fifteen

▶ •••••••••••••••••••••• ◀

Future Directions in Justice System Policy and Practice

C. Aaron McNeece

The number of Americans under some form of correctional supervision is staggering: more than one in one hundred (Bureau of Justice Statistics, 1994)! The impact of the justice system on the lives of our citizens seems even more profound when we consider that as many as one of ten juveniles comes under the jurisdiction of the juvenile court (McNeece, 1983), and that three percent to five percent of males born in the United States today are likely to serve a sentence in an adult prison at some time during their lives (BJS, 1994). With so many persons in the justice system, one might wonder why more social workers aren't employed in this field. Given our generally negative perceptions of the correctional system in this country, we should be concerned with the potential harm to so many people.

In chapter 11, Alexander traced the involvement of social workers in corrections and justice system social work for more than a hundred years. The very name of one of the earliest social work organizations, the National Conference of Charities and Correction, recognized the crucial role that the social work profession played in prisons, reform schools, and other correctional programs (Hollis & Taylor, 1951). Unfortunately, as social work became more "professional" in the 1920s and 1930s, it gradually strayed from its commitment to justice system issues (Miller, 1995). When the federal and state correctional systems began abandoning rehabilitative goals in the 1970s, many of the remaining social workers left to work in other fields. These developments also made it much more difficult to recruit new social work graduates into justice system employment. By 1972 only one percent of NASW's members were employed in the justice system, while mental health attracted one of every three members (Gibelman & Schervish, 1993). As our social and political system became more conservative in the 1990s, social workers appeared to have "fallen in step with the prevailing ideology" (Miller, 1995, p. 656).

Social workers have some special problems in assisting clients in the justice system. The major difficulty is that these clients are in the system involuntarily. Coercion is a way of life for them, and they are likely to view everyone who is employed by or is part of the justice system as an enemy—as an agent of control, not as a helper. Glasser (1978) recommended that clients treat social workers, psychologists, and other "helpers" as they would treat a police officer. Be polite and civil but expect that anything you say might be used against you. Nevertheless, the social worker must often perform certain services for the client, whether or not the client desires them. Keeping in mind our traditional attachment to the client's right of self-determination, it is understandable that many social workers have difficulty working in the justice system. By working in an authoritarian system with unmotivated, involuntary clients, the correctional social worker is also frequently shunned by colleagues in other branches of the profession as a coercer of clients and a violator of professional ethics. This situation is further exacerbated by the movement of state, local, and federal correctional agencies away from rehabilitation and toward control.

Yet the need has never been greater for social work skills to be used in assisting clients in the legal system. With increasing crime rates and the widening net of social control being spread by diversion programs, more of our population will probably come into contact with the system. One way to deal with this situation is to return to our original role in working outside the correctional system—as reformers. Another is to work within the system to make it more humane. Still another is to become involved in prevention programs at all levels. Perhaps if we were more successful in other areas of social work, the need for social workers in the legal system would be greatly reduced!

Adult Programs

Probation and Parole

The move toward determinate sentencing for adults in most jurisdictions has redefined parole and the social worker's role in the justice system. The new postrelease system, known as supervised release in the federal system, lacks the focus on rehabilitation and emphasizes protection of the community. Similarly, redefining probation in the federal system as a sentence will most likely shift its mission away from rehabilitation and toward punishment, deterrence, and "justice." The changes made in federal probation under the Comprehensive Crime Control Act of 1984 transformed probation from a suspension of incarceration to a sentence in its own right (Allen, 1995).

All of these changes portend not a decreased need but a decreased likelihood that in the foreseeable future, many new social workers will be employed in adult probation or parole, where Chandler and Kassebaum (chapter 10, this volume) predict a greater emphasis on surveillance and enforcement of the orders of the court and more use of chemical testing for drug use. If liberty is conditional on a positive urinalysis and compliance with service orders of the court such as child support, employment, and participation in training and abstinence programs, then social workers will de facto be a part of a wide social control network. Social workers must consider the implications of a relapse report for parole or probation revocation for their client. NASW will have to become familiar with the implications of these new issues, and the profession will have to take a position on social workers' social control functions.

Prisons

Social work and the other helping professions are meeting with a moderate degree of success in staging a come-back in adult institutional programs. The Federal Bureau of Prisons now operates a number of chemical dependency programs and family counseling programs in federal prisons (BJS, 1994), and, as Hairston (chapter 9) described, state prison systems are also beginning to recognize the need for maintaining and strengthening family relationships during incarceration. Chandler and Kassebaum (chapter 10) clearly document the need for social workers to become involved in women's correctional programs where, because of their smaller numbers, female inmates are routinely provided inferior treatment.

The largest growth in institutional populations for both genders is due directly to the impact of our state and federal policies on drugs. As long as we continue to incarcerate people for drug use and drug sales, our prisons will have to maintain "revolving door" policies. The additional impact of "mandatory minimum" sentencing laws for drug offenses will further bloat our prisons. For those inmates suffering from an addiction, it would be logical to offer them treatment. Otherwise we will most likely simply continue to recycle them. Most of the inmates would probably benefit from a number of other social work services, ranging from mental health to advocacy and case management.

New Directions

There are a number of new directions in the adult system that hold some promise for social work practice. The Anti-Drug Abuse Act of 1988 made available a considerable amount of federal funding for local treatment programs for drug-involved criminal offenders (see chapter 5). Much of that money has been used by local governments to contract with private, usually not-for-profit agencies to treat this group of clients. Perhaps some of the hesitancy of professional social workers to accept public employment in the justice system may be overcome by this approach. Several types of programs are being funded in this manner.

Pretrial Intervention

The most basic pretrial intervention program simply assesses offenders and determines whether they need to be kept in jail or detention, or whether they can safely be released back into the community. Ties to the community, the seriousness of the crime, and the degree of drug involvement, if any, are all factors that can influence this decision. Where there is drug involvement, the offender may be referred to a treatment agency, kept under probation supervision, and required to drop a periodic urine sample. Not having to maintain these offenders in a secure facility is almost always more cost effective.

Drug Court

One of the most interesting new approaches has been the drug court. It is usually designed for first-time drug offenders who are given the opportunity to bypass the traditional criminal court. Successful completion of the drug court program in many cases results in expungement of the criminal record, thereby providing a powerful incentive for many people. The offender is typically in treatment for nine to twelve months, reports to a probation officer, and undergoes regular urinalysis.

Drug Screening/Assessment/Treatment

Drug-involved offenders may be screened in jail or detention and begin treatment while there. However, the in-jail treatment components rarely amount to more than AA meetings or a few hours of drug education.

Victimology and Victim Assistance

Although scholarly interest in the study of crime-victim relationships emerged more than fifty years ago (Mendelsohn, 1940), the widespread acceptance and adoption of victim assistance programs has been relatively new (Roberts, 1990). The passage of the Violence Against Women Act of 1994 may provide additional resources to recruit, hire, and train social workers to expand victim assistance programs.

Juvenile Programs

Nonsecure Programs

Prospects are perhaps a little brighter in juvenile probation and aftercare than in adult probation and parole. As Ashford (chapter 3) pointed out, however, there is also a lack of clarity in the juvenile aftercare system about the appropriate balance between protecting the community and helping the offender. The jury is still out on the appropriate degree of case load specialization (sex offenders, violent offenders, etc.) and the proper role of "due process" in juvenile aftercare. Intensive supervision has become quite common for juvenile probationers, giving the probation officer a reduced case load and an opportunity to see clients much more often, sometimes daily. It is relatively unusual for social work educational programs at either the undergraduate or graduate level to offer courses or field placements either in adult probation/parole or juvenile aftercare.

Secure Programs

Training School and Detention Facilities

Few social workers would mourn the demise of juvenile training schools if it weren't for the possibility of juveniles ending up in even worse facilities. Although allegedly a disposition of last resort for chronic, serious offenders, a majority of juveniles are not sent there for serious felonies (Schwartz, Willis, & Battle, 1991). Despite attempts to phase out training schools in a number of states, 28,535 youths were in public training schools in 1991 (OJJDP, 1994). Adding the number of youth in public detention facilities brings the total for public facilities to over 54,000. Another 36,190 were in private secure programs (BJS, 1993).

Boot Camps and "Shock Incarceration"

Shock incarceration or shock probation growing out of the "Scared Straight" model, provides juvenile offenders with a brief period of incarceration or confinement (Parent, 1989). Boot camps are a somewhat longer variant based on a military model applied to juvenile training schools. Usually small in size, boot camps stress discipline, physical conditioning, and strict authoritarian control. They are generally thought to be cheaper alternatives than jail or prison, and they are harsh enough to satisfy the public's retributive desire.

Adventure Programs

Adventure programs use physical challenges to help juveniles develop self-confidence and learn teamwork. Often called challenge or wilderness programs, Outward Bound is one of the best known models. Sometimes stirring controversy because of their demanding nature and occasional unavoidable injury to clients, studies have indicated some promise, at least in lower recidivism rates than institutional programs (Rollin & Sarri, 1992).

Diversion Programs

The pros and cons of diversion programs have been debated for at least two decades, and the jury is still out (Blomberg, 1983). Social workers with reformist tendencies applaud the effort to keep juveniles out of the justice system altogether, but there is considerable fear that the "net-widening" effects of diversion programs may have actually *increased* the number of juveniles in the justice system. The fear is founded on a belief that, once organized, diversion programs will automatically find clients. Some of those clients will be juveniles who probably never would have gotten far into the system. However, their identification as "diversion clients" makes them eligible for further processing. While it would be difficult to prove that diversion has backfired and increased juvenile court cases, it is quite clear there has *not* been a decrease in officially processed juvenile cases that corresponds with the growth of diversion programs (McNeece, 1994).

Conclusion

In the late nineteenth century, before social work became a profession, reform-minded social workers attempted to put their ideals into action in reforming one particular aspect of the justice system: the handling of juvenile offenders (Miller, 1995). In the 1990s, the moral and ethical strength of those early social workers is needed more than ever. As Sarri recently wrote (1995) about the problem of crime, solutions are more likely to be found in interventions designed to improve and support families and communities than in law enforcement. It is time for us to recognize that social workers should be an integral part of these interventions. With multiple crises occurring in the justice system—dramatic increases in drug arrests, overcrowding in jails and prisons, the explosion in HIV/AIDS, and so on—the time may be ripe for social workers to step forward with a renewed dedication to justice system clients and new ideas for resolving their problems.

References

Allen, G. (1995). Probation and parole. In *Encyclopedia of social work* (19th ed.). Washington, DC: NASW Press.

Blomberg, T. (1983). Diversion's disparate results and unresolved questions—An integrative evaluation perspective. *Journal of Research in Crime and Delinquency, 20*, 24–38.

Hollis, E., & Taylor, A. (1951). An expanded role for social work. In E. Hollis and A. Taylor (Eds.), *Social work education in the United States: The report of a study made for the National Council on Social Work Education*. New York: Columbia University Press.

Gibelman, M. & Schervish, P. (1993). *Who we are: The social work labor force as reflected in the NASW membership*. Washington, DC: NASW Press.

Glasser, I. (1978). Prisoners of benevolence: Power vs. liberty in the welfare state. In W. Gaylin, I. Glasser, S. Marcus, & D. Rothman (Eds.), *Doing good: The limits of benevolence*. New York: Pantheon Books.

McNeece, C. A. (1983). Juvenile Justice Policy. In A. R. Roberts (Ed.), *Social work in juvenile and criminal justice settings* (pp. 18–43). Springfield, IL: Charles C. Thomas.

McNeece, C. (1994). National trends in offenses and case dispositions. In A. R. Roberts (Ed.), *Critical issues in crime and justice*. Thousand Oaks, CA: Sage.

Mendelsohn, B. (1940). *Rape in criminology*. Giustizia Penale.

Miller, J. (1995). Criminal justice: Social work roles. In *Encyclopedia of social work* (19th ed., pp. 653–659). Washington, DC: NASW Press.

Parent, D. (1989). *Shock incarceration: An overview of existing programs*. Washington, DC: Dept. of Justice, National Institute of Justice.

Roberts, A. (1990). *Helping crime victims: Research, policy, and practice*. Thousand Oaks, CA: Sage.

Rollin, J., & Sarri, R. (1992). *New directions for youth: A follow-up report on Pioneer Work and Learn Center of Wolverine Human Services*. Ann Arbor: University of Michigan, Institute for Social Research.